COMMON SENSE AND OTHER POLITICAL WRITINGS

The American Heritage Series
OSKAR PIEST, FOUNDER

COMMON SENSE

AND OTHER
POLITICAL WRITINGS

THOMAS PAINE

Edited, with an introduction, by
NELSON F. ADKINS

The Library of Liberal Arts
published by
THE BOBBS-MERRILL COMPANY, INC.
INDIANAPOLIS · NEW YORK

Thomas Paine: 1737-1809

COMMON SENSE was originally published in 1776

. . . .

COPYRIGHT © 1953
THE LIBERAL ARTS PRESS, INC.
A Division of
THE BOBBS-MERRILL COMPANY, INC.
Printed in the United States of America
Library of Congress Catalog Card Number 53-11326
ISBN 0-672-60004-8 (pbk)
Eighth Printing

CONTENTS

THOMAS PAINE'S POLITICAL WRITINGS

PAINE'S LIFE AND WORKS: A CHRONOLOGY

1737   Born January 29, at Thetford, Norfolk, England.
        Educated at the Thetford Grammar School.

1750–74 Employed by his father as a staymaker; served as a
        sailor on a privateer; taught school. Employed by the
        government as a collector of the excise; dismissed, but
        re-employed.

1759   Married.

1760   Death of his wife.

1771   Remarried.

1774   Separated from his second wife.
        Dismissed from his excise post a second time. Went bank-
        rupt.
        Met Benjamin Franklin and emigrated to America bear-
        ing a letter of introduction to Franklin's son-in-law,
        Richard Bache.

1775   March 8, publication of "African Slavery in America,"
        an attack on the slavery of Negroes in the Colonies.
        This won him the friendship of Benjamin Rush and
        others.
        October 18, publication in *The Pennsylvania Journal* of
        "A Serious Thought," espousing the cause of inde-
        pendence for the Colonies.
        Contributor to various other periodicals.
        Served as editor of *The Pennsylvania Magazine* for
        eighteen months.

1776   January 10, publication of the pamphlet, *Common Sense.*
        Served in the Continental Army as aide-de-camp to
        General Greene.

December 19, publication of the first of the *American Crisis* papers, the last of which, "A Supernumerary Crisis," was published December 9, 1783.

1777–79 Served as Secretary of the Committee of Foreign Affairs in Congress.

1779 Dismissed from that post as a result of a public controversy with Silas Deane, during the course of which Paine published secret material.

1779–80 Served as clerk to the Pennsylvania Assembly.

1780 Received a Master of Arts degree from the University of Pennsylvania.

Instrumental in forming the bank which later became the Bank of North America.

December 30, publication of the pamphlet, *Public Good*, concerning the right of the United States to certain territory claimed by the state of Virginia.

1781 Short trip to France with Col. John Laurens to solicit French aid for America.

1782–83 December–February, publication in the *Providence Gazette* of six letters attempting to persuade Rhode Island to ratify the five per cent duty on imported articles passed by Congress.

1786 Publication of *Dissertations on Government; the Affairs of the Bank; and Paper Money*, a defense of the bank formed in 1780 and an attack on the use of paper money.

1787 Went to France to promote his design of a single-arch iron bridge.

Saw much of Jefferson in Paris.

August 30, left for England, where he visited his mother, published *Prospects on the Rubicon*, and corresponded with Jefferson.

1789 In Paris, September to March. Aided in drawing up the "Declaration of the Rights of Man and of Citizens."

1791   February, publication in England of *Rights of Man*,
        Part I. Translated and published in France in May.

        July 1, with Achille Duchâtelet, nailed to the door of the
        French Assembly "A Republican Manifesto," calling
        for the abolition of monarchy.

        With Condorcet, Bonneville, and others, founded the "So-
        ciété Républicaine," and the journal, *Le Républicain*.

        August, publication of "Address and Declaration of the
        Friends of Universal Peace and Liberty."

1792   February, publication in England of *Rights of Man*,
        Part II.

        June 8, as a result of the publication, charged with sedi-
        tion; trial set for December.

        Wrote *Letter Addressed to the Addressers on the Late
        Proclamation*, inciting the British people to form a
        republic.

        September 12, made a revolutionary speech to the society
        of the "Friends of Liberty" and the next day escaped
        to France, arriving in Paris on September 19.

        Almost immediately after arrival in Paris, took a seat in
        the Convention.

        As a result of *Rights of Man* and the *Address*, Paine
        burned in effigy throughout Britain, and, on Decem-
        ber 18, officially outlawed from that country.

1793   Member of a nine-man committee—with Condorcet,
        Brissot, Sieyès, and others—to write a constitution for
        France. The resulting document not adopted.

        Alienated the Jacobins by his opposition to the execution
        of Louis XVI.

        Arrested in December and held in prison until Novem-
        ber, 1794, as an Englishman.

1794   Publication of *The Age of Reason*, Part I, in Paris, New
        York, and London.

        Released, November, from prison at the request of the
        American ambassador, James Monroe, on the grounds
        that Paine was an American citizen.

Lived at Monroe's home for 18 months, recuperating from the effects of his confinement in prison.

1795   Readmitted to the Convention.
Published, in Paris, *Dissertation on First Principles of Government*.

1796   Published *Age of Reason,* Part II.
Published *Decline and Fall of the English System of Finance* and *Letter to Washington*.

1797   Publication of *Agrarian Justice* and *Discourse to the Theophilanthropists*.

1802   Returned to America after receiving an offer of assistance from Jefferson.
Attacked the Federalists in eight *Letters to the Citizens of the United States*.

1809   Died June 8, and buried in New Rochelle, New York.

INTRODUCTION

I

Thomas Paine was one of those great humanitarian spirits who illuminate with rare intensity the age into which they are born. In any study of the man's political and social thinking, we must therefore regard him above all a lover of mankind. By temperament Paine, throughout life, was revolted by human suffering, and with a mind to a large degree pragmatic he diligently sought out the causes of injustice. Never a pessimistic determinist, Paine, even in the darkest periods of his life, retained at least some faith in his fellow man; and it was his firm conviction that human suffering might be mitigated by bringing men more fully to understand the principles of good government. Paine saw clearly that "a great portion of mankind, in what are called civilized countries, are in a state of poverty and wretchedness." [1] To oppressive governments he laid the blame for this "disgustful picture of human wretchedness." [2] "Why is it," he asks, "that scarcely any are executed but the poor? The fact is a proof, among other things, of a wretchedness in their condition." [3] So far as government is concerned, he felt that monarchy violates the spirit of humanitarianism, operating as a monarchy must always operate for the good of the few. No clearer declaration may be found of Paine's belief in the close relation of government and the betterment of mankind than in his assertion that "the true greatness of a nation is founded on the principles of humanity." [4] It is in part the purpose of this Introduction to trace out in Paine's life and works what he believed the proper functioning of these principles.

[1] *Rights of Man* in *The Writings of Thomas Paine,* ed. by Moncure Daniel Conway (New York, G. P. Putnam's Sons, 1894-96), II, 454. Hereafter in the footnotes this collected edition of Paine's writings will be referred to as "Conway."   [2] P. 114.

[3] *Rights of Man,* Conway, II, 462.

[4] *Prospects on the Rubicon,* Conway, II, 195.

If we may say that a great humanitarian like Paine must have been born rather than made, we should not fail also to take into account innumerable factors which served to strengthen and, indeed, to condition the humanitarian temperament of the man. Paine, we need always remember, possessed the incalculable advantage of living in the eighteenth century. Yet in undertaking a brief survey of the ideological backgrounds of the era, we should observe at the outset that Paine seems never to have been an exhaustive reader—never a learned man like his friend, Thomas Jefferson. What learning he did possess he often picked up on the run. But for Paine to have been generally informed regarding the great principles that made the latter half of the eighteenth century a hot-bed of radicalism and reform, he need not have been an avid reader. As Professor Gilbert Chinard has so rightly pointed out:

We shall have to admit that there are times when ideas are "in the air," when they seem common property, and when the attribution to any one man of the paternity of any particular idea is well nigh impossible. The eighteenth century was undoubtedly such a period.[5]

If we consider the bulk of Paine's writings, we are surprised how seldom the great thinkers of the seventeenth and eighteenth centuries are mentioned. Occasionally the physiocrats, Quesnay and Turgot, as well as the philosopher, Montesquieu, are mentioned in the pages of Paine's works, though the impact of their ideas on Paine seems to have been slight. The writings of Rousseau and the Abbé Raynal he regarded as possessing "a loveliness of sentiment in favor of liberty, that excites respect and elevates the human faculties; but having raised [the reader's] animation, they do not direct its operation, and leave the mind in love with an object, without describing the means of possessing it." [6] In Paine's thinking there is, indeed, little to suggest the sentimental idealism of Rousseau—little that can be interpreted as a return to nature in the Rousseauistic sense. Essentially a

[5] *The Correspondence of Jefferson and DuPont de Nemours,* ed. by Gilbert Chinard (Baltimore, 1931), p. xi. The publisher of the work, Johns Hopkins Press, has kindly granted permission to use this quotation.

[6] Conway, II, 334.

rationalist, Paine may be more accurately associated with two seventeenth-century thinkers whose work exerted a profound influence on the following century: Newton and Locke.

Strange to say, these writers, too, are infrequently mentioned in Paine's published writings, and we are naturally led to question his firsthand acquaintance with their work. Yet we do know that at the age of twenty Paine attended lectures on Newtonian astronomy delivered by Benjamin Martin and James Ferguson; and Professor Clark has pointed out certain parallels in thought between Paine and these two popularizers of Newtonian principles.[7] The influence here is at best religious; the political influence of Newtonianism is more difficult to demonstrate. In concluding the eighth of the *Crisis* papers, Paine expresses the conviction that

Natural philosophy, mathematics and astronomy, carry the mind from the country to the creation, and give it a fitness suited to the extent. It was not Newton's honor, neither could it be his pride, that he was an Englishman, but that he was a philosopher: the heavens had liberated him from the prejudices of an island, and science had expanded his soul as boundless as his studies. [8]

Of the handful of specific references to Newton, this is most nearly concerned with political theory, though the connection is even here remote and tenuous. Of course, Paine's works contain more passages that, without mentioning Newton, seek to draw an analogy between Newtonian physics and government. In the second part of the *Rights of Man* Paine asserts,

We must shut our eyes against reason, we must basely degrade our understanding, not to see the folly of what is called monarchy. Nature is orderly in all her works, but this is a mode of government that counteracts nature.[9]

In asserting that "Nature is orderly in all her works" Paine is, of course, alluding to the order and design of the Newtonian universe, but it is not immediately evident how monarchy violates

<hr>

[7] Harry H. Clark, "An Historical Interpretation of Thomas Paine's Religion," *University of California Chronicle*, XXXV (1933), 56-87.

[8] Conway, I, 300. [9] P. 132.

the Newtonian design of the universe. Even more fanciful is Paine's assertion that "It is only by organizing civilization upon such principles as to act like a system of pulleys that the whole weight of misery can be removed." [10] Although we may acknowledge Paine's indebtedness to a Newtonian concept of the universe in his deistic thinking (especially in the *Age of Reason*), his application of this line of reasoning to politics and government leaves us almost wholly unconvinced. At best his acceptance of a Newtonian universe, far from having played a major role in shaping his political theories, served mainly as an indirect means of supporting, through analogy, social and governmental ideas arrived at by wholly different means.

Again Paine refers little to John Locke in his writings, and the few references to the English thinker made during the close of Paine's life are in refutation of James Cheetham's assertion that Paine had drawn heavily upon Locke in writing *Common Sense* and the *Rights of Man*. "It may be so for what I know," Paine replied to Cheetham, who was both a personal and political enemy, "for I never read Locke, nor even had the work in my hand." Paine further claims to have been informed of some of Locke's ideas by Horne Tooke, the English politician; and on this basis Paine condemns Locke's writings as speculative and impractical. Then with an irrelevance at times so characteristic of Paine, he proceeds to note what he insists originally turned his attention to the theory of government:

So far from taking any ideas from Locke or from anybody else, it was the absurd expression of a mere John Bull, in England, about the year 1773, that first caused me to turn my mind to systems of government. In speaking of the then king of Prussia, called the Great Frederick, he said, "He is the right sort of man for a king, for he has a deal of the devil in him." This set me to think if a system of government could not exist that did not require the devil, and I succeeded without any help from anybody.[11]

[10] *Agrarian Justice,* Conway, III, 337.

[11] "Reply to Cheetham" in *The Political Writings of Thomas Paine* (Granville, Middletown, N. J., 1839), II, 491-492. Hereafter this edition of Paine's works will be referred to as "1839 ed."

That Paine had never read any of Locke seems an absurdity, yet had he been a deep student of the English theorist, it seems improbable that he would have disclaimed all knowledge of the English thinker. The truth probably lies somewhere between the two extremes. But despite parallels in phrasing which have at times been noted by scholars, it is safe to assume that much of Paine's knowledge of the "rights of man" and the "social compact" must have come to him by devious and indirect sources. Paine, for example, was acquainted with the writings of Dr. Richard Price, whose political theory rested heavily on the doctrine of natural rights. For some of his ideas on popular government Paine may well have been indebted to a work by James Burgh entitled *Political Disquisitions: or, an Enquiry into Public Errors, Defects, and Abuses* (1774-75). This treatise in three volumes, mentioned in *Common Sense,* appears to have derived in part from Locke.

Indeed, Locke himself was not the originator of these liberal principles of government to which we have just referred. It was rather Locke's distinction to have given "clear and reasonable expression to beliefs that were the product of centuries of political experience and the stock-in-trade of liberty-loving Englishmen and Americans." [12] These beliefs stood in marked contrast to another ideology, again centuries in the making, but for the seventeenth century made popularly available in Hobbes' *Leviathan* (1651). Hobbes based his case for monarchical government on the assumption that man in a state of nature is essentially bad, and that society without a strong restraining hand can never hope to emerge from a condition of anarchy or war. The state therefore becomes an artificial contrivance by which men, clearly perceiving the dangers of isolated existence, agree, for the maintenance of their own happiness, to submit themselves to the will of an individual or group of individuals who will maintain law and order.

Locke in his *Two Treatises of Government* (1690) presents a theory of the state diametrically opposed to Hobbes', and possess-

[12] John Locke, *The Second Treatise of Government,* ed. by Thomas P. Peardon (N. Y., The Liberal Arts Press, 1952), p. xiii.

ing liberal and even democratic implications unknown to the author of *Leviathan*. The essential reason for the difference in the political thinking of the two writers lies in their assumptions regarding human nature. To Hobbes man's nature was inherently bad and warlike; to Locke it was essentially good and peaceful. To be sure, men and nations have at times fought among themselves, and have shown themselves to be anything but peaceful. But may not this discord spring from man's failure to act in strict accord with the laws of nature? Of the truth of this assumption Locke had no doubt. Man is a rational being, and the laws of nature should at all times be his guide. As Professor Peardon has said:

. . . the chief lesson John Locke learned from the law of nature was that even before government existed men were free, independent, and equal in the enjoyment of inalienable rights, chief among them being life, liberty and property.[13]

But, after all, Locke was no more an advocate of a state of nature than was Hobbes; and Locke insisted that if man is to secure his natural rights in the midst of civilization, he must meet his neighbors on equal terms. That is, natural rights must be implemented by contract. The primary object of this political agreement is to keep intact, so far as possible, the natural liberties of mankind; and men must therefore surrender only so much freedom as will make the maintenance of these liberties possible. Locke's contract concerned only free persons, and did not include the rulers. Unlike Hobbes, who thought of the sovereign's power as being absolute, Locke regarded the ruler as holding his power solely in trust. This "fiduciary power" is exercised "for the good of the community." Such, in brief, is Locke's doctrine of natural rights, with the concomitant theory of the social contract. And even if Paine, as he asserted, had never read a word of Locke, it may readily be seen that his writings are veined with expressions of, and allusions to, these political principles.

One further ideology presents itself to our attention as a factor contributing to Paine's political thinking. Since Paine's father

[13] *Ibid.*, p. xv.

was a Quaker, and Paine himself at times spoke with approbation of the sect, Moncure Conway has placed much emphasis on the possible impact which the doctrines of the Society of Friends had on Paine's democratic thought. Of the Pennsylvania Quakers during the war, Paine had no illusions. In the third *Crisis* paper and elsewhere he condemned them without reservations for their pacifism—and by implication for their Tory sympathies. Yet after the war, and especially with his return to America in 1802, Paine wrote of the Quakers as "a people more moral and regular in their conduct than the people of other sectaries." [14] Indeed, he was to recall that he himself was "a descendant of a family of that profession," especially commending the Quakers "for their care of the poor of their Society" and "for the education of their children." [15] Finally, in his will he expressed the wish that he be interred in their burial ground if they would permit someone not a member of their Society to be buried there.[16] The broad humanitarianism, as well as the equalitarianism of the Quakers, must early have responded to Paine's democratic imagination, and the Quaker beliefs are assuredly a factor to be reckoned with in surveying the liberal and democratic influences exerted upon him. But Paine was too much a rationalist to accept the full mystical import of the Quaker faith, so that as a stimulus to his liberal thinking, the principles of the Friends must have been limited to that expansive humanitarianism for which in general the eighteenth century so clearly stood.

In concluding this review of the backgrounds of Paine's political speculations, we should not forget some of the facts of his early life in England which had encouraged his thinking along liberal, not to say radical, lines. Born of parents who with only the greatest difficulty could send their son to school, Paine at the age of thirteen began to work at the side of his father as a staymaker. During the years which were to follow, Paine, in the midst of numerous attempts to improve his condition, was perpetually brought face to face with misery and poverty. At the age of twenty-five, he became an excise man. Discharged three years

[14] *Prospect Papers,* Conway, IV, 340.

[15] *Worship and Church Bells,* Conway, IV, 252.   [16] Conway, IV, 509.

later, he served as a teacher in a school located in Kensington. But he was reappointed an excise officer in 1768. Now firmly convinced that excisemen were underpaid, Paine, at the instigation of his fellow officers, wrote his first pamphlet, which he addressed to Parliament: *Case of the Officers of Excise* (1772). This pamphlet contains words prophetic of Paine's later humanitarianism:

> If the increase of money in the kingdom is one cause of the high price of provisions, the case of the excise officers is peculiarly pitiable. No increase comes to them—they are shut out from the general blessing—they behold it like a map of *Peru*. The answer of Abraham to Dives is somewhat applicable to them, *"There is a great gulf fixed."* [17]

Paine even sought personally to influence members of Parliament on behalf of the excisemen, with the result that he was dismissed in 1774 by the government as a troublemaker. Further misfortune overtook Paine when later in the same year he went into bankruptcy. Franklin, then in London, fortunately came to Paine's assistance, and by the close of the same year Paine was in America, ready, at the age of thirty-seven, to embark upon a new life.

II

Always a refuge for the oppressed, America came at once to Paine's rescue, as, within a brief period, he was himself to come to the rescue of America. Paine, as we have seen, had already become thoroughly convinced of the wrongs that perpetually beset mankind. It now remained only for his experiences in America to sharpen his humanitarian and democratic outlook on life. As we look back upon Paine's earliest political writing done in America and follow the course which his writing took through the ensuing years, we may discern a major impulse motivating his thinking. This impulse, closely allied to his humanitarianism and best stated years later in the *Rights of Man*, is now worth a moment's thought. A deep-seated inertia, pervading both individuals and nations, is eternally threatening the liberty and happi-

[17] *Ibid.*, IV, 500.

ness which is by nature man's. Man must therefore learn to assert and reassert his natural rights. "There is existing in man," asserts Paine, "a mass of sense lying in a dormant state and which, unless something excites it to action, will descend with him, in that condition, to the grave." [1] Why, after all, allow ourselves to pass into a somnolent state in which we fail to observe how enslaved we have become. Strangely enough, even in Burke's *Reflections on the Revolution in France* Paine discovered at least one redeeming virtue. Some of Burke's assertions serve "to demonstrate how necessary it is at all times to watch against the attempted encroachment of power and to prevent its running to excess." [2]

Possibly Paine's Quaker background directed his attention to the evils of Negro slavery soon after he reached America. In any case, one of his first essays published in this country bore the title "African Slavery in America" (1775). There is little in this brief piece to suggest that Paine had personally observed the miseries of the Southern Negroes. But it was addressed "To Americans," and was plainly intended to fulfill that purpose which was to lie in the background of so much of his writing—to keep mankind aware of the principle of natural rights. The humanitarianism of his approach to the subject is suggested by the concluding sentence: "These are the sentiments of Justice and Humanity." [3] Yet in submitting to the reader his arguments for the abolition of slavery, he was not unaware of the slavery from which America itself was then suffering. Indeed, he entreats the "Americans to consider"

. . . With what consistency, or decency they complain so loudly of attempts to enslave them, while they hold so many hundred thousands in slavery; and annually enslave many thousands more, without any pretence of authority, or claim upon them? [4]

Paine, of course, arrived in America at a moment of grave political danger for the Colonies, and he was never without an eye for the dramatic. England's attempts to enslave America had been more than evident to all but the Tories since the Stamp Act of 1765. The growing irritation between the Colonies and the

[1] P. 126.   [2] P. 78.   [3] Conway, I, 9.   [4] *Ibid.*, I, 7.

mother country had reached another crisis with the Boston Massacre of 1770; and more recently the Boston Tea Party had resulted in the imposition upon America of the so-called "Intolerable Acts," which included the closing of the Boston harbor and the curtailing of certain liberties provided by the Massachusetts charter. These acts had been passed earlier in the same year that Paine came to America, and there was something strange and sinister in the air. Rebellion and sedition lurked in every corner; and the King's proclamation of October, 1775, declaring that "all our officers, civil and military, are obliged to exert their utmost endeavours to suppress such rebellion," [5] only added to the political tension throughout the Colonies.

Stirred by this mounting spirit of rebellion, Paine wrote *Common Sense*. The pamphlet was published in January, 1776, with a "New Edition" containing some additions and an "Appendix" appearing the following month. Seventeen years later, in looking back upon the inception of this famous pamphlet, Paine wrote:

. . . I saw an opportunity, in which I thought I could do some good, and I followed exactly what my heart dictated. I neither read books, nor studied other people's opinions. I thought for myself. The case was this:

During the suspension of the old governments in America, both prior to and at the breaking out of hostilities, I was struck with the order and decorum with which everything was conducted; and impressed with the idea, that a little more than what society naturally performed, was all the government that was necessary, and that monarchy and aristocracy were frauds and impositions upon mankind.

On these principles I published the pamphlet *Common Sense*. [6]

The principles here alluded to are obviously those summarized so eloquently by Locke and others who had preceded Paine. If we may take at its face value Paine's early impression of the "order and decorum" with which the American Revolution in its early stages had been conducted, we may readily accept the sincerity of

[5] *New-York Gazette and Weekly Mercury*, Nov. 6, 1775.
[6] *Rights of Man*, Conway, II, 463.

the attending reflection that "a little more than what society naturally performed, was all the government that was necessary."
Thus Paine early in *Common Sense* cast doubt upon the benefi-
cence of complex government, and turned to society regulated by
the law of nature as the source of man's contentment and happiness. Indeed, Paine asks his readers to "suppose a small number
of persons settled in some sequestered part of the earth, unconnected with the rest; they will then represent the first peopling of
any country, or of the world. In this state of natural liberty, society will be their first thought." [7] In succeeding paragraphs, he
describes the virtues of an elective system of government, still
operating, however, as closely as possible in accordance with
nature's simple plan. "I draw my idea of the form of government," he asserts, "from a principle in nature which no art can
overturn, viz., that the more simple anything is, the less liable it
is to be disordered and the easier repaired when disordered." [8]
Having placed this ideal clearly before the reader, Paine presents,
by way of contrast, the evils of the constitution of England, "so
exceedingly complex," he avers, "that the nation may suffer for
years together without being able to discover in which part the
fault lies." [9] And in a long section on the disadvantages of monarchy and hereditary succession, looking forward to the *Rights of
Man,* he gives numerous illustrations of the wrongs arising from
complex government—evils that spring from a violation of the
principle of natural rights.

With the theory of natural rights clearly established, Paine
reveals how foolish it is for America longer to maintain an allegiance to England. In presenting his arguments for immediate
separation, he offers "nothing more than simple facts, plain arguments, and common sense." [10] "It is repugnant to reason," he
avers, "to the universal order of things, to all examples from
former ages, to suppose that this continent can long remain subject to any external power." [11] Sooner or later independence must
come to pass. Our distance from England militates against a continued union with the mother country. A connection with Eng-

[7] P. 5.   [8] P. 7.   [9] *Loc. cit.*   [10] P. 18.   [11] P. 25.

land may involve us in foreign wars—may affect our trade adversely. As for reconciliation, it is now no more than "a fallacious dream." [12] Some still speak kindly of the parent country; but England has always persecuted her children; and now that mother, in declaring war on her colonies, has declared "war against the natural rights of all mankind." [13] But perhaps the outstanding reason for demanding separation lies in the tyranny of King George himself, that "hardened, sullen-tempered Pharaoh of England." Unrelenting "wretch," "with the pretended title of Father of his People," the King "can unfeelingly hear of their slaughter, and composedly sleep with their blood upon his soul." This demand for separation on the basis of the faithlessness of the sovereign suggests one of Locke's conditions whereby a government may be dissolved—"when the legislative or the prince, either of them, act contrary to their trust." [14] Foolish, indeed, now to seek peace with England!

Much of Paine's invective against England undoubtedly should be called the rhetoric of a propagandist. Yet a saner, sturdier vein of thought inspires those passages wherein he seeks to unite the Colonies in their common task of resisting England. Seldom does Paine leave his readers wholly to founder in a sea of fascinating generalizations. And in *Common Sense* he lays before us his blueprint for a colonial organization with a congress, president, and charter (i.e., constitution). Most striking, indeed, is his call for a "Declaration for Independence." This he insists must be an "open and determined" document—"a manifesto . . . setting forth the miseries we have endured." [15]

The "Appendix" to the "New Edition" of the pamphlet reiterates the importance of immediate independence. Especially worthy of note is the significance which Paine discovers for America in the Quebec Act (one of the "Intolerable Acts" of 1774). This act, by extending the boundaries of Canada, had deprived several colonies of their "backlands"—frontier territories of inestimable value in the economic development of the country. Paine at least dimly recognized in 1776 what he was to see more clearly

[12] *Loc. cit.*   [13] P. 3.   [14] Peardon, p. 123.   [15] P. 43.

a few years later—the importance of the West in the building of the new nation. Finally, the "Appendix" concludes with an exhortation for unity as the first step toward independence.

Let the names of Whig and Tory be extinct, and let none other be heard among us than those of a good citizen, an open and resolute friend, and a virtuous supporter of the rights of mankind and of the free and independent states of America.[16]

Common Sense met with a success that probably astonished even Paine himself. He had, indeed, caught up the spirit of rebellion then prevailing in the land, and had embodied that spirit in the clear, forceful language of the people. Years later he referred extravagantly to the popularity of *Common Sense* as "beyond anything since the invention of printing." We know that he relinquished all rights of authorship to the work, giving, as he said, "copyright to every State in the union"; but his statement that the demand for the pamphlet "ran to not less than one hundred thousand copies" [17] would, indeed, be difficult to verify. This is not to cast doubt on the tremendous force which *Common Sense* had in giving the Revolution, already under way, a momentum that was to carry it to a successful conclusion. Paine's eloquent call for a "Declaration" must have helped to focus the efforts of the Continental Congress on the drafting of the famous document. But unquestionably Paine's own stress on the popular appeal made by *Common Sense* should stand as the paramount significance of the book. It was one of several outstanding media that were to bring the Revolution close to the hearts of every American. More formal evidence of the influence which *Common Sense* had on Paine's contemporaries lies in the several replies which were written to the work. Perhaps the most important of these was a series of letters which appeared in the *Pennsylvania Gazette* and were signed "Cato." Written by an Anglican clergyman, Dr. William Smith, these letters, with more than common brilliance, sought to disclose the danger of growing republicanism in America, and the folly of attempted independence. Paine, undoubtedly realizing the cogency of Smith's arguments, pub-

[16] P. 52.   [17] *Rights of Man*, Conway, II, 463.

lished in the *Pennsylvania Journal* "The Forester's Letters," four
in number, in which he defended his earlier demands for independence.

Paine himself was to link *Common Sense* to his next series of
pamphlets. "I continued the subject" of American Independence,
he wrote, "under the title of the 'Crisis,' till the complete establishment of the Revolution." [18] This was the group of papers originally published as "The American Crisis." There were thirteen
of these pamphlets, together with one "extraordinary" and two
"supernumerary" issues, each signed "Common Sense." All these
are marked by the outspokenness so characteristic of all Paine's
writings. Again not without a feeling for the dramatic, Paine
spoke as one who feels himself in the midst of history in the making. Seizing in his first paper upon one of the darkest moments
of the Revolution, Paine penned the line that was to become so
famous—the line which he took so affectionately to his own heart,
years later still cherishing its memory: "These are the times which
try men's souls." The American army had suffered several severe
defeats in the vicinity of New York and had retreated through
New Jersey. To many the cause of independence now seemed
doomed. "Tyranny, like hell, is not easily conquered," wrote
Paine in a mood of defiance; "yet we have this consolation with
us that, the harder the conflict, the more glorious the triumph." [19]
Paine further described graphically his own experiences in the
war under General Greene; and he attacked the Tories merci-
lessly:

And what is a Tory? Good God! what is he? I should not be
afraid to go with a hundred Whigs against a thousand Tories,
were they to attempt to get into arms. Every Tory is a coward;
for servile, slavish, self-interested fear is the foundation of Toryism, and a man under such influence, though he may be cruel,
never can be brave.[20]

At the conclusion of his first paper, Paine reviews the destruction and suffering that must come to America if cowardice gains
mastery over the people. He exclaims: "Look on this picture and

[18] *Loc. cit.*   [19] P. 55.   [20] P. 58.

weep over it! and if there yet remains one thoughtless wretch
who believes it not, let him suffer it unlamented." [21]

We may briefly note some of the crises of the war that Paine
covered in the succeeding issues of his famous series of pamphlets.
In the papers that followed, Paine repeatedly warned the Americans against appeasement. General Howe in 1776 had twice issued
proclamations offering clemency to those who would submit or
lay down their arms. Paine realized the danger that lurked in
such enticements and addressed his second *Crisis* "To Lord Howe"
and the New York Tories. The fourth *Crisis* was written directly
after the battle of Brandywine in June of 1777. This defeat of
the American army caused consternation in Philadelphia, and
many felt that the city was lost. There is no reason to believe
that Paine failed to view the defeat realistically, but he had
learned from experience how to make a bad situation appear as
good if only to encourage his fellow countrymen to action. "Our
strength," Paine asserts, "is yet reserved; and it is evident that
Howe does not think himself a gainer by the affair." [22] "The
nearer any disease approaches to a crisis," spoke the optimist,
"the nearer it is to a cure. Danger and deliverance make their
advances together, and it is only the last push, in which one or
the other takes the lead." [23]

As the war progressed, certain political factions in England
became increasingly aware not only of the debt into which the
war with America was leading the British, but of the uncertainty
regarding the outcome of the war. Alert in taking advantage of
the murmuring among the English people, Paine addressed his
seventh and eighth *Crisis* papers "To the People of England,"
reminding them, among other things, of the debts the British government was daily incurring, and of the high taxes in which they
would shortly be involved. Here Paine anticipated at some points
his attack on a monarchical form of government in the *Rights
of Man.* "To what persons or to whose system of politics you owe
your present state of wretchedness, is a matter of total indiffer-
ence to America." [24]

[21] P. 63.   [22] Conway, I, 231.   [23] *Ibid.,* I, 231.   [24] *Ibid.,* I, 298.

As the war came to an end in April of 1783, Paine in a mood of romantic expansiveness penned the last regular issue of the *Crisis* papers. His success as a pamphleteer had, indeed, gone to his head. "The times that tried men's souls" were not over; even Paine in his momentary exultation must have realized that fact, although there was a sense in which this *was* "the greatest and completest revolution the world" had ever known.[25] With some truth too he declared near the close, "It was the cause of America that made me an author." Yet with the same heady enthusiasm that pervades much of the pamphlet he could allude, without reserve, to the services he had rendered the country, and to the belief that he had "likewise added something to the reputation of literature." In the light of Paine's later diversified career the note of prophecy struck in his final paragraph—both a valedictory and prelude to the years of controversy and suffering in other lands—is moving:

But as the scenes of war are closed and every man preparing for home and happier times, I therefore take my leave of the subject. I have most sincerely followed it from beginning to end and through all its turns and windings; and whatever country I may hereafter be in, I shall always feel an honest pride at the part I have taken and acted, and a gratitude to nature and providence for putting it in my power to be of some use to mankind.[26]

In glancing at a few of the more important ideas embodied in the *Crisis* papers, we have passed over one conviction that grew steadily upon Paine during the years of the Revolution: the need for greater union among the states. It will be recalled that the Articles of Confederation, which had been presented to the Colonies for ratification in 1777, but which had not been finally adopted until 1781, granted to the central government a minimum of power needed to execute the affairs of the nation. All other powers resided in the states. Such a plan for governing the nation conforms in some measure to the suggestions for organizing the provinces which Paine had made in *Common Sense*, although he observes in that pamphlet that "our strength is con-

25 P. 64.   26 P. 70.

tinental, not provincial." [27] In any case, both Paine's simple blue-print for colonial organization and the Articles of Confederation obviously avoided political control by a strong federal govern-ment, and no doubt were felt to embody, as well as might be for the moment, the natural rights of man. As we know, the Articles failed to provide sufficient central control for the Colonies, and numerous political crises arose which threatened the integrity of the nation. Naturally in the early eighties a movement for a stronger union began more and more to make itself felt. Washing-ton, Hamilton, and Madison became the chief proponents of a revised constitution; and Paine, contrary to what one might per-haps expect, joined in the same movement for a stronger union.

Years later in the *Rights of Man* Paine was to describe the essential fault which he and other American politicians (usually called conservative) had found with the Act of Confederation.

The powers vested in the governments of the several states by the state constitutions were found, upon experience, to be too great; and those vested in the Federal Government by the Act of Confederation too little. The defect was not in the principle, but in the distribution of power.[28]

Though avowedly connected with no political party,[29] Paine as early as 1780 supported a federalist point of view as opposed to states' rights. In that year he published the pamphlet entitled *Public Good*, which argued for the rights of the United States to the vacant western territory then claimed by Virginia. Since Maryland, because her frontier boundaries were limited by her charter, could lay claim to no western territory, she refused to ratify the Articles until Virginia had relinquished her frontier lands to the federal government. In *Public Good* Paine examines in some detail the original charter and other documents on which Virginia laid her own claims, and declares these claims "unreason-able." [30] Furthermore, since "The hand of providence has cast us into one common lot, and accomplished the independence of America," [31] these vacant lands belong logically to the federal gov-

[27] P. 32.　　[28] P. 138.　　[29] P. 4.　　[30] Conway, II, 58.
[31] *Ibid.*, II, 33.

ernment. Even more distinctly than in *Common Sense,* Paine now foresees the value of these western lands in the expansion of the new country.

The United States now standing on the line of sovereignty, the vacant territory is their property collectively, but the persons by whom it may hereafter be peopled will also have an equal right with ourselves; and, therefore, as new States shall be laid off and incorporated with the present, they will become partakers of the remaining territory with us who are already in possession.[32]

But Paine felt that the implementation of America's future growth must lie in the hands of a stronger legislative body than that provided by the Articles of Confederation. In concluding his pamphlet, therefore, he calls upon America to elect "a Continental convention, for the purpose of forming a Continental constitution, defining and describing the powers and authority of Congress." [33] Thus Paine was among the first to advocate the calling of a constitutional convention. Virginia finally yielded the greater part of her vacant territory to the federal government, and Maryland belatedly ratified the Articles of Confederation.

During the early eighties Paine continued to direct his attention toward the need which he constantly saw for a stronger federal government. In the last regular issue of the *Crisis* he declared that "It is with confederated states as with individuals in society: something must be yielded up to make the whole secure. . . . Our citizenship in the United States is our national character." [34] And in "A Supernumerary Crisis," addressed "To the People of America" at the end of 1783, he closed with the assertion that "it is only by acting in union, that the usurpations of foreign nations on the freedom of trade can be counteracted, and security extended to the commerce of America." [35] Further economic implications of Paine's conviction that the strength and greatness of the nation lie in union may be studied in the six letters to Rhode Island which he contributed to the *Providence Gazette* in 1782 and 1783. Under the Articles of Confederation the passage

[32] *Ibid.,* II, 65.   [33] *Ibid.,* II, 66.   [34] Pp. 68f.
[35] Conway, I, 380.

of a law by Congress became contingent on the unanimous approval of the thirteen states. Rhode Island refused to give her consent to the passage of a five per cent duty on imported articles which Congress had proposed. With his usual fearlessness and confidence, Paine through these letters sought to bring about Rhode Island's acceptance of the measure. Interesting, indeed, is the way in which he seeks to define Congress not as "a body of men," but as "an Assembly of States." "Those States, thus assembled," he continues, "have, as the most eligible and easy mode of payment, proposed a duty of five per cent on imported goods. Twelve of the States have adopted the measure, and passed laws for that purpose. Rhode-Island alone is delinquent." [36] Nothing could be clearer to Paine; for their own good the thirteen states must act in concert. Whether Paine regarded his advocacy of a stronger central government in full agreement with the theory of natural rights, it would be impossible now to say. Yet his pragmatic mind for the moment saw in "the Union of the States" "the most important of all subjects." [37] Eight years of experience in American politics had revealed to Paine "that the confederation is not adapted to fit all cases which the empire of the United States, in the course of her sovereignty, may experience." [38] In this group of letters Paine sheds further light on the predicament in which Rhode Island had unhappily placed the nation. In doing so, Paine seeks to define the citizen's relation first to his native state, and then to the United States.

Every man in America stands in a two-fold order of citizenship. He is a citizen of the State he lives in, and of the United States; and without justly and truly supporting his citizenship in the latter, he will inevitably sacrifice the former. By his rank in the one, he is made secure with his neighbors; by the other, with the world.[39]

Paine's involvement in American politics between 1775 and 1787, when he sailed for Europe, has been but partially covered

---

[36] *Six New Letters of Thomas Paine*, ed. by Harry H. Clark (Madison Wisconsin, 1939), p. 10.   [37] *Ibid.*, p. 12.   [38] *Ibid.*, p. 23.
[39] *Ibid.*, p. 22.

in our survey. Certain gaps may now be briefly filled in. In "Thoughts on Defensive War" and in an "Epistle to Quakers" (added to the "New Edition" of *Common Sense*) Paine condemned the pacifism of the Quakers, which he felt a serious impediment to the prosecution of the war. Of greater historical significance was Paine's defense, in several essays, of the Pennsylvania Constitution of 1776. Actual participation in colonial politics, however, led Paine in 1777 to be elected by Congress to the post of Secretary of the Committee of Foreign Affairs. Tact was never a part of Paine's mental equipment; and he soon came into serious controversy with Silas Deane, American Commissioner to France, who, Paine claimed, had benefited financially from his transactions with the French government. Paine undoubtedly acted from ingenuous motives in desiring to save Congress the loss of money of which he believed it had been defrauded by Deane, but Paine proved overzealous in publishing information from documents which, as Secretary of the Committee of Foreign Affairs, he should have regarded as secret and confidential. He exposed Deane in a series of letters published in the *Pennsylvania Packet* in 1778 and 1779. Paine's dismissal from his post rankled in his bosom until shortly before his death. As late as 1808 he penned letters to Congress defending his part in the Deane affair, and asking for the salary which he believed was then rightfully owing him.

Paine's political activities play so intimately into the economic problems of the country during the Revolution that we must not wholly ignore his part in reorganizing the financial affairs of the nation. Toward the close of 1779 Paine had been elected clerk of the Pennsylvania Assembly; and in the performance of his official duties, he read to the Assembly the letter of Washington (1780) in which the general vigorously expressed himself on the "combination of circumstances" which were rapidly exhausting "the patience of the soldiery." Washington added that "we see in every line of the army the most serious features of mutiny and sedition." [40] In the ninth issue of the *Crisis* (1780) Paine, in

[40] *Basic Writings of George Washington*, ed. by Saxe Commins (N. Y., 1948), p. 391.

bringing before his fellow countrymen the conditions so vividly described by Washington, noted that "an association has been entered into by the merchants, tradesmen, and principal inhabitants" of Philadelphia, "to receive and support the new state money at the value of gold and silver." [41] Paine, who had himself contributed the sum of five hundred dollars, became instrumental along with his erstwhile political opponent, Robert Morris, in founding the Bank of North America with the expressed purpose of financing the Revolution. After the war, in 1786, those who advocated paper money as opposed to specie sought the repeal of the Bank's charter; and in that year Paine came to the defense of the Bank in a pamphlet—his last before leaving America— entitled *Dissertations on Government; the Affairs of the Bank; and Paper Money.* Paine's position in regard to paper money had not changed since the formation of the Bank. Paper money "is at best a bubble. Considered as property, it is inconsistent to suppose that the breath of an assembly, whose authority expires with the year, can give to paper the value and duration of gold." [42] Paine had clearly aligned himself with men of wealth. Public opinion broke sharply regarding his economic stand—some insisting that he had forsaken the cause of the common man. This is a question too complex for our present discussion. Suffice it to say that again, as in his espousal of a strong central government, Paine here sought to meet the financial exigencies of the moment. He clearly recognized, as did Hamilton, that only by maintaining a gold or silver standard could the new nation as a whole grow and prosper. If this be desertion of the cause of the common people, Paine's opponents then or now may make the most of their case.

III

With the close of the Revolution Paine believed his work in America mainly done. And in the valedictory with which the final issue of the *Crisis* closed, it will be recalled that he alluded to "whatever country I may hereafter be in." As Henry D. Thoreau

[41] Conway, I, 305.   [42] *Ibid.*, II, 181.

regarded his experience at Walden as but a single experiment in living, which left him "several more lives to live," so Paine appears now to have looked to other lands for fresh experiences in the cause of liberty—an expectation in which he was not disappointed. An examination of his first sojourn in America reveals the ever widening scope of the man's preoccupation with humanity. The *Letter to the Abbé Raynal,* a pamphlet published a year before the close of the Revolution, suggests something of the world of brotherhood and cooperation that Paine had already begun to envisage. Ostensibly an attempt to correct numerous errors in the Abbé's account of the Revolution as set forth in his *Révolution d'Amérique,* Paine looked forward to a world harmoniously knit by commerce and science. "The wants of the individual," he asserts, "which first produced the idea of society, are now augmented into the wants of the nation, and he is obliged to seek from another country what before he sought from the next person." And "Science, the partisan of no country, but the beneficent patroness of all, has liberally opened a temple where all may meet." [1]

With his newly acquired leisure after the Revolution, Paine turned to several inventions, the most important of which was an iron bridge without piers. A model of the bridge safely stowed away in his trunk, Paine, in April, 1787, sailed for France. The bridge, it is true, attracted some attention abroad, but more significant for our study is the fact that Paine found himself almost at once involved in the politics of France and England. After the outbreak of the French Revolution, Edmund Burke published in 1790 *Reflections on the Revolution in France.* Paine had earlier been on terms of friendship with Burke, but Burke's attack upon the French Revolution with his defense of the British monarchy aroused Paine's indignation, and called forth his *Rights of Man,* published in two parts, 1791-1792. This brilliant refutation of Burke probably concentrates in one work more of Paine's political and social thinking than may be found in any other single publication of the author. The *Rights of Man* is mainly concerned with the politics of England and France. Yet today one reads

[1] Conway, II, 103.

the book with the keen realization that it could not have been
written if Paine had not had back of him twelve years of political
experience in America, during which he had followed with intense
interest every crisis of the Revolution, as well as many political
and economic crises that had occurred thereafter. Paine had, indeed, been in the midst of democracy in the making. As one of
the "people of America" he felt privileged to speak with authority
to England, still in the chains of monarchy. To Paine "America
was the only spot in the political world where the principles of
universal reformation could begin." [2]   America was the great
mother of democracy that had given birth to Washington. In fact,
the first part of the *Rights of Man* was dedicated to the "President
of the United States of America": "I present you a small treatise
in defense of those principles of freedom which your exemplary
virtue has so eminently contributed to establish." At least for
Paine the American Revolution had cleared the air of tradition
and conformity, and had laid the groundwork for the political
reformation of the world.

Despite annoying repetitions and even occasional bits of bad
grammar, the *Rights of Man* is a skillful attack on Burke, in
which the author not only employs uncompromising logic but
introduces humor and even enlivens his argument with at least
one bit of scandal. Burke's *Reflections* Paine regards as a tissue
of romantic nonsense. He laughs at Burke's assertions that "The
age of chivalry" is gone—"the glory of Europe is extinguished
forever!" [3] Paine further observes: "When Mr. Burke, in a speech
last winter in the British parliament, 'cast his eyes over the map
of Europe, and saw a chasm that once was France,' he talked
like a dreamer of dreams." [4] Paine believes that Burke knows
nothing of the real principles motivating the French Revolution;
he is impassive even before the evils of the Bastille. The practical
humanitarianism of Paine is outraged at Burke's pompous rhetoric:
"In the rhapsody of his imagination he has discovered a world
of wind mills, and his sorrows are that there are no Quixotes to
attack them." [5] Thus Paine matches rhetoric with rhetoric in his

[2] P. 112.   [3] Conway, II, 287.   [4] *Ibid.*, II, 379.
[5] *Ibid.*, II, 287.

reply to Burke. Nor is Paine lacking in humor while disposing of Burke's romantic rhapsodies:

The farce of monarchy and aristocracy, in all countries, is following that of chivalry, and Mr. Burke is dressing for the funeral. Let it then pass quietly to the tomb of all other follies, and the mourners be comforted.[6]

But Burke's defense of the English system of monarchy rests upon an argument which may in part have been suggested to him by his early training as a lawyer. With the English revolution of 1688, Parliament made a declaration to William and Mary that " 'The Lords Spiritual and Temporal, and Commons, do, in the name of the people aforesaid' (meaning the people of England then living) 'most humbly and faithfully *submit* themselves, their *heirs* and *posterities, forever*.' "[7] Thus, argues Burke, the English people had made what was virtually a legal contract, binding to their sovereigns not only themselves but their heirs *forever*. Here was a contract that could never be broken. Years after Paine had written the *Rights of Man*, he expressed the belief that he was the first to attack and expose "hereditary succession on the ground of illegality, which is the strongest of all grounds to attack it upon; for if the right to set it up [does] not exist, and that it does not is certain, because it is establishing a form of government, *not for themselves*, but for a future race of people, all discussion upon the subject ends at once."[8] The illegality of Burke's position lay for Paine in the British statesman's declaration that one generation could make a contract with their sovereign that would be binding upon posterity. In reality Paine in the *Rights of Man* sought to reveal not only the illegality but the foolishness of attempting to make the law of contract, essentially designed to protect property, into a principle of government. Paine summarizes his contention in words now justly famous:

Every age and generation must be as free to act for itself, *in all cases*, as the ages and generations which preceded it. The vanity and presumption of governing beyond the grave is the most ridiculous and insolent of all tyrannies.

[6] *Ibid.*, II, 508.   [7] P. 75.   [8] 1839 ed., II, 498.

Man has no property in man; neither has any generation a property in the generations which are to follow. . . .

Every generation is and must be competent to all the purposes which its occasions require. It is the living and not the dead that are to be accommodated.[9]

Paine, of course, believed that all systems of monarchy and aristocracy rest on an unsound and insecure basis; in short they violate the law of nature. The rights of man are natural rights. But we must move cautiously at this point in ascribing directly to Locke's treatises on government the principles on which Paine's rights of man rest. Locke's treatises, one should recall, were written in large part to defend the Revolution of 1688—"to establish the throne of our great restorer, our present King William—to make good his title in the consent of the people. . . ."[10] If we recall that Paine's avowed purpose in the *Rights of Man* was to prove the illegality of the Revolution, we may perhaps have discovered one of the reasons for his denial of ever having read Locke. Another deviation from Locke lies in the relative importance attributed by each to a sovereign or reigning power. Locke clearly provides for such a power—fiduciary though it be. Paine in the *Rights of Man* reduces the significance and importance of a nation's executive to a minimum. Thus Paine perhaps follows more closely Rousseau's *Contrat Social,* in which sovereignty rests essentially in the people, and the people themselves are bound together by the principle of fraternity. Yet one is scarcely convinced either that Paine had studied Rousseau's book profoundly.

But whether it was Rousseau, Locke, or Paine, the underpinning of the political thought of each was the doctrine of natural rights. In Paine's earlier works on government a belief in this theory is sometimes implied, sometimes briefly expressed, but nowhere in these writings is the theory fully defined. In the *Rights of Man* he elaborates on the doctrine as the background for his condemnation of monarchy; and in view of this more extended discussion one must assume that Paine had done much thinking and probably some reading on the subject since he wrote *Common Sense.* Now Paine points out that so far as we may care

[9] PD. 76f.   [10] Peardon, p. x.

to go into the past, there has always been oppression, and the only way in which we can think of man as unoppressed by his fellows is to go back in thought to the creation of the world. Thus we arrive "at the origin of man"—man as he came "from the hand of his Maker." [11] So Paine insists that "all men are born equal, and with equal natural rights"; [12] and that "whatever appertains to the nature of man cannot be annihilated by man." [13] Nothing can, indeed, destroy "the natural dignity of man." [14] "The artificial noble shrinks into a dwarf before the noble of nature." [15]

In seeking to embody the theory of natural rights in the form of social contract set forth in the *Rights of Man,* Paine drew deeply on his own political experiences in America.

One of the great advantages of the American Revolution has been that it led to a discovery of the principles and laid open the imposition of governments. All the revolutions till then had been worked within the atmosphere of a court, and never on the great floor of a nation. The parties were always of the class of courtiers; and whatever was their rage for reformation, they carefully preserved that fraud of the profession.

In all cases they took care to represent government as a thing made up of mysteries, which only themselves understood; and they hid from the understanding of the nation the only thing that was beneficial to know, namely, *that government is nothing more than a national association acting on the principles of society.*[16]

To understand what Paine here calls "a national association," we should examine the distinction which he makes between "natural rights" and "civil rights." "Natural rights," he affirms, "are those which appertain to man in right of his existence. Of this kind are all the intellectual rights, or rights of the mind, and also all those rights of acting as an individual for his own comfort and happiness which are not injurious to the natural rights of others. Civil rights," he continues, "are those which appertain to man in right of his being a member of society." [17] A man unquestionably possesses certain natural rights, but he is often powerless by him-

[11] P. 81.   [12] P. 82.   [13] P. 79.   [14] P. 86.   [15] P. 91.
[16] P. 120.   [17] P. 84.

self to make these active or effective. So he joins with his fellows to make everyday living possible. Every civil right, according to Paine, grows out of a natural right. By nature a man has the right to protect himself and to make possible his own security, but if left to himself he may find he cannot obtain what is naturally or rightfully his own. So there arises the social contract or compact, which, by means of concerted effort, is intended to make living possible. Yet Paine believed that at no time must the social compact invade the natural rights of the individual. For "All the great laws of society are laws of nature." [18]

To Paine no nation need be denied the happiness that springs from a "national association." "The instant formal government is abolished," he asserts, "society begins to act. A general association takes place, and common interest produces common security." [19] England was plainly denying itself the felicities inherent in representative government, and Burke had argued so brilliantly for the glories of the monarchy. Ever since Paine's clash with government officials in his early days as an exciseman, he had come to dislike England—a dislike that increased as American resistance to England developed into rebellion and rebellion developed into war. Now as he viewed what he felt to be Burke's wretched attempts to defend the very monarchy that Paine had done so much to resist while in America, his dislike of the "mother country" turned to Anglophobia. The nonsense of the English people in bringing William of Orange from Holland in 1688 or George I from Hanover in 1714 to assume the throne of England! As foreigners, neither monarch could understand the English mind or could possibly administer justice. ". . . what is called monarchy," says Paine, "always appears to me a silly, contemptible thing." [20] And the hereditary side of monarchy appeared to Paine offensively contemptible when a child or a man, feeble in body and mind, ascended the throne. Furthermore, the House of Commons, he felt, did not represent the people of England; and he refused even to acknowledge that England possessed a real constitution. There was the English government with its innumerable laws; there were documents, such as the Magna Charta,

[18] P. 118.   [19] P. 117.   [20] P. 132.

which assert the liberties of specified groups. But nowhere, as in the case of America or France, was there a constitution drawn up by the representatives of the people—a document embodying the liberties of the people as a whole. Finally the cost of maintaining a monarchy militates against humanitarianism and the administration of justice.

It is inhuman to talk of a million sterling a year, paid out of the public taxes of any country, for the support of any individual, whilst thousands, who are forced to contribute thereto, are pining with want, and struggling with misery.[21]

But why need the mass of mankind suffer at the expense of the privileged few? Consider, says Paine, the example of the French Revolution and the overwhelming benefits it has brought to France. Paine insists that Burke in his horror of the French Revolution has either suppressed or distorted the facts of that great uprising of the people. In his account of the Revolution, derived partly from his own experiences and partly from what had been related to him by Lafayette and others, Paine is bent upon revealing the truth as he sees it, with regard to the early stages of the Revolution. Thus Paine traces the growth of the French Revolution which, like the American Revolution, he regards as no more than "a renovation of the natural order of things." [22] He notes the dignity of the National Assembly, as well as the relative restraint with which the Revolution had been effected. As opposed to the "musty records and mouldy parchments" on which rested the archaic arguments of Burke, Paine offers the *living* words which Lafayette employed in proposing a declaration of rights to the National Assembly:

Call to mind the sentiments which nature has engraved in the heart of every citizen, and which take a new force when they are solemnly recognized by all: For a nation to love liberty, it is sufficient that she knows it; and to be free, it is sufficient that she wills it.[23]

"The Declaration of the Rights of Man and of Citizens," which Lafayette here proposed, Paine prints entire, with copious com-

[21] Conway, II, 448.   [22] P. 109.   [23] Conway, II, 282.

ment.[24] Here is a declaration—a constitution in miniature—made by the representatives of the people. England, as Paine repeatedly avers, has nothing comparable to this great republican document which had its origin in the people, and which was designed solely to benefit the people as a whole. In this Declaration the Assembly acknowledges the "sacred rights of men and citizens," and asserts that "Men are born and always continue free and equal in respect to rights"; that "The end of all political associations is the preservation of the natural and imprescriptible rights of man."

In the first part of the *Rights of Man* American independence, though clearly in the background of Paine's thinking, seldom enters directly into the author's arguments. The second part of the book, however, in which Paine is less concerned with a refutation of Burke, though no less committed to a demolition of the principles of the British monarchy, uses America chiefly as his great example of primal democratic sanity. Nature in all her magnitude has made America the great nursing ground of democracy; and America has demonstrated "to the artificial world that man must go back to nature for information." [25] Thus Paine is associating America with that "original simple democracy" [26] —that voluntary association of men which he feels to be the essence of all true government. But owing to the vastness of America, even this simple democracy must remain inactive without that other great principle—representation. "By ingrafting representation upon democracy, we arrive at a system of government capable of embracing and confederating all the various interests and every extent of territory and population." [27] Paine here clearly recognizes the close kinship of "The Declaration of the Rights" and "The Declaration of Independence." As Paine elsewhere asserts, "The Declaration of Rights of France and America are but one and the same thing in principles and almost in expressions." [28] In the second part of the *Rights of Man* he reviews in detail the method of framing the Constitution of Pennsylvania, the Articles of Confederation, and the Federal Constitution; and he points out the significance of these documents in the making of a rep-

[24] See pp. 96 ff.   [25] P. 113.   [26] P. 130.   [27] P. 130.
[28] "To the Abbé Sieyès," Conway, III, 9.

resentative government. Paine especially notes that in these constitutions "there is no such thing as the idea of a compact between
the people on one side and the government on the other. The
compact was that of the people with each other, to produce and
constitute a government." [29] President Washington was virtually
the unanimous choice of the people. "He accepted no pay as
Commander-in-Chief; he accepts none as President of the United
States." He is a "gentleman . . . sufficient to put all those men
called kings to shame." [30] How different from having as king a
stadholder from Holland or a German elector! Thus, in reviewing
the establishment of a representative democracy, Paine drew heavily upon personal observations and experiences.

The *Rights of Man*, not always clearly or logically organized,
is in reality a great repository of materials concerned, as we have
seen, not simply with destruction of monarchy, but with bringing
justice and happiness to men through representative government.
In this brief analysis of Paine's work two remaining points only
can be touched on. In the second part, he devotes several pages
to a discussion of a possible alliance between England, France,
and America, developing more fully the broader understanding
among nations at which he had hinted in his *Letter to the Abbé
Raynal*. More significant is the humanitarian and pragmatic turn
which Paine's thinking takes near the close of the work. In both
parts of the *Rights of Man* Paine has indicated how in countless
ways the English people have been misruled—how the rich and
privileged have been maintaining themselves chiefly at the expense
of the poor. Now Paine asks, How can this injustice be abolished?
And his answer is, Only by liquidating the monarchy, and reorganizing the financial resources of England. With those monies
which have been devoted so religiously to maintaining an aristo-
cratic form of government, material aid may be given to the poor
and underprivileged. "Public money," he writes in the mood of
humanitarianism with which the book ends, "ought to be touched
with the most scrupulous consciousness of honor. It is not the
produce of riches only, but of the hard earnings of labor and
poverty. It is drawn even from the bitterness of want and misery.

[29] P. 138.   [30] P. 140.

Not a beggar passes, or perishes in the streets, whose mite is not
in that mass." [31] Paine finally makes specific proposals to help
financially the poor and to make their living easier and happier.
A few of these proposals—two strikingly contemporary for Americans—may be noted:

. . . Annuity of ten pounds each for life for all poor persons,
decayed tradesmen, and others (supposed seventy thousand) of
the age of sixty years.
Donation of twenty shillings each for fifty thousand births.
Donation of twenty shillings each for twenty thousand mar-
riages. . . .
Employment at all times for the casual poor in the cities of
London and Westminster. [32]

Both parts of the *Rights of Man* obtained a wide circulation,
finding special popularity among those societies organized for the
promotion of English liberties. [33] Yet mobs, presumably inspired
by the government, burned Tom Paine in effigy and indulged in
other demonstrations against him. Finally in June of 1792 Paine
was formally charged by the government with sedition, and a date
was set for his trial. Tradition says that the English poet William
Blake warned Paine in September of his impending arrest. In any
case, Paine immediately escaped to France. During the summer,
however, he had penned a slashing denunciation of his prosecu-
tors. This pamphlet, a *Letter Addressed to the Addressers on the
Late Proclamation,* was Paine's last stand against the English
monarchy, written under what was probably momentary dangei
of arrest. If the *Rights of Man* had contained the seeds of sedition, the "Address" was sedition itself. Here Paine takes a final
thrust at "Mr. Burke's incoherent rhapsodies, and distorted
facts," [34] and makes a plea for the freedom of the press:

. . . If the press be free only to flatter Government, as Mr.
Burke has done, and to cry up and extol what certain Court sycophants are pleased to call a "glorious Constitution," and not
free to examine into its errors or abuses, or whether a Constitu-

[31] Conway, II, 481-482.   [32] *Ibid.,* II, 502.
[33] See *Rights of Man,* note 2, p. 180.   [34] Conway, III, 46.

tion really exist or not, such freedom is no other than that of Spain, Turkey, or Russia. . . .[35]

But perhaps the most important item in the "Address" is Paine's suggestion that "a national convention" be called which "would bring together the sense and opinions of every part of the nation, fairly taken." [36] The English government could take no more.

In bringing to a close Paine's attacks on the English monarchy, it may be wise to observe that he sometimes failed fully to foresee the power which tradition has over the minds of men—a failure which he shared with the natural rights theorists in general. He too often felt that if only men could be brought to a knowledge of right political principles, they would at once throw off oppressive forms of government. Unlike many an eighteenth-century perfectionist, who was waiting patiently for the millennium, Paine desired and often expected immediate results. In dedicating the second part of the *Rights of Man* to Lafayette, Paine observed that he and his friend differed in but one point, which did not concern the "principles of government" but "time." "That which you suppose accomplishable in fourteen or fifteen years," Paine triumphantly declares, "I may believe practicable in a much shorter period." [37] This was plainly written before the Reign of Terror in France—before the rise to power of Napoleon Bonaparte. Indeed, Paine's optimism in the *Rights of Man* led him at moments to believe that most of the monarchies of Europe were on the very point of falling. With an inconsistency after all so typical of the thinking of his age this man, whose political theory could exhibit such marked pragmatic values, could also assert, "I do not believe that monarchy and aristocracy will continue seven years longer in any of the enlightened countries in Europe." [38] But then again this sentence was penned before the Reign of Terror!

IV

The years between Paine's going to France in 1787 and his confinement in the Luxembourg prison in 1793 must have been

[35] *Ibid.*, III, 68.   [36] *Ibid.*, III, 91.   [37] *Ibid.*, II, 392.
[38] *Ibid.*, II, 398.

an interlude punctuated by moments of enthusiasm and even happiness. During this period he made several trips between France and England. In France he had ample opportunity to talk with Jefferson, minister to that country until 1789. Soon Paine was eyewitness of the early events of the French Revolution. He was on terms of familiarity with Lafayette, who gave Paine the key to the Bastille to present to Washington. It is said that he even helped to draft the "Declaration of Rights." And so Paine, who loved always to be in the midst of history in the making, played his inconspicuous part in the French Revolution. After King Louis' attempted flight in June, 1791, he wrote "A Republican Manifesto," probably issued as a broadside, denouncing the King's "abdication" and arousing the people to continued rebellion. Looking forward to the conclusion of the second part of the *Rights of Man*, to be published the following year, Paine presents his familiar argument for the abolition of monarchy when he speaks of "The thirty millions [of francs] which it costs to support a King in the éclat of stupid brutal luxury. . . ."[1] Tradition has it that Paine and Duchâtelet placarded the buildings of Paris with the "Manifesto" and even nailed a copy to the door of the building where the Assembly convened.

The second phase of his participation in the Revolution, beginning in 1792, after he had escaped from England, was fraught with grave consequences for Paine. Earlier in the same year the Assembly had bestowed upon him the title of citizen and he was later elected a representative to the Convention. In an "Address," now in his collected works, Paine accepted with gratitude these honors and reminded his "fellow citizens" that it had been his fate to bear a part "in the commencement and complete establishment of one revolution (I mean the Revolution of America)."[2] But Paine soon found himself enmeshed in French politics which, owing partly to his slender knowledge of the language, but perhaps even more to his ignorance of the French mind, he failed fully to understand. He was mainly allied to the Girondists, who some of Paine's biographers believe used him as a political tool. Among other conservative measures he advocated sparing the life

[1] Conway, III, 2.   [2] *Ibid.*, III, 98.

of the King. With the coming into power of Robespierre and the Jacobins, Paine shortly found himself in disfavor. He now attended less frequently the meetings of the Convention; and by the end of 1793 he was imprisoned. Gouverneur Morris, the American minister, who was one of Paine's bitter enemies, seems to have taken no measures to effect his release, though giving the impression to the American government that he had done all in his power. In any case, Paine remained in prison for a period of ten months, suffering, during much of that time, from serious illness. Finally James Monroe, the new ambassador, after much diplomatic maneuvering, secured his release.

For eighteen months Paine remained at Monroe's home endeavoring to regain his health. In 1795 he tried once again to occupy his seat in the French National Convention, which was then considering the adoption of a constitution. Among other things, Paine disapproved of certain property restrictions which it was proposed to place on suffrage. In preparation for a speech he intended to be delivered for him at the Convention, he wrote and apparently had distributed among the members a pamphlet entitled *Dissertation on First Principles of Government*, which was published in Paris in 1795. This work, which is reprinted entire in the present volume, brings together in brief compass much of the essential political thinking of Paine. In part a digest of some of his major ideas on government set forth in the *Rights of Man*, Paine stresses what he calls "the principle of equal rights,"[3] insisting that "The right of voting for representatives is the primary right by which other rights are protected."[4] With the Convention thus prepared, in July, 1795, he stood before the body while a secretary read his speech in French. Paine here pointed out that the proposed limitations on suffrage violated the "Declaration of Rights." No one is said to have spoken in support of Paine's plea, nor was his suggestion heeded in the final adoption of the Constitution. He did not again appear before the Convention.

These days spent in Monroe's home must have been sad for Paine. Distressed by bodily disease, he was manifestly disap-

[3] P. 170.   [4] P. 165.

pointed by the inadequate functioning of republicanism in France. But all was far from right in America too. Disappointment turned to disillusion and bitterness as he contemplated his imprisonment in the Luxembourg, not as the act of a few political fanatics in France, but, owing mainly to the meanness and defection of one man in America—George Washington—to whose rescue he had come in the ninth *Crisis* and on whom he had lavished so much extravagant praise in print. The "Letter to George Washington" (1796) is a difficult document for an American to read with complete objectivity. Yet if we may for the moment look squarely at the facts, it is impossible not to see that, in failing to investigate personally Paine's imprisonment, Washington had been negligent in performing his duties as President of the United States. The fact that Gouverneur Morris, the minister to France, had given Washington the impression that all possible influence had been exerted to effect Paine's release does not excuse Washington, since he was fully aware of the enmity between Morris and Paine. But the letter, though penned in a mood of bitterness sharply accentuated by ill health, was plainly the product of indiscretion and tactlessness. By the time this letter was penned, America had broken politically into two sharply opposed parties—the Federalists and the Republicans (or Anti-Federalists). Paine now found it necessary to align himself with the latter group; yet, as he observes early in the letter, although he was opposed to certain things in the Federal Constitution, he was among the first, as we have seen, to advocate the consolidating of "the States into a Federal Government." [5] Hence there was a real sense in which the term "Anti-Federalist" could not justly be applied to him; and he and Washington (whatever the latter might think) did not necessarily stand at opposite political poles. "The part I acted in the American Revolution," Paine asserts, "is well known"; [6] and, as we have amply shown, Paine was right in his assertion that he had "had America constantly in mind" in all the political writing which he did abroad. [7] He had never denied America; and the "Washington of politics" [8] was responsible for Paine's undoing.

[5] Conway, III, 214.   [6] *Ibid.*, III, 217.   [7] *Ibid.*, III, 216.
[8] *Ibid.*, III, 213.

Paine's denunciations in the letter presently became more personal: "Elevated to the chair of the Presidency, you assumed the merit of everything to yourself, and the natural ingratitude of your constitution began to appear." [9] Surely "it was the duty of the Executive Department in America, to have made (at least) some inquiries about me, as soon as it heard of my imprisonment." [10]

After a lengthy attack on the Jay Treaty,[11] Paine concluded his letter with a burst of rhetorical passion for which many an American will find it difficult to forgive the author of *Common Sense*:

And as to you, Sir, treacherous in private friendship (for so you have been to me, and that in the day of danger) and a hypocrite in public life, the world will be puzzled to decide whether you are an apostate or an impostor; whether you have abandoned good principles, or whether you ever had any.[12]

We now move with some relief to a saner work—indeed the last important pamphlet done by Paine abroad—*Agrarian Justice* (1797). Here he returns to the humanitarian vein which he had developed so effectively near the close of the *Rights of Man*—a plan for alleviating the condition of the poor of England. The title of the work is at first misleading since nowhere does Paine advocate an agrarian economy. The concept of agrarianism enters the work only in Paine's recognition that man in his original state had been close to the soil and had been dependent on the land for his existence. "It is a position not to be controverted," he notes, "that the earth, in its natural, uncultivated state was, and ever would have continued to be, *the common property of the human race*. In that state every man would have been born to property." [13] But the land for centuries has been slowly coming into the hands of the few, who now possess estates that threaten

[9] *Ibid.*, III, 217.   [10] *Ibid.*, III, 220.

[11] The first treaty with England after the peace treaty of 1783, negotiated in 1795 by John Jay. This treaty marked the beginning of regular diplomatic and commercial relations with Britain.   [12] *Ibid.*, III, 252.

[13] *Ibid.*, III, 329.

the well-being of England. Paine, it must be noted, is far from advocating a return to nature. "It is always possible to go from the natural to the civilized state, but it is never possible to go from the civilized to the natural state." [14] The problem facing the poor lies in a complicated dispossession involved in the gradual development of civilization. How, then, can the dispossessed ever be given justice? Paine's answer is to place an inheritance tax on personal property and on land. Part of his plan for the distribution among the poor of the monies thus acquired by the government Paine puts into these words:

> To create a national fund, out of which there shall be paid to every person, when arrived at the age of twenty-one years, the sum of fifteen pounds sterling, as a compensation in part, for the loss of his or her natural inheritance, by the introduction of the system of landed property.[15]

V

It seems proper to assume that Paine by the close of the eighteenth century recognized that he no longer had anything to contribute to the political progress of England and France. His thoughts once more returned to America. While Jefferson was still the Republican nominee, Paine had written to Jefferson expressing the wish that he be given passage to America "in a public vessel." Upon his election Jefferson replied in a cordial letter, offering Paine convoy in the sloop of war, *Maryland*. In addition, the President replied that he was in hopes that Paine would find the country "returned generally to sentiments worthy of former times. In these it will be your glory to have steadily labored and with as much effect as any man living. That you may long live to continue your useful labors and to reap the reward in the thankfulness of nations is my sincere prayer." [1] Later in 1801 Paine wrote to Jefferson congratulating him on his election, though for the time being declining his invitation to use the *Maryland*. In September of the following year, however, Paine arrived in Baltimore.

[14] *Ibid.*, III, 328.   [15] *Ibid.*, III, 331.
[1] Conway, III, 428.

Because of his notorious letter to Washington and of his attacks on formal religion in the *Age of Reason* (1794-96), he returned for the most part a man hated and despised. For a time he felt that even Jefferson was shunning him, but Jefferson was not long in assuring Paine of his friendship and admiration. Besides Jefferson, Robert Fulton and John Wesley Jarvis, the painter, in whose home Paine resided for five months, proved staunch friends.

With his return to America Paine had no other course but to choose a political party and to fight as best he still could for the principles of that party. His most significant political writing done during Jefferson's administration consisted of public letters, eight in number, addressed "To the Citizens of the United States" (1802, 1803, 1805). Though somewhat rambling and incoherent, these letters were obviously an attempt to strengthen Jefferson's hand in the difficult task which that statesman had taken upon himself in the face of an opposing political party. Paine still contended that essentially he was a Federalist if by Federalist was "to be understood one who was for cementing the Union by a general government operating equally over all the States, in all matters that embraced the common interest." [2] And Paine has much to say about "Those who once figured as leaders under the assumed and fraudulent name of *federalism.*" [3] Indeed, America had had her own "Reign of Terror"—"the latter end of the Washington Administration, and the whole of that of Adams." [4] These letters were unquestionably of assistance in paving the way for Jefferson's re-election.

In numerous other essays and letters Paine now sought to support the Republican cause. Among these is "A Challenge to the Federalists to Declare their Principles." In this paper he asserts that the principles of the Republicans are well known and incontrovertible—"that sovereignty resides in the great mass of the people, and that the persons they elect are the representatives of that sovereignty itself." But the Federalists "have no principles, and are mere *snarlers*, or . . . their principles are too bad to be

---

[2] *Ibid.,* III, 386.   [3] Philadelphia *Aurora,* June 7, 1805.

[4] Conway, III, 392. Reference here is to John Adams, second President of the United States (1796-1800).

told." "As to the inconsistencies, contradictions, and falsehoods of the Federal faction, they are too numerous to be counted." [5] Let the Federalists, therefore, declare their principles if they can! Just before his death Paine became involved in a political controversy with James Cheetham, editor of the New York *American Citizen,* a newspaper of strong Federalist, not to say monarchical, leanings. A portion of this controversy centered about some of Paine's recent comments on the English monarchy made in the same spirit of Anglophobia characteristic of the *Rights of Man.* By the time of his death Paine had come to identify Federalism with a devotion to England. Cheetham undertook to answer these aspersions on England; and Paine penned several replies quite in the manner of the eighteenth-century satirists sparing no offensive or coarse detail. He describes Cheetham as "an ugly-tempered man," who "carries the evidence of it in the vulgarity and forbiddingness of his countenance—God has set a mark upon Cain." [6] Cheetham finally retaliated with a scathing biography of Paine published the year of Paine's death.

Alas for the Reign of Terror! Paine was never the same man after his imprisonment in the Luxembourg and the defection of Washington, exaggerated beyond all normal proportions. Born always to enjoy the very breath of liberty, Paine had met with a doom so very wretched. In writing *Common Sense,* he had asserted that he espoused no political party; elsewhere he had declared himself "a citizen of the world." Now in old age he became unpleasantly partisan and was a man almost without a country. Not even Jefferson's strong friendship could redeem him in the eyes of his countrymen. Soured and disillusioned he went to the grave.

Yet this must not be our final appraisal of Thomas Paine. It is our hope to have demonstrated that, despite the human frailties that attend ever upon genius, Paine was one of those great humanitarian spirits who illuminate with rare intensity the age into which they are born. Remember him, then, as the apostle of political liberty and the spokesman of the common man in America—in England—and in France!

[5] 1839 ed., II, 460-461.   [6] *Ibid.,* II, 490-491.

SELECTED BIBLIOGRAPHY

Paine's Major Political Works

Common Sense (1776).

The American Crisis (15 papers published during the war, 1770-1783; the last paper, number 16, published after the war, December 9, 1783).

Public Good (1780).

Dissertations on Government; the Affairs of the Bank; and Paper Money (1786).

Rights of Man (Part I, 1791; Part II, 1792).

Dissertation on First Principles of Government (1795).

Agrarian Justice (1797).

Collected Works

The Political Writings of Thomas Paine. 2 vols. Charlestown, Mass., 1824.

Clark, Harry H., ed., *Six New Letters of Thomas Paine.* Madison, Wisconsin, 1939.

Conway, Moncure D., ed., *The Writings of Thomas Paine.* 4 vols. New York, 1894-1896.

Foner, Philip S., ed., *The Complete Writings of Thomas Paine.* 2 vols. New York, 1945.

Van der Weyde, William M., ed., *The Life and Works of Thomas Paine.* 10 vols. New York, 1925.

Collateral Reading

Blunk, R., *Thomas Paine, Ein Leben für Amerika.* Berlin, 1936.

Bradford, Gamaliel, "Damaged Souls," *Harper's Magazine,* CXLVI, 369-378, Feb., 1923.

Brailsford, H. N., *Shelley, Godwin, and Their Circle.* New York, 1913.

Brinton, Crane, "Thomas Paine." *Dictionary of American Biography*, Vol. XIV. New York, 1934.

Burke, Edmund, *Reflections on the French Revolution*, edited by W. Alison Phillips and C. B. Phillips. Cambridge, England, 1912; revised, 1929.

Clark, Harry H., "Thomas Paine," Introduction to *Representative Selections*, published in "American Writers Series." New York, 1944

Conway, Moncure D., *The Life of Thomas Paine*. 2 vols. New York, 1892.

Davidson, Philip, *Propaganda and the American Revolution, 1763-1783*. Chapel Hill, N. C., 1941.

Dorfman, H., "The Economic Philosophy of Thomas Paine," *Political Science Quarterly*, LIII, 372-386, Sept., 1938.

Hall, W. P., *British Radicalism, 1791-97*. New York, 1912.

Link, E. P., *Democratic-Republican Societies, 1790-1800*. New York, 1942.

Merriam, C. E., Jr., "Thomas Paine's Political Theories," *Political Science Quarterly*, XIV, 389-404, Sept., 1899.

Parrington, Vernon L., *The Colonial Mind, 1620-1800*. New York, 1927.

Pearson, Hesketh, *Tom Paine, Friend of Mankind*. New York, 1936.

Penniman, Howard, "Thomas Paine—Democrat," *American Political Science Review*, XXXVII, 244-262, April, 1943.

Persinger, C. E., "The Political Philosophy of Thomas Paine," *Graduate Bulletin* of The University of Nebraska, series VI, no. 3, July, 1901.

Sheldon, Frederick, "Tom Paine's First Appearance in America," *Atlantic Monthly*, IV, 565-575, Nov., 1859.

—— "Thomas Paine's Second Appearance in the United States," *Atlantic Monthly*, IV, 1-17, July, 1859.

—— "Thomas Paine in England and in France," *Atlantic Monthly*, IV, 690-709, Dec., 1859.

Smith, Frank, "New Light on Thomas Paine's First Year in America, 1775," *American Literature*, I, 347-371, Jan., 1930.

—— "The Date of Thomas Paine's First Arrival in America," *American Literature*, III, 317-318, Nov., 1931.

Stephen, Leslie, "Thomas Paine," *Dictionary of National Biography*, Vol. XLIII.

Tyler, M. C., *Literary History of the American Revolution—1763-1783*. 2 vols. New York, 1897.

Van Doren, Carl, "Thomas Paine," *American Writers on American Literature*, edited by John Macy. New York, 1931.

Woodward, W. E., *Tom Paine; America's Godfather*. New York. 1945.

COMMON SENSE

ADDRESSED TO
INHABITANTS OF AMERICA

{ A NEW EDITION, 1776 }

COMMON SENSE

INTRODUCTION

PERHAPS THE SENTIMENTS CONTAINED IN THE FOLLOWING pages are not *yet* sufficiently fashionable to procure them general favor; a long habit of not thinking a thing *wrong* gives it a superficial appearance of being *right*, and raises at first a formidable outcry in defense of custom. But the tumult soon subsides. Time makes more converts than reason.

As a long and violent abuse of power is generally the means of calling the right of it in question (and in matters, too, which might never have been thought of, had not the sufferers been aggravated into the inquiry), and as the King of England has undertaken in his *own right* to support the Parliament in what he calls *theirs*, and as the good people of this country are grievously oppressed by the combination, they have an undoubted privilege to inquire into the pretensions of both and equally to reject the usurpation of either.

In the following sheets, the author has studiously avoided everything which is personal among ourselves. Compliments as well as censure to individuals make no part thereof. The wise and the worthy need not the triumph of a pamphlet; and those whose sentiments are injudicious or unfriendly will cease of themselves, unless too much pains are bestowed upon their conversion.

The cause of America is in a great measure the cause of all mankind. Many circumstances have and will arise which are not local but universal, and through which the principles of all lovers of mankind are affected and in the event of which their affections are interested. The laying a country desolate with fire and sword, declaring war against the natural rights of all mankind, and extirpating the defenders thereof from the face of the earth is the concern of every man to whom nature has given the power of feeling, of which class, regardless of party censure, is the

AUTHOR

3

P. S. [a] The publication of this new edition has been delayed, with a view of taking notice (had it been necessary) of any attempt to refute the doctrine of independence. As no answer has yet appeared, it is now presumed that none will, the time needful for getting such a performance ready for the public being considerably past.

Who the author of this production is, is wholly unnecessary to the public, as the object for attention is the *doctrine itself*, not the *man*. Yet it may not be unnecessary to say that he is unconnected with any party and under no sort of influence, public or private, but the influence of reason and principle.

Philadelphia, February 14, 1776

COMMON SENSE

OF THE ORIGIN AND DESIGN OF GOVERNMENT IN GENERAL. WITH CONCISE REMARKS ON THE ENGLISH CONSTITUTION

SOME WRITERS have so confounded society with government as to leave little or no distinction between them, whereas they are not only different but have different origins. Society is produced by our wants, and government by our wickedness; the former promotes our happiness *positively* by uniting our affections, the latter *negatively* by restraining our vices. The one encourages intercourse, the other creates distinctions. The first is a patron, the last a punisher.

Society in every state is a blessing, but government even in its best state is but a necessary evil, in its worst state an intolerable one; for when we suffer or are exposed to the same miseries *by a government* which we might expect in a country *without government*, our calamity is heightened by reflecting that we furnish the means by which we suffer. Government, like dress, is the badge of lost innocence; the palaces of kings are built on the ruins of the bowers of paradise. For were the impulses of conscience clear, uniform, and irresistibly obeyed, man would need no other lawgiver; but that not being the case, he finds it necessary to

[a] [The following is Paine's postscript to the Preface in the New Edition.]

surrender up a part of his property to furnish means for the protection of the rest, and this he is induced to do by the same prudence which in every other case advises him out of two evils to choose the least. Wherefore, security being the true design and end of government, it unanswerably follows that whatever form thereof appears most likely to ensure it to us, with the least expense and greatest benefit, is preferable to all others.

In order to gain a clear and just idea of the design and end of government, let us suppose a small number of persons settled in some sequestered part of the earth, unconnected with the rest; they will then represent the first peopling of any country, or of the world. In this state of natural liberty, society will be their first thought. A thousand motives will excite them thereto; the strength of one man is so unequal to his wants and his mind so unfitted for perpetual solitude that he is soon obliged to seek assistance and relief of another, who in his turn requires the same. Four or five united would be able to raise a tolerable dwelling in the midst of a wilderness, but one man might labor out the common period of life without accomplishing anything; when he had felled his timber, he could not remove it, nor erect it after it was removed; hunger in the meantime would urge him from his work and every different want call him a different way. Disease, nay even misfortune, would be death; for though neither might be mortal, yet either would disable him from living and reduce him to a state in which he might rather be said to perish than to die.

Thus necessity, like a gravitating power, would soon form our newly arrived emigrants into society, the reciprocal blessings of which would supersede and render the obligations of law and government unnecessary while they remained perfectly just to each other; but as nothing but Heaven is impregnable to vice, it will unavoidably happen that in proportion as they surmount the first difficulties of emigration, which bound them together in a common cause, they will begin to relax in their duty and attachment to each other, and this remissness will point out the necessity of establishing some form of government to supply the defect of moral virtue.

Some convenient tree will afford them a statehouse, under the branches of which the whole colony may assemble to deliberate on public matters. It is more than probable that their first laws will have the title only of regulations and be enforced by no other penalty than public disesteem. In this first parliament every man by natural right will have a seat.

But as the colony increases, the public concerns will increase likewise, and the distance at which the members may be separated will render it too inconvenient for all of them to meet on every occasion as at first, when their number was small, their habitations near, and the public concerns few and trifling. This will point out the convenience of their consenting to leave the legislative part to be managed by a select number chosen from the whole body, who are supposed to have the same concerns at stake which those have who appointed them and who will act in the same manner as the whole body would act were they present. If the colony continue increasing, it will become necessary to augment the number of representatives; and that the interest of every part of the colony may be attended to, it will be found best to divide the whole into convenient parts, each part sending its proper number; and that the *elected* might never form to themselves an interest separate from the *electors,* prudence will point out the propriety of having elections often, because as the *elected* might by that means return and mix again with the general body of the *electors* in a few months, their fidelity to the public will be secured by the prudent reflection of not making a rod for themselves. And as this frequent interchange will establish a common interest with every part of the community, they will mutually and naturally support each other, and on this (not on the unmeaning name of king) depends the *strength of government and the happiness of the governed*.

Here then is the origin and rise of government, namely, a mode rendered necessary by the inability of moral virtue to govern the world; here too is the design and end of government, viz., freedom and security. And however our eyes may be dazzled with show or our ears deceived by sound, however prejudice may warp our wills or interest darken our understanding, the simple voice of nature and reason will say it is right.

I draw my idea of the form of government from a principle in nature which no art can overturn, viz., that the more simple anything is, the less liable it is to be disordered and the easier repaired when disordered; and with this maxim in view I offer a few remarks on the so much boasted constitution of England. That it was noble for the dark and slavish times in which it was erected is granted. When the world was overrun with tyranny, the least remove therefrom was a glorious rescue. But that it is imperfect, subject to convulsions, and incapable of producing what it seems to promise is easily demonstrated.

Absolute governments (though the disgrace of human nature) have this advantage with them: that they are simple; if the people suffer, they know the head from which their suffering springs, know likewise the remedy, and are not bewildered by a variety of causes and cures. But the constitution of England is so exceedingly complex that the nation may suffer for years together without being able to discover in which part the fault lies; some will say in one and some in another, and every political physician will advise a different medicine.

I know it is difficult to get over local or long-standing prejudices; yet if we will suffer ourselves to examine the component parts of the English constitution, we shall find them to be the base remains of two ancient tyrannies, compounded with some new republican materials:

First, the remains of monarchical tyranny in the person of the king.

Secondly, the remains of aristocratical tyranny in the persons of the peers.

Thirdly, the new republican materials in the persons of the Commons, on whose virtue depends the freedom of England.

The two first, by being hereditary, are independent of the people; wherefore, in a *constitutional sense,* they contribute nothing toward the freedom of the state.

To say that the constitution of England is a *union* of three powers, reciprocally *checking* each other, is farcical; either the words have no meaning or they are flat contradictions.

To say that the Commons is a check upon the king presupposes two things:

First, that the king is not to be trusted without being looked after, or, in other words, that a thirst for absolute power is the natural disease of monarchy.

Secondly, that the Commons, by being appointed for that purpose, are either wiser or more worthy of confidence than the crown.

But as the same constitution which gives the Commons a power to check the king by withholding the supplies gives afterward the king a power to check the Commons by empowering him to reject their other bills, it again supposes that the king is wiser than those whom it has already supposed to be wiser than him. A mere absurdity!

There is something exceedingly ridiculous in the composition of monarchy; it first excludes a man from the means of information, yet empowers him to act in cases where the highest judgment is required. The state of a king shuts him from the world, yet the business of a king requires him to know it thoroughly; wherefore the different parts, by unnaturally opposing and destroying each other, prove the whole character to be absurd and useless.

Some writers have explained the English constitution thus: the king, say they, is one, the people another; the peers are a house in behalf of the king, the Commons in behalf of the people; but this has all the distinctions of a house divided against itself, and though the expressions be pleasantly arranged, yet when examined they appear idle and ambiguous; and it will always happen that the nicest construction that words are capable of, when applied to the description of something which either cannot exist or is too incomprehensible to be within the compass of description, will be words of sound only, and though they may amuse the ear, they cannot inform the mind; for this explanation includes a previous question, viz., *how came the king by a power which the people are afraid to trust and always obliged to check?* Such a power could not be the gift of a wise people, neither can any power *which needs checking* be from God; yet the provision which the constitution makes supposes such a power to exist.

But the provision is unequal to the task; the means either cannot or will not accomplish the end, and the whole affair is a Felo-de-se; for as the greater weight will always carry up the less, and as all the wheels of a machine are put in motion by one, it only remains to know which power in the constitution has the most weight, for that will govern; and though the others, or a part of them, may clog or, as the phrase is, check the rapidity of its motion, yet so long as they cannot stop it, their endeavors will be ineffectual. The first moving power will at last have its way, and what it wants in speed is supplied by time.

That the crown is this overbearing part in the English constitution needs not be mentioned, and that it derives its whole consequence merely from being the giver of places and pensions is self-evident; wherefore, though we have been wise enough to shut and lock a door against absolute monarchy, we at the same time have been foolish enough to put the crown in possession of the key.

The prejudice of Englishmen in favor of their own government by king, lords, and Commons arises as much or more from national pride than reason. Individuals are undoubtedly safer in England than in some other countries; but the will of the king is as much the law of the land in Britain as in France, with this difference, that instead of proceeding directly from his mouth, it is handed to the people under the more formidable shape of an act of Parliament. For the fate of Charles the First [1] has only made kings more subtle—not more just.

Wherefore, laying aside all national pride and prejudice in favor of modes and forms, the plain truth is that *it is wholly owing to the constitution of the people, and not to the constitution of the government,* that the crown is not as oppressive in England as in Turkey.

An inquiry into the *constitutional errors* in the English form of government is at this time highly necessary; for as we are never in proper condition of doing justice to others while we continue under the influence of some leading partiality, so neither are we capable of doing it to ourselves while we remain fettered by any obstinate prejudice. And as a man who is attached to a prostitute is unfitted to choose or judge of a wife, so any prepossession in favor of a rotten constitution of government will disable us from discerning a good one.

Of Monarchy and Hereditary Succession

Mankind being originally equals in the order of creation, the equality could only be destroyed by some subsequent circumstance; the distinctions of rich and poor may in a great measure be accounted for, and that without having recourse to the harsh, ill-sounding names of oppression and avarice. Oppression is often the *consequence* but seldom or never the *means* of riches; and though avarice will preserve a man from being necessitously poor, it generally makes him too timorous to be wealthy.

But there is another and greater distinction for which no truly natural or religious reason can be assigned, and that is the distinction of men into kings and subjects. Male and female are the distinctions of nature, good and bad the distinctions of heaven; but how a race of men came into the world so exalted above the rest, and distinguished like some new species, is worth inquiring into, and whether they are the means of happiness or of misery to mankind.

In the early ages of the world, according to the scripture chronology, there were no kings, the consequence of which was there were no wars; it is the pride of kings which throws mankind into confusion. Holland, without a king, has enjoyed more peace for this last century than any of the monarchical governments in Europe. Antiquity favors the same remark, for the quiet and rural lives of the first patriarchs have a happy something in them which vanishes when we come to the history of Jewish royalty.

Government by kings was first introduced into the world by the heathens, from whom the children of Israel copied the custom. It was the most prosperous invention the devil ever set on foot for the promotion of idolatry. The heathens paid divine honors to their deceased kings, and the Christian world has improved on the plan by doing the same to their living ones. How impious is the title of sacred majesty applied to a worm, who in the midst of his splendor is crumbling into dust!

As the exalting one man so greatly above the rest cannot be justified on the equal rights of nature, so neither can it be defended on the authority of scripture; for the will of the Almighty, as declared by Gideon and the prophet Samuel, expressly disapproves of government by kings. All antimonarchical parts of scripture have been very smoothly glossed over in monarchical governments, but they undoubtedly merit the attention of countries which have their governments yet to form. "Render unto Caesar the things which are Caesar's" [2] is the scripture doctrine of courts; yet it is no support of monarchical government, for the Jews at that time were without a king and in a state of vassalage to the Romans.

Near three thousand years passed away, from the Mosaic account of the creation, till the Jews under a national delusion requested a king. Till then their form of government (except in extraordinary cases where the Almighty interposed) was a kind of republic, administered by a judge and the elders of the tribes. Kings they had none, and it was held sinful to acknowledge any being under that title but the Lord of Hosts. And when a man seriously reflects on the idolatrous homage which is paid to the persons of kings, he need not wonder that the Almighty, ever jealous of his honor, should disapprove of a form of government which so impiously invades the prerogative of heaven.

Monarchy is ranked in scripture as one of the sins of the Jews, for which a curse in reserve is denounced against them. The history of that transaction is worth attending to.

The children of Israel being oppressed by the Midianites, Gideon [3] marched against them with a small army, and victory through the divine interposition decided in his favor. The Jews, elate with success and attributing it to the generalship of Gideon, proposed making him a king, saying, "Rule thou over us, thou and thy son, and thy son's son." Here was temptation in its fullest extent—not a kingdom only, but a hereditary one—but Gideon, in the piety of his soul, replied, "I will not rule over you, neither shall my son rule over you. *The Lord shall rule over you*." Words need not be more explicit; Gideon does not decline the honor, but denies their right to give it; neither does he compliment them with invented declarations of his thanks, but in the positive style of a prophet charges them with disaffection to their proper sovereign, the King of Heaven.

About one hundred and thirty years after this, they fell again into the same error. The hankering which the Jews had for the idolatrous customs of the heathens is something exceedingly unaccountable; but so it was that, laying hold of the misconduct of Samuel's [4] two sons, who were entrusted with some secular concerns, they came in an abrupt and clamorous manner to Samuel, saying, "Behold thou art old, and thy sons walk not in thy ways, now make us a king to judge us like all the other nations." And here we cannot but observe that their motives were bad, viz., that they might be like unto other nations, i.e., the heathens, whereas their true glory lay in being as much unlike them as possible. "But the thing displeased Samuel when they said, Give us a king to judge us; and Samuel prayed unto the Lord, and the Lord said unto Samuel, Hearken unto the voice of the people in all that they say unto thee, for they have not rejected thee, but they have rejected me, *that I should not reign over them.* According to all the works which they have done since the day that I brought them up out of Egypt even unto this day, wherewith they have forsaken me, and served other Gods: so do they also unto thee. Now therefore hearken unto their voice, howbeit, protest solemnly unto them and show them the manner of the king that shall reign over them," i.e., not of any particular king, but the general manner of the kings of the earth whom Israel was so eagerly copying after. And notwithstanding the great distance of time and difference of manners, the character is still in fashion. "And Samuel told all the words of the Lord unto the people, that asked of him a king. And he said, This shall be the manner of the king that shall reign over you; he will take your sons and appoint them for himself for his chariots and to be his horsemen, and some shall run before his chariots" (this description agrees with the present mode of impressing men); "and he will appoint him captains over thousands and captains over fifties, and will set them to ear his ground and to reap his harvest, and to make his instruments of war, and instruments of his chariots; and he will take your daughters to be confectionaries, and to be cooks, and to be bakers" (this describes the expense and luxury as well as the oppression of kings); "and he will take your fields and your olive yards, even the best of them, and give them to his servants; and he will take the tenth of your seed and of your vineyards, and give them to his officers and to his servants" (by which we see that bribery, corruption, and favoritism are the standing vices of kings); "and he will take the tenth of your men servants, and your maid servants, and your goodliest young men, and your asses, and put them to his work; and he will take the tenth of your sheep, and ye shall be his servants, and ye shall cry out in that day because of your king which ye shall have chosen, *and the Lord will not hear you in that day.*" This accounts for the continuation of monarchy; neither do the characters of the few good kings which have lived since either sanctify the title or blot out the sinfulness of the origin; the high encomium given of David takes no notice of him *officially as a king,* but only as a *man* after God's own heart. "Nevertheless the people refused to obey the voice of Samuel, and they said, Nay but we will have a king over us, that we may be like all the nations, and that our king may judge us, and go out before us and fight our battles." Samuel continued to reason with them, but to no purpose; he set before them their ingratitude, but all would not avail; and seeing them fully bent on their folly, he cried out, "I will call unto the Lord, and he shall send thunder and rain" (which was then a punishment, being in the time of wheat harvest) "that ye may perceive and see that your wickedness is great which ye have done in the sight of the Lord, *in asking you a king.* So Samuel called unto the Lord, and the Lord sent thunder and rain that day, and all the people greatly feared the Lord and Samuel. And all the people said unto Samuel, Pray for thy servants unto the Lord thy God that we die not, for *we have added unto our sins this evil, to ask a king.*" These portions of scripture are direct and positive. They admit of no equivocal construction. That the Almighty has here entered his protest against monarchical government is true, or the scripture is false. And a man has good reason to believe that there is as much of kingcraft as priestcraft in withholding the scripture from the public in popish countries. For monarchy in every instance is the popery of government.

To the evil of monarchy we have added that of hereditary succession; and as the first is a degradation and lessening of ourselves, so the second, claimed as a matter of right, is an insult and an imposition on posterity. For all men being originally equals, no one by birth could have a right to set up his own family in perpetual preference to all others forever; and though himself might deserve some decent degree of honors of his co-temporaries, yet his descendants might be far too unworthy to inherit them. One of the strongest natural proofs of the folly of hereditary right in kings is that nature disapproves it; otherwise she would not so frequently turn it into ridicule by giving mankind an *ass for a lion*.

Secondly, as no man at first could possess any other public honors than were bestowed upon him, so the givers of those honors could have no power to give away the right of posterity, and though they might say "We choose you for our head," they could not without manifest injustice to their children say "that your children and your children's children shall reign over ours forever." Because such an unwise, unjust, unnatural compact might (perhaps) in the next succession put them under the government of a rogue or a fool. Most wise men in their private sentiments have ever treated hereditary right with contempt; yet it is one of those evils which when once established is not easily removed; many submit from fear, others from superstition, and the more powerful part shares with the king the plunder of the rest.

This is supposing the present race of kings in the world to have had an honorable origin; whereas it is more than probable that, could we take off the dark covering of antiquity and trace them to their first rise, that we should find the first of them nothing better than the principal ruffian of some restless gang, whose savage manners or pre-eminence in subtilty obtained him the title of chief among plunderers and who, by increasing in power and extending his depredations, overawed the quiet and defenseless to purchase their safety by frequent contributions. Yet his electors could have no idea of giving hereditary right to his descendants, because such a perpetual exclusion of themselves was incompatible with the free and unrestrained principles they professed to live by. Wherefore hereditary succession in the early ages of monarchy could not take place as a matter of claim, but as something casual or complemental; but as few or no records were extant in those days, and traditionary history stuffed with fables, it was very easy, after the lapse of a few generations, to trump up some superstitious tale conveniently timed, Mahometlike, to cram hereditary right down the throats of the vulgar. Perhaps the disorders which threatened, or seemed to threaten, on the decease of a leader and the choice of a new one (for elections among ruffians could not be very orderly) induced many at first to favor hereditary pretensions; by which means it happened, as it has happened since, that what at first was submitted to as a convenience was afterward claimed as a right.

England since the conquest has known some few good monarchs, but groaned beneath a much larger number of bad ones; yet no man in his senses can say that their claim under William the Conqueror [5] is a very honorable one. A French bastard landing with an armed banditti and establishing himself king of England against the consent of the natives is in plain terms a very paltry, rascally original. It certainly has no divinity in it. However, it is needless to spend much time in exposing the folly of hereditary right; if there are any so weak as to believe it, let them promiscuously worship the ass and lion, and welcome. I shall neither copy their humility nor disturb their devotion.

Yet I should be glad to ask how they suppose kings came at first? The question admits but of three answers, viz., either by lot, by election, or by usurpation. If the first king was taken by lot, it establishes a precedent for the next, which excludes hereditary succession. Saul was by lot, yet the succession was not hereditary; neither does it appear from that transaction that there was any intention it ever should. If the first king of any country was by election, that likewise establishes a precedent for the next; for to say that the right of all future generations is taken away by the act of the first electors in their choice, not only of a king but of a family of kings, forever, has no parallel in or out of scripture but the doctrine of original sin, which supposes the free will of all men lost in Adam; and from such comparison, and it will admit of no other, hereditary succession can derive no glory. For as in Adam all sinned and as in the first electors all men obeyed, as in the one all mankind were subjected to Satan and in the other to sovereignty, as our innocence was lost in the first and our authority in the last, and as both disable us from reassuming some former state and privilege, it unanswerably follows that original sin and hereditary succession are parallels. Dishonorable rank! inglorious connection! yet the most subtle sophist cannot produce a juster simile.

As to usurpation, no man will be so hardy as to defend it; and that William the Conqueror was a usurper is a fact not to be contradicted. The plain truth is that the antiquity of English monarchy will not bear looking into.

But it is not so much the absurdity as the evil of hereditary succession which concerns mankind. Did it insure a race of good and wise men, it would have the seal of divine authority; but as it opens a door to the *foolish,* the *wicked,* and the *improper,* it has in it the nature of oppression. Men who look upon themselves born to reign and others to obey soon grow insolent. Selected from the rest of mankind, their minds are early poisoned by importance; and the world they act in differs so materially from the world at large that they have but little opportunity of knowing its true interests and, when they succeed to the government, are frequently the most ignorant and unfit of any throughout the dominions.

Another evil which attends hereditary succession is that the throne is subject to be possessed by a minor at any age, all which time the regency, acting under the cover of a king, have every opportunity and inducement to betray their trust. The same national misfortune happens when a king, worn out with age and infirmity, enters the last stage of human weakness. In both these cases the public becomes a prey to every miscreant who can tamper successfully with the follies either of age or infancy.

The most plausible plea which has ever been offered in favor of hereditary succession is that it preserves a nation from civil wars; and were this true it would be weighty, whereas it is the most barefaced falsity ever imposed upon mankind. The whole history of England disowns the fact. Thirty kings and two minors have reigned in that distracted kingdom since the conquest, in which time there have been (including the Revolution [b]) no less than eight civil wars and nineteen rebellions. Wherefore, instead of making for peace, it makes against it and destroys the very foundation it seems to stand on.

The contest for monarchy and succession between the houses of York and Lancaster [6] laid England in a scene of blood for many years. Twelve pitched battles besides skirmishes and sieges were fought between Henry and Edward. Twice was Henry prisoner to Edward, who in his turn was prisoner to Henry. And so uncertain is the fate of war and the temper of a nation, when nothing but personal matters are the ground of a quarrel, that Henry was taken in triumph from a prison to a palace, and Edward obliged to fly from a palace to a foreign land; yet, as sudden transitions of temper are seldom lasting, Henry in his turn was driven from the throne, and Edward recalled to succeed him. The Parliament always following the strongest side.

This contest began in the reign of Henry the Sixth and was not entirely extinguished till Henry the Seventh,[7] in whom the families were united. Including a period of sixty-seven years, viz., from 1422 to 1489.

In short, monarchy and succession have laid (not this or that kingdom only) but the world in blood and ashes. 'Tis a form of government which the word of God bears testimony against, and blood will attend it.

If we inquire into the business of a king, we shall find that in some countries they have none; and after sauntering away their lives without pleasure to themselves or advantage to the nation, withdraw from the scene and leave their successors to tread the same idle round. In absolute monarchies the whole weight of business, civil and military, lies on the king; the children of Israel in their request for a king urged this plea, "that he may judge us, and go out before us and fight our battles." But in the countries where he is neither a judge nor a general, as in England, a man would be puzzled to know what *is* his business.

[b] [Reference here is to the Revolution of 1688.]

The nearer any government approaches to a republic, the less business there is for a king. It is somewhat difficult to find a proper name for the government of England. Sir William Meredith [8] calls it a republic; but in its present state it is unworthy of the name, because the corrupt influence of the crown, by having all the places in its disposal, has so effectually swallowed up the power and eaten out the virtue of the House of Commons (the republican part in the constitution) that the government of England is nearly as monarchical as that of France or Spain. Men fall out with names without understanding them. For it is the republican and not the monarchical part of the constitution of England which Englishmen glory in, viz., the liberty of choosing a House of Commons from out of their own body—and it is easy to see that when republican virtues fail, slavery ensues. Why is the constitution of England sickly but because monarchy has poisoned the republic; the crown has engrossed the Commons.

In England a king has little more to do than to make war and give away places, which, in plain terms, is to impoverish the nation and set it together by the ears. A pretty business indeed for a man to be allowed eight hundred thousand sterling a year for, and worshiped into the bargain! Of more worth is one honest man to society, and in the sight of God, than all the crowned ruffians that ever lived.

THOUGHTS ON THE PRESENT STATE OF AMERICAN AFFAIRS

In the following pages I offer nothing more than simple facts, plain arguments, and common sense; and have no other preliminaries to settle with the reader than that he will divest himself of prejudice and prepossession, and suffer his reason and his feelings to determine for themselves; that he will put on, or rather that he will not put off, the true character of a man, and generously enlarge his views beyond the present day.

Volumes have been written on the subject of the struggle between England and America. Men of all ranks have embarked in the controversy, from different motives and with various designs; but all have been ineffectual, and the period of debate is closed. Arms as the last resource decide the contest; the appeal was the choice of the king, and the continent has accepted the challenge.

It has been reported of the late Mr. Pelham [9] (who, though an able minister, was not without his faults) that, on his being attacked in the House of Commons on the score that his measures were only of a temporary kind, replied, "they will last my time." Should a thought so fatal and unmanly possess the colonies in the present contest, the name of ancestors will be remembered by future generations with detestation.

The sun never shined on a cause of greater worth. 'Tis not the affair of a city, a county, a province, or a kingdom, but of a continent—of at least one-eighth part of the habitable globe. 'Tis not the concern of a day, a year, or an age; posterity are virtually involved in the contest, and will be more or less affected even to the end of time by the proceedings now. Now is the seed-time of continental union, faith, and honor. The least fracture now will be like a name engraved with the point of a pin on the tender rind of a young oak; the wound would enlarge with the tree, and posterity read it in full-grown characters.

By referring the matter from argument to arms, a new era for politics is struck—a new method of thinking has arisen. All plans, proposals, etc., prior to the nineteenth of April, i.e., to the commencement of hostilities,[10] are like the almanacs of the last year, which, though proper then, are superseded and useless now. Whatever was advanced by the advocates on either side of the question then terminated in one and the same point, viz., a union with Great Britain; the only difference between the parties was the method of effecting it—the one proposing force, the other friendship; but it has so far happened that the first has failed, and the second has withdrawn her influence.

As much has been said of the advantages of reconciliation, which, like an agreeable dream, has passed away and left us as we were, it is but right that we should examine the contrary side of the argument and inquire into some of the many material injuries which these colonies sustain, and always will sustain, by being connected with and dependent on Great Britain. To examine that connection and dependence on the principles of nature and common sense; to see what we have to trust to, if separated, and what we are to expect, if dependent.

I have heard it asserted by some that, as America has flourished under her former connection with Great Britain, the same connection is necessary toward her future happiness and will always have the same effect. Nothing can be more fallacious than this kind of argument. We may as well assert that because a child has thrived upon milk that it is never to have meat, or that the first twenty years of our lives is to become a precedent for the next twenty. But even this is admitting more than is true; for I answer roundly that America would have flourished as much, and probably much more, had no European power had anything to do with her. The commerce by which she has enriched herself are the necessaries of life and will always have a market while eating is the custom of Europe.

But she has protected us, say some. That she has engrossed us is true, and defended the continent at our expense as well as her own is admitted; and she would have defended Turkey from the same motive, viz., for the sake of trade and dominion.

Alas! we have been long led away by ancient prejudices and made large sacrifices to superstition. We have boasted the protection of Great Britain without considering that her motive was *interest,* not *attachment;* and that she did not protect us from *our enemies* on *our account* but from *her enemies* on *her own account,* from those who had no quarrel with us on any *other account* and who will always be our enemies on the *same account.* Let Britain waive her pretensions to the continent or the continent throw off the dependence, and we should be at peace with France and Spain, were they at war with Britain. The miseries of Hanover's last war [11] ought to warn us against connections.

It has lately been asserted in Parliament that the colonies have no relation to each other but through the parent country, i.e., that Pennsylvania and the Jerseys, and so on for the rest, are sister colonies by the way of England; this is certainly a very roundabout way of proving relationship, but it is the nearest and only true way of proving enemyship, if I may so call it. France and Spain never were, nor perhaps ever will be, our enemies as *Americans,* but as our being the *subjects of Great Britain.*

But Britain is the parent country, say some. Then the more shame upon her conduct. Even brutes do not devour their young nor savages make war upon their families; wherefore the assertion, if true, turns to her reproach; but it happens not to be true, or only partly so, and the phrase "parent" or "mother country" has been jesuitically adopted by the king and his parasites with a low papistical design of gaining an unfair bias on the credulous weakness of our minds. Europe, and not England, is the parent country of America. This New World has been the asylum for the persecuted lovers of civil and religious liberty from *every part* of Europe. Hither have they fled, not from the tender embraces of the mother, but from the cruelty of the monster; and it is so far true of England that the same tyranny which drove the first emigrants from home pursues their descendants still.

In this extensive quarter of the globe, we forget the narrow limits of three hundred and sixty miles (the extent of England) and carry our friendship on a larger scale; we claim brotherhood with every European Christian, and triumph in the generosity of the sentiment.

It is pleasant to observe by what regular gradations we surmount the force of local prejudices as we enlarge our acquaintance with the world. A man born in any town in England divided into parishes will naturally associate most with his fellow parishioners (because their interests in many cases will be common) and distinguish him by the name of "neighbor"; if he meet him but a few miles from home, he drops the narrow idea of a street and salutes him by the name of "townsman"; if he travel out of the county and meet him in any other, he forgets the minor divisions of street and town, and calls him "countryman," i.e., "countyman"; but if in their foreign excursions they should associate in France, or any other part of *Europe,* their local remembrance would be enlarged into that of "Englishmen." And by a just parity of reasoning, all Europeans meeting in America, or any other quarter of the globe, are "countrymen"; for England, Holland,

Germany, or Sweden, when compared with the whole, stand in the same places on the larger scale which the divisions of street, town, and county do on the smaller ones—distinctions too limited for continental minds. Not one third of the inhabitants, even of this province,[c] are of English descent. Wherefore I reprobate the phrase of parent or mother country applied to England only as being false, selfish, narrow, and ungenerous.

But, admitting that we were all of English descent, what does it amount to? Nothing. Britain, being now an open enemy, extinguishes every other name and title; and to say that reconciliation is our duty is truly farcical. The first king of England of the present line (William the Conqueror) was a Frenchman, and half the peers of England are descendants from the same country; wherefore, by the same method of reasoning, England ought to be governed by France.

Much has been said of the united strength of Britain and the colonies, that in conjunction they might bid defiance to the world. But this is mere presumption; the fate of war is uncertain, neither do the expressions mean anything; for this continent would never suffer itself to be drained of inhabitants to support the British arms in either Asia, Africa, or Europe.

Besides, what have we to do with setting the world at defiance? Our plan is commerce, and that, well attended to, will secure us the peace and friendship of all Europe; because it is the interest of all Europe to have America a free port. Her trade will always be a protection, and her barrenness of gold and silver secure her from invaders.

I challenge the warmest advocate for reconciliation to show a single advantage that this continent can reap by being connected with Great Britain. I repeat the challenge; not a single advantage is derived. Our corn will fetch its price in any market in Europe, and our imported goods must be paid for, buy them where we will.

But the injuries and disadvantages we sustain by that connection are without number, and our duty to mankind at large, as well as to ourselves, instruct us to renounce the alliance; because any submission to or dependence on Great Britain tends

[c] [Pennsylvania.]

directly to involve this continent in European wars and quarrels and sets us at variance with nations who would otherwise seek our friendship and against whom we have neither anger nor complaint. As Europe is our market for trade, we ought to form no partial connection with any part of it. It is the true interest of America to steer clear of European contentions, which she never can do while, by her dependence on Britain, she is made the makeweight in the scale of British politics.

Europe is too thickly planted with kingdoms to be long at peace; and whenever a war breaks out between England and any foreign power, the trade of America goes to ruin *because of her connection with Britain.* The next war may not turn out like the last; and should it not, the advocates for reconciliation now will be wishing for separation then, because neutrality in that case would be a safer convoy than a man-of-war. Everything that is right or natural pleads for separation. The blood of the slain, the weeping voice of nature cries, *" 'Tis time to part."* Even the distance at which the Almighty has placed England and America is a strong and natural proof that the authority of the one over the other was never the design of heaven. The time likewise at which the continent was discovered adds weight to the argument, and the manner in which it was peopled increases the force of it. The Reformation was preceded by the discovery of America—as if the Almighty graciously meant to open a sanctuary to the persecuted in future years, when home should afford neither friendship nor safety.

The authority of Great Britain over this continent is a form of government which sooner or later must have an end. And a serious mind can draw no true pleasure by looking forward, under the painful and positive conviction that what he calls "the present constitution" is merely temporary. As parents, we can have no joy, knowing that this government is not sufficiently lasting to insure anything which we may bequeath to posterity. And by a plain method of argument, as we are running the next generation into debt, we ought to do the work of it; otherwise we use them meanly and pitifully. In order to discover the line of our duty rightly, we should take our children in our hand and fix our station a few years farther into life; that eminence will present a prospect which a few present fears and prejudices conceal from our sight.

Though I would carefully avoid giving unnecessary offense, yet I am inclined to believe that all those who espouse the doctrine of reconciliation may be included within the following descriptions. Interested men, who are not to be trusted, weak men who *cannot* see, prejudiced men who *will not* see, and a certain set of moderate men who think better of the European world than it deserves; and this last class, by an ill-judged deliberation, will be the cause of more calamities to this continent than all the other three.

It is the good fortune of many to live distant from the scene of sorrow; the evil is not sufficiently brought to *their* doors to make *them* feel the precariousness with which all American property is possessed. But let our imaginations transport us a few moments to Boston; that seat of wretchedness will teach us wisdom and instruct us forever to renounce a power in whom we can have no trust. The inhabitants of that unfortunate city who, but a few months ago, were in ease and affluence have now no other alternative than to stay and starve or turn out to beg.[12] Endangered by the fire of their friends if they continue within the city, and plundered by the soldiery if they leave it. In their present condition they are prisoners without the hope of redemption; and in a general attack for their relief they would be exposed to the fury of both armies.

Men of passive tempers look somewhat lightly over the offenses of Great Britain and, still hoping for the best, are apt to call out, "Come, come, we shall be friends again for all this." But examine the passions and feelings of mankind, bring the doctrine of reconciliation to the touchstone of nature, and then tell me whether you can hereafter love, honor, and faithfully serve the power that has carried fire and sword into your land? If you cannot do all these, then are you only deceiving yourselves, and by your delay bringing ruin upon posterity. Your future connection with Britain, whom you can neither love nor honor, will be forced and unnatural, and being formed only on the plan of present convenience will, in a little time, fall into a relapse more wretched than the first. But if you say you still can pass the violations over, then I ask, has your house been burned? Has your property been destroyed before your face? Are your wife and children destitute of a bed to lie on or bread to live on? Have you lost a parent or a child by their hands, and yourself the ruined and wretched survivor? If you have not, then are you not a judge of those who have. But if you have and can still shake hands with the murderers, then are you unworthy the name of husband, father, friend, or lover; and whatever may be your rank or title in life, you have the heart of a coward and the spirit of a sycophant.

This is not inflaming or exaggerating matters, but trying them by those feelings and affections which nature justifies and without which we should be incapable of discharging the social duties of life or enjoying the felicities of it. I mean not to exhibit horror for the purpose of provoking revenge, but to awaken us from fatal and unmanly slumbers, that we may pursue determinately some fixed object. It is not in the power of Britain or Europe to conquer America, if she do not conquer herself by delay and timidity. The present winter is worth an age if rightly employed, but if lost or neglected the whole continent will partake of the misfortune; and there is no punishment which that man will not deserve, be he who or what or where he will, that may be the means of sacrificing a season so precious and useful.

It is repugnant to reason, to the universal order of things, to all examples from former ages, to suppose that this continent can longer remain subject to any external power. The most sanguine in Britain does not think so. The utmost stretch of human wisdom cannot, at this time, compass a plan, short of separation, which can promise the continent even a year's security. Reconciliation is *now* a fallacious dream. Nature has deserted the connection, and art cannot supply her place. For, as Milton wisely expresses, "never can true reconcilement grow where wounds of deadly hate have pierced so deep." [13]

Every quiet method for peace has been ineffectual. Our prayers have been rejected with disdain, and only tended to convince us that nothing flatters vanity or confirms obstinacy in kings more than repeated petitioning—and nothing has contributed more than that very measure to make the kings of Europe absolute. Witness Denmark and Sweden. Wherefore, since nothing but blows will do, for God's sake let us come to a final separation, and not leave the next generation to be cutting throats under the violated unmeaning names of parent and child.

To say they will never attempt it again is idle and visionary; we thought so at the repeal of the Stamp Act,[14] yet a year or two undeceived us; as well may we suppose that nations which have been once defeated will never renew the quarrel.

As to government matters, it is not in the power of Britain to do this continent justice. The business of it will soon be too weighty and intricate to be managed with any tolerable degree of convenience by a power so distant from us and so very ignorant of us; for if they cannot conquer us, they cannot govern us. To be always running three or four thousand miles with a tale or a petition, waiting four or five months for an answer, which, when obtained, requires five or six more to explain it in, will in a few years be looked upon as folly and childishness. There was a time when it was proper, and there is a proper time for it to cease.

Small islands not capable of protecting themselves are the proper objects for kingdoms to take under their care, but there is something very absurd in supposing a continent to be perpetually governed by an island. In no instance has nature made the satellite larger than its primary planet; and as England and America, with respect to each other, reverse the common order of nature, it is evident they belong to different systems—England to Europe, America to itself.

I am not induced by motives of pride, party, or resentment to espouse the doctrine of separation and independence; I am clearly, positively, and conscientiously persuaded that it is the true interest of this continent to be so; that everything short of *that* is mere patchwork, that it can afford no lasting felicity—that it is leaving the sword to our children, and shrinking back at a time when a little more, a little further, would have rendered this continent the glory of the earth.

As Britain has not manifested the least inclination toward a compromise, we may be assured that no terms can be obtained worthy the acceptance of the continent, or any ways equal to the expense of blood and treasure we have been already put to.

The object contended for ought always to bear some just proportion to the expense. The removal of North,[15] or the whole detestable junto, is a matter unworthy the millions we have expended. A temporary stoppage of trade was an inconvenience which would have sufficiently balanced the repeal of all the acts complained of, had such repeals been obtained; but if the whole continent must take up arms, if every man must be a soldier, it is scarcely worth our while to fight against a contemptible ministry only. Dearly, dearly do we pay for the repeal of the acts, if that is all we fight for; for in a just estimation it is as great a folly to pay a Bunker Hill price for law as for land.[16] As I have always considered the independence of this continent as an event which sooner or later must arrive, so from the late rapid progress of the continent to maturity, the event cannot be far off. Wherefore, on the breaking out of hostilities, it was not worth the while to have disputed a matter which time would have finally redressed, unless we meant to be in earnest; otherwise it is like wasting an estate on a suit at law to regulate the trespasses of a tenant whose lease is just expiring. No man was a warmer wisher for a reconciliation than myself before the fatal nineteenth of April, 1775,[d] but the moment the event of that day was made known I rejected the hardened, sullentempered Pharaoh of England [17] forever and disdain the wretch that, with the pretended title of father of his people, can unfeelingly hear of their slaughter and composedly sleep with their blood upon his soul.

But admitting that matters were now made up, what would be the event? I answer, the ruin of the continent. And that for several reasons:

First. The powers of governing still remaining in the hands of the king, he will have a negative over the whole legislation of this continent. And as he has shown himself such an inveterate enemy to liberty and discovered such a thirst for arbitrary power, is he or is he not a proper man to say to these colonies, "You shall

[d] Massacre at Lexington.

make no laws but what I please!"? And is there any inhabitant of America so ignorant as not to know that, according to what is called the "present Constitution," that this continent can make no laws but what the king gives leave to; and is there any man so unwise as not to see that (considering what has happened) he will suffer no law to be made here but such as suits *his* purpose? We may be as effectually enslaved by the want of laws in America as by submitting to laws made for us in England. After matters are made up (as it is called), can there be any doubt but the whole power of the crown will be exerted to keep this continent as low and humble as possible? Instead of going forward we shall go backward, or be perpetually quarrelling, or ridiculously petitioning. We are already greater than the king wishes us to be, and will he not hereafter endeavor to make us less? To bring the matter to one point, is the power who is jealous of our prosperity a proper power to govern us? Whoever says "No" to this question is an independent, for independence means no more than whether we shall make our own laws or whether the king, the greatest enemy this continent has or can have, shall tell us "there shall be no laws but such as I like."

But the king, you will say, has a negative in England; the people there can make no laws without his consent. In point of right and good order, there is something very ridiculous that a youth of twenty-one (which has often happened) shall say to several millions of people older and wiser than himself, "I forbid this or that act of yours to be law." But in this place I decline this sort of reply, though I will never cease to expose the absurdity of it, and only answer that England being the king's residence, and America not so, makes quite another case. The king's negative *here* is ten times more dangerous and fatal than it can be in England; for *there* he will scarcely refuse his consent to a bill for putting England into as strong a state of defense as possible, and in America he would never suffer such a bill to be passed.

America is only a secondary object in the system of British politics. England consults the good of *this* country no farther than it answers her *own* purpose. Wherefore her own interest leads her to suppress the growth of *ours* in every case which does not pro-

mote her advantage or in the least interferes with it. A pretty state
we should soon be in under such a secondhand government, considering what has happened! Men do not change from enemies to
friends by the alteration of a name. And in order to show that
reconciliation now is a dangerous doctrine, I affirm *that it would
be policy in the king at this time to repeal the acts, for the sake of
reinstating himself in the government of the provinces,* in order
that *he may accomplish by craft and subtlety in the long run what
he cannot do by force and violence in the short one.* Reconciliation
and ruin are nearly related.

Secondly. That as even the best terms which we can expect to
obtain can amount to no more than a temporary expedient, or a
kind of government by guardianship, which can last no longer than
till the colonies come of age, so the general face and state of things
in the interim will be unsettled and unpromising. Emigrants of
property will not choose to come to a country whose form of government hangs but by a thread, and who is every day tottering on
the brink of commotion and disturbance; and numbers of the present inhabitants would lay hold of the interval to dispose of their
effects and quit the continent.

But the most powerful of all arguments is that nothing but independence, i.e., a continental form of government, can keep the
peace of the continent and preserve it inviolate from civil wars. I
dread the event of a reconciliation with Britain now, as it is more
than probable that it will be followed by a revolt somewhere or
other, the consequences of which may be far more fatal than all
the malice of Britain.

Thousands are already ruined by British barbarity (thousands
more will probably suffer the same fate). Those men have other
feelings than us who have nothing suffered. All they now possess is
liberty; what they before enjoyed is sacrificed to its service, and
having nothing more to lose they disdain submission. Besides, the
general temper of the colonies toward a British government will be
like that of a youth who is nearly out of his time; they will care
very little about her. And a government which cannot preserve the
peace is no government at all, and in that case we pay our money

for nothing; and pray what is it that Britain can do, whose power will be wholly on paper, should a civil tumult break out the very day after reconciliation? I have heard some men say, many of whom I believe spoke without thinking, that they dreaded an independence, fearing that it would produce civil wars. It is but seldom that our first thoughts are truly correct, and that is the case here; for there are ten times more to dread from a patched-up connection than from independence. I make the sufferer's case my own, and I protest that, were I driven from house and home, my property destroyed, and my circumstances ruined, that as a man, sensible of injuries, I could never relish the doctrine of reconciliation or consider myself bound thereby.

The colonies have manifested such a spirit of good order and obedience to continental government as is sufficient to make every reasonable person easy and happy on that head. No man can assign the least pretense for his fears on any other grounds than such as are truly childish and ridiculous, viz., that one colony will be striving for superiority over another.

Where there are no distinctions, there can be no superiority; perfect equality affords no temptation. The republics of Europe are all (and we may say always) in peace. Holland and Switzerland are without wars, foreign or domestic. Monarchical governments, it is true, are never long at rest; the crown itself is a temptation to enterprising ruffians at home; and that degree of pride and insolence ever attendant on regal authority swells into a rupture with foreign powers in instances where a republican government, by being formed on more natural principles, would negotiate the mistake.

If there is any true cause of fear respecting independence, it is because no plan is yet laid down. Men do not see their way out. Wherefore, as an opening into that business, I offer the following hints, at the same time modestly affirming that I have no other opinion of them myself than that they may be the means of giving rise to something better. Could the straggling thoughts of individuals be collected, they would frequently form materials for wise and able men to improve into useful matter.

Let the assemblies be annual, with a president only. The representation more equal, their business wholly domestic, and subject to the authority of a Continental Congress.

Let each colony be divided into six, eight, or ten convenient districts, each district to send a proper number of delegates to Congress, so that each colony send at least thirty. The whole number in Congress will be at least 390. Each Congress to sit and to choose a president by the following method: When the delegates are met, let a colony be taken from the whole thirteen colonies by lot, after which let the whole Congress choose (by ballot) a president from out of the delegates of *that* province. In the next Congress, let a colony be taken by lot from twelve only, omitting that colony from which the president was taken in the former Congress, and so proceeding on till the whole thirteen shall have had their proper rotation. And in order that nothing may pass into a law but what is satisfactorily just, not less than three fifths of the Congress to be called a majority. He that will promote discord under a government so equally formed as this would have joined Lucifer in his revolt.

But as there is a peculiar delicacy from whom or in what manner this business must first arise, and as it seems most agreeable and consistent that it should come from some intermediate body between the governed and the governors, that is, between the Congress and the people, let a continental conference be held in the following manner and for the following purpose:

A committee of twenty-six members of Congress, viz., two for each colony. Two members from each House of Assembly or Provincial Convention and five representatives of the people at large, to be chosen in the capital city or town of each province for and in behalf of the whole province, by as many qualified voters as shall think proper to attend from all parts of the province for that purpose; or, if more convenient, the representatives may be chosen in two or three of the most populous parts thereof. In this conference, thus assembled, will be united the two grand principles of business, *knowledge* and *power*. The members of Congress, Assemblies, or Conventions, by having had experience in national concerns, will be able and useful counselors, and the whole, being empowered by the people, will have a truly legal authority.

The conferring members being met, let their business be to frame a Continental Charter or Charter of the United Colonies (answering to what is called the Magna Charta [18] of England), fixing the number and manner of choosing members of Congress, members of Assembly, with their date of sitting, and drawing the line of business and jurisdiction between them. (Always remembering that our strength is continental, not provincial.) Securing freedom and property to all men, and above all things the free exercise of religion, according to the dictates of conscience, with such other matter as it is necessary for a charter to contain. Immediately after which, the said conference to dissolve, and the bodies which shall be chosen conformable to the said charter to be the legislators and governors of this continent for the time being: Whose peace and happiness may God preserve. *Amen.*

Should any body of men be hereafter delegated for this or some similar purpose, I offer them the following extracts from that wise observer on governments, Dragonetti.[19] "The science," says he, "of the politician consists in fixing the true point of happiness and freedom. Those men would deserve the gratitude of ages, who should discover a mode of government that contained the greatest sum of individual happiness, with the least national expense." Dragonetti on *Virtues and Reward.*

But where, says some, is the king of America? I'll tell you, friend, he reigns above, and does not make havoc of mankind like the royal brute of Britain. Yet that we may not appear to be defective even in earthly honors, let a day be solemnly set apart for proclaiming the charter; let it be brought forth placed on the divine law, the word of God; let a crown be placed thereon, by which the world may know that, so far as we approve of monarchy, that in America *the law is king.* For as in absolute governments the king is law, so in free countries the law *ought* to be king; and there ought to be no other. But lest any ill use should afterward arise, let the crown at the conclusion of the ceremony be demolished and scattered among the people, whose right it is.

A government of our own is our natural right; and when a man seriously reflects on the precariousness of human affairs, he will become convinced that it is infinitely wiser and safer to form a Constitution of our own in a cool, deliberate manner while we have it in our power than to trust such an interesting event to time and chance. If we omit it now, some Massanello [e] may hereafter arise, who, laying hold of popular disquietudes, may collect together the desperate and the discontented, and by assuming to themselves the powers of government may sweep away the liberties of the continent like a deluge. Should the government of America return again into the hands of Britain, the tottering situation of things will be a temptation for some desperate adventurer to try his fortune, and in such a case what relief can Britain give? Ere she could hear the news, the fatal business might be done, and ourselves suffering like the wretched Britons under the oppression of the conqueror. Ye that oppose independence now, ye know not what ye do; ye are opening a door to eternal tyranny by keeping vacant the seat of government. There are thousands and tens of thousands who would think it glorious to expel from the continent that barbarous and hellish power which has stirred up the Indians and the Negroes to destroy us; the cruelty has a double guilt: it is dealing brutally by us and treacherously by them.

To talk of friendship with those in whom our reason forbids us to have faith and our affections, wounded through a thousand pores, instruct us to detest is madness and folly. Every day wears out the little remains of kindred between us and them; and can there be any reason to hope that, as the relationship expires, the affection will increase, or that we shall agree better when we have ten times more and greater concerns to quarrel over than ever?

Ye that tell us of harmony and reconciliation, can ye restore to us the time that is past? Can ye give to prostitution its former innocence? Neither can ye reconcile Britain and America. The last cord now is broken, the people of England are presenting addresses against us. There are injuries which nature cannot forgive; she

[e] Thomas Anello, otherwise Massanello, a fisherman of Naples, who after spiriting up his countrymen in the public market place against the oppression of the Spaniards, to whom the place was then subject, prompted them to revolt and in the space of a day became king.

would cease to be nature if she did. As well can the lover forgive the ravisher of his mistress as the continent forgive the murders of Britain. The Almighty has implanted in us these unextinguishable feelings for good and wise purposes. They are the guardians of his image in our hearts. They distinguish us from the herd of common animals. The social compact would dissolve and justice be extirpated [from] the earth, or have only a casual existence, were we callous to the touches of affection. The robber and the murderer would often escape unpunished did not the injuries which our tempers sustain provoke us into justice.

O ye that love mankind! Ye that dare oppose not only the tyranny but the tyrant, stand forth! Every spot of the Old World is overrun with oppression. Freedom has been hunted round the globe. Asia and Africa have long expelled her. Europe regards her like a stranger, and England has given her warning to depart. O! receive the fugitive, and prepare in time an asylum for mankind.

OF THE PRESENT ABILITY OF AMERICA, WITH SOME MISCELLANEOUS REFLECTIONS

I have never met with a man, either in England or America, who has not confessed his opinion that a separation between the countries would take place one time or other. And there is no instance in which we have shown less judgment than in endeavoring to describe what we call the ripeness or fitness of the continent for independence.

As all men allow the measure and vary only in their opinion of the time, let us, in order to remove mistakes, take a general survey of things and endeavor, if possible, to find out the *very* time. But we need not go far; the inquiry ceases at once, for the *time has found us*. The general concurrence, the glorious union of all things prove the fact.

It is not in numbers but in unity that our great strength lies; yet our present numbers are sufficient to repel the force of all the world. The continent has at this time the largest body of armed and disciplined men of any power under heaven, and is just arrived at that pitch of strength in which no single colony is able to support itself, and the whole, when united, can accomplish the matter, and either more or less than this might be fatal in its effects. Our land force is already sufficient; and as to naval affairs, we cannot be insensible that Britain would never suffer an American man-of-war to be built while the continent remained in her hands. Wherefore we should be no forwarder a hundred years hence in that branch than we are now; but the truth is we should be less so, because the timber of the country is every day diminishing, and that which will remain at last will be far off and difficult to procure.

Were the continent crowded with inhabitants, her sufferings under the present circumstances would be intolerable. The more seaport towns we had, the more should we have both to defend and to lose. Our present numbers are so happily proportioned to our wants that no man need be idle. The diminution of trade affords an army, and the necessities of an army create a new trade. Debts we have none, and whatever we may contract on this account will serve as a glorious memento of our virtue. Can we but leave posterity with a settled form of government, an independent constitution of its own, the purchase at any price will be cheap. But to expend millions for the sake of getting a few vile acts repealed, and routing the present ministry only, is unworthy the charge and is using posterity with the utmost cruelty, because it is leaving them the great work to do and a debt upon their backs from which they derive no advantage. Such a thought is unworthy a man of honor and is the true characteristic of a narrow heart and a peddling politician.

The debt we may contract does not deserve our regard if the work be but accomplished. No nation ought to be without a debt. A national debt is a national bond, and when it bears no interest is in no case a grievance. Britain is oppressed with a debt of upward of one hundred and forty millions sterling, for which she pays upward of four millions interest. And as a compensation for her debt, she has a large navy. America is without a debt and without a navy, yet for the twentieth part of the English national debt could have a navy as large again. The navy of England is not worth at this time more than three millions and a half sterling.

The first and second editions of this pamphlet were published without the following calculations, which are now given as a proof that the above estimation of the navy is a just one. See Entic's *Naval History*,[20] Intro., p. 56.

The charge of building a ship of each rate and furnishing her with masts, yards, sails, and rigging, together with a proportion of eight months boatswain's and carpenter's sea stores, as calculated by Mr. Burchett,[21] Secretary to the navy:

For a ship of 100 guns	35,553 *l*.
90	29,886
80	23,638
70	17,785
60	14,197
50	10,606
40	7,558
30	5,846
20	3,710

And from hence it is easy to sum up the value, or cost rather, of the whole British navy, which in the year 1757, when it was at its greatest glory, consisted of the following ships and guns:

Ships	Guns	Cost of One	Cost of All
6	100	35,553 *l*.	213,318 *l*.
12	90	29,886	358,632
12	80	23,638	283,656
43	70	17,785	764,755
35	60	14,197	496,895
40	50	10,606	424,240
45	40	7,558	340,110
58	20	3,710	215,180
85	Sloops, bombs, and fireships, one with another, at	2,000	170,000

Cost	3,266,786 *l*.
Remains for guns	233,214
Total	3,500,000 *l*.

No country on the globe is so happily situated or so internally capable of raising a fleet as America. Tar, timber, iron, and cordage are her natural produce. We need go abroad for nothing. Whereas the Dutch, who make large profits by hiring out their ships of war to the Spaniards and Portuguese, are obliged to import most of the materials they use. We ought to view the building a fleet as an article of commerce, it being the natural manufactory of this country. It is the best money we can lay out. A navy when finished is worth more than it cost. And is that nice point in national policy in which commerce and protection are united. Let us build; if we want them not, we can sell; and by that means replace our paper currency with ready gold and silver.

In point of manning a fleet, people in general run into great errors; it is not necessary that one fourth part should be sailors. The terrible privateer, Captain Death, stood the hottest engagement of any ship last war,[22] yet had not twenty sailors on board, though her complement of men was upward of two hundred. A few able and social sailors will soon instruct a sufficient number of active landmen in the common work of a ship. Wherefore we never can be more capable to begin on maritime matters than now while our timber is standing, our fisheries blocked up, and our sailors and shipwrights out of employ. Men-of-war, of seventy and eighty guns, were built forty years ago in New England, and why not the same now? Shipbuilding is America's greatest pride and in which she will, in time, excel the whole world. The great empires of the east are mostly inland, and consequently excluded from the possibility of rivaling her. Africa is in a state of barbarism, and no power in Europe has either such an extent of coast or such an internal supply of materials. Where nature has given the one, she has withheld the other; to America only has she been liberal of both. The vast empire of Russia is almost shut out from the sea, wherefore her boundless forests, her tar, iron, and cordage are only articles of commerce.

In point of safety, ought we to be without a fleet? We are not the little people now which we were sixty years ago; at that time we might have trusted our property in the streets, or fields rather, and slept securely without locks or bolts to our doors or windows.

The case is now altered, and our methods of defense ought to improve with our increase of property. A common pirate, twelve months ago, might have come up the Delaware [23] and laid the city of Philadelphia under instant contribution for what sum he pleased, and the same might have happened to other places. Nay, any daring fellow, in a brig of fourteen or sixteen guns, might have robbed the whole continent and carried off half a million of money. These are circumstances which demand our attention and point out the necessity of naval protection.

Some perhaps will say that, after we have made it up with Britain, she will protect us. Can they be so unwise as to mean that she shall keep a navy in our harbors for that purpose? Common sense will tell us that the power which has endeavored to subdue us is, of all others, the most improper to defend us. Conquest may be effected under the pretense of friendship, and ourselves, after a long and brave resistance, be at last cheated into slavery. And if her ships are not to be admitted into our harbors, I would ask, how is she to protect us? A navy three or four thousand miles off can be of little use, and on sudden emergencies none at all. Wherefore, if we must hereafter protect ourselves, why not do it for ourselves? Why do it for another?

The English list of ships of war is long and formidable, but not a tenth part of them are at any one time fit for service, numbers of them not in being; yet their names are pompously continued in the list if only a plank be left of the ship, and not a fifth part of such as are fit for service can be spared on any one station at one time. The East and West Indies, Mediterranean, Africa, and other parts over which Britain extends her claim, make large demands upon her navy. From a mixture of prejudice and inattention, we have contracted a false notion respecting the navy of England and have talked as if we should have the whole of it to encounter at once, and for that reason supposed that we must have one as large, which not being instantly practicable has been made use of by a set of disguised Tories to discourage our beginning thereon. Nothing can be farther from truth than this, for if America had only a twentieth part of the naval force of Britain she would be by far an overmatch for her; because, as we neither have nor claim any foreign dominion, our whole force would be employed on our own coast, where we should, in the long run, have two to one the advantage of those who had three or four thousand miles to sail over before they could attack us and the same distance to return in order to refit and recruit. And although Britain, by her fleet, has a check over our trade to Europe, we have as large a one over her trade to the West Indies, which, by laying in the neighborhood of the continent, lies entirely at its mercy.

Some method might be fallen on to keep up a naval force in time of peace, if we should not judge it necessary to support a constant navy. If premiums were to be given to merchants to build and employ in their service ships mounted with twenty, thirty, forty, or fifty guns (the premiums to be in proportion to the loss of bulk to the merchants), fifty or sixty of those ships, with a few guardships on constant duty, would keep up a sufficient navy, and that without burdening ourselves with the evil so loudly complained of in England, of suffering their fleet in time of peace to lie rotting in the docks. To unite the sinews of commerce and defense is sound policy; for when our strength and our riches play into each other's hand, we need fear no external enemy.

In almost every article of defense we abound. Hemp flourishes even to rankness, so that we need not want cordage. Our iron is superior to that of other countries. Our small arms equal to any in the world. Cannon we can cast at pleasure. Saltpeter and gunpowder we are every day producing. Our knowledge is hourly improving. Resolution is our inherent character, and courage has never yet forsaken us. Wherefore, what is it that we want? Why is it that we hesitate? From Britain we can expect nothing but ruin. If she is once admitted to the government of America again, this continent will not be worth living in. Jealousies will be always arising, insurrections will be constantly happening, and who will go forth to quell them? Who will venture his life to reduce his own countrymen to a foreign obedience? The difference between Pennsylvania and Connecticut, respecting some unlocated lands, shows the insignificance of a British government and fully proves that nothing but continental authority can regulate continental matters.

Another reason why the present time is preferable to all others is that the fewer our numbers are, the more land there is yet unoccupied, which, instead of being lavished by the king on his worthless dependents, may be hereafter applied, not only to the discharge of the present debt, but to the constant support of government. No nation under heaven has such an advantage as this.

The infant state of the Colonies, as it is called, so far from being against, is an argument in favor of independence. We are sufficiently numerous, and were we more so we might be less united. It is a matter worthy of observation that the more a country is peopled, the smaller their armies are. In military numbers, the ancients far exceeded the moderns; and the reason is evident, for trade being the consequence of population, men become too much absorbed thereby to attend to anything else. Commerce diminishes the spirit both of patriotism and military defense. And history sufficiently informs us that the bravest achievements were always accomplished in the nonage of a nation. With the increase of commerce, England has lost its spirit. The city of London, notwithstanding its numbers, submits to continued insults with the patience of a coward. The more men have to lose, the less willing are they to venture. The rich are, in general, slaves to fear and submit to courtly power with the trembling duplicity of a spaniel.

Youth is the seedtime of good habits, as well in nations as in individuals. It might be difficult, if not impossible, to form the continent into one government half a century hence. The vast variety of interests, occasioned by an increase of trade and population, would create confusion. Colony would be against colony. Each being able might scorn each other's assistance; and while the proud and foolish gloried in their little distinctions, the wise would lament that the union had not been formed before. Wherefore the present time is the true time for establishing it. The intimacy which is contracted in infancy and the friendship which is formed in misfortune are, of all others, the most lasting and unalterable. Our present union is marked with both these characters; we are young and we have been distressed, but our concord has withstood our troubles and fixes a memorable era for posterity to glory in.

The present time, likewise, is that peculiar time which never happens to a nation but once, viz., the time of forming itself into a government. Most nations have let slip the opportunity, and by that means have been compelled to receive laws from their conquerors instead of making laws for themselves. First they had a king and then a form of government, whereas the articles or charter of government should be formed first and men delegated to execute them afterward; but from the errors of other nations let us learn wisdom and lay hold of the present opportunity *to begin government at the right end.*

When William the Conqueror subdued England, he gave them law at the point of the sword; and until we consent that the seat of government in America be legally and authoritatively occupied, we shall be in danger of having it filled by some fortunate ruffian who may treat us in the same manner, and then where will be our freedom? where our property?

As to religion, I hold it to be the indispensable duty of all government to protect all conscientious professors thereof, and I know of no other business which government has to do therewith. Let a man throw aside that narrowness of soul, that selfishness of principle, which the niggards of all professions are so unwilling to part with, and he will be at once delivered of his fears on that head. Suspicion is the companion of mean souls and the bane of all good society. For myself, I fully and conscientiously believe that it is the will of the Almighty that there should be diversity of religious opinions among us. It affords a larger field for our Christian kindness. Were we all of one way of thinking, our religious dispositions would want matter for probation; and on this liberal principle I look on the various denominations among us to be like children of the same family, differing only in what is called their Christian names.

In pages [30-31] I threw out a few thoughts on the propriety of a Continental Charter (for I only presume to offer hints, not plans), and in this place I take the liberty of rementioning the subject by observing that a charter is to be understood as a bond of solemn obligation, which the whole enters into to support the right of every separate part, whether of religion, personal freedom, or property. A firm bargain and a right reckoning make long friends.

I have heretofore likewise mentioned the necessity of a large and equal representation, and there is no political matter which more deserves our attention. A small number of electors or a small number of representatives are equally dangerous. But if the number of the representatives be not only small but unequal, the danger is increased. As an instance of this I mention the following: when the associators' petition was before the House of Assembly of Pennsylvania, twenty-eight members only were present; all the Bucks County members, being eight, voted against it; and had seven of the Chester members done the same this whole province had been governed by two counties only, and this danger it is always exposed to. The unwarrantable stretch, likewise, which that house made in their last sitting to gain an undue authority over the delegates of that province ought to warn the people at large how they trust power out of their own hands. A set of instructions for the delegates were put together which, in point of sense and business, would have dishonored a schoolboy, and, after being approved by a few—a very few—withoutdoors, were carried into the house and there passed *in behalf of the whole colony;* whereas did the whole colony know with what ill will that house had entered on some necessary public measures, they would not hesitate a moment to think them unworthy of such a trust.

Immediate necessity makes many things convenient which, if continued, would grow into oppressions. Expedience and right are different things. When the calamities of America required a consultation, there was no method so ready or at that time so proper as to appoint persons from the several houses of Assembly for that purpose, and the wisdom with which they have proceeded has preserved this continent from ruin. But as it is more than probable that we shall never be without a Congress, every well-wisher to good order must own that the mode for choosing members of that body deserves consideration. And I put it as a question to those who make a study of mankind, whether representation and election is not too great a power for one and the same body of men to possess? When we are planning for posterity, we ought to remember that virtue is not hereditary.

It is from our enemies that we often gain excellent maxims

and are frequently surprised into reason by their mistakes. Mr. Cornwall [24] (one of the Lords of the Treasury) treated the petition of the New York Assembly with contempt because *that* house, he said, consisted but of twenty-six members, which trifling number, he argued, could not with decency be put for the whole. We thank him for his involuntary honesty.[f]

To conclude, however strange it may appear to some or however unwilling they may be to think so matters not, but many strong and striking reasons may be given to show that nothing can settle our affairs so expeditiously as an open and determined declaration for independence. Some of which are:

Firstly. It is the custom of nations, when any two are at war, for some other powers, not engaged in the quarrel, to step in as mediators and bring about the preliminaries of a peace. But while America calls herself the subject of Great Britain, no power, however well disposed she may be, can offer her mediation. Wherefore, in our present state, we may quarrel on forever.

Secondly. It is unreasonable to suppose that France or Spain will give us any kind of assistance if we mean only to make use of that assistance for the purpose of repairing the breach and strengthening the connection between Britain and America, because those powers would be sufferers by the consequences.

Thirdly. While we profess ourselves the subjects of Britain, we must, in the eye of foreign nations, be considered as rebels. The precedent is somewhat dangerous to their peace for men to be in arms under the name of subjects; we, on the spot, can solve the paradox, but to unite resistance and subjection requires an idea much too refined for common understanding.

Fourthly. Were a manifesto to be published and dispatched to foreign courts, setting forth the miseries we have endured and the peaceable methods which we have ineffectually used for redress; declaring at the same time that, not being able any longer to live happily or safely under the cruel disposition of the British court,

---

[f] Those who would fully understand of what great consequence a large and equal representation is to a state should read Burgh's *Political Disquisitions*. [James Burgh, *Political Disquisitions: or, an Enquiry into Public Errors, Defects and Abuses.* 3 vols. London, 1774-5.]

we had been driven to the necessity of breaking off all connections with her; at the same time assuring all such courts of our peaceable disposition toward them and of our desire of entering into trade with them—such a memorial would produce more good effects to this continent than if a ship were freighted with petitions to Britain.

Under our present denomination of British subjects, we can neither be received nor heard abroad; the custom of all courts is against us, and will be so until, by an independence, we take rank with other nations.

These proceedings may at first appear strange and difficult, but like all other steps which we have already passed over will in a little time become familiar and agreeable; and until an independence is declared, the continent will feel itself like a man who continues putting off some unpleasant business from day to day, yet knows it must be done, hates to set about it, wishes it over, and is continually haunted with the thoughts of its necessity.

APPENDIX

Since the publication of the first edition of this pamphlet, or rather, on the same day on which it came out, the King's speech [25] made its appearance in this city.[g] Had the spirit of prophecy directed the birth of this production, it could not have brought it forth at a more seasonable juncture or at a more necessary time. The bloody-mindedness of the one shows [h] the necessity of pursuing the doctrine of the other. Men read by way of revenge. And the speech, instead of terrifying, prepared a way for the manly principles of independence.

Ceremony, and even silence, from whatever motive they may arise, have a hurtful tendency when they give the least degree of countenance to base and wicked performances; wherefore, if this maxim be admitted, it naturally follows that the King's speech, as being a piece of finished villainy, deserved and still deserves a

---

[g] [Philadelphia.]
[h] [The New Edition has "show."]

Cursing

general execration, both by the Congress and the people. Yet, as the domestic tranquillity of a nation depends greatly on the *chastity* of what may properly be called "national manners," it is often better to pass some things over in silent disdain than to make use of such new methods of dislike as might introduce the least innovation on that guardian of our peace and safety. And perhaps it is chiefly owing to this prudent delicacy that the King's speech has not before now suffered a public execution. The speech, if it may be called one, is nothing better than a willful audacious libel against the truth, the common good, and the existence of mankind; and is a formal and pompous method of offering up human sacrifices to the pride of tyrants. But this general massacre of mankind is one of the privileges and the certain consequence of kings; for as nature knows them *not* they know *not her*, and although they are beings of our *own* creating they know not *us*, and are become the gods of their creators. The speech has one good quality, which is that it is not calculated to deceive; neither can we, even if we would, be deceived by it. Brutality and tyranny appear on the face of it. It leaves us at no loss. And every line convinces, even in the moment of reading, that he who hunts the woods for prey, the naked and untutored Indian, is less savage than the king of Britain.

Sir John Dalrymple, the putative father of a whining jesuitical piece, fallaciously called "*The address of the people* of England *to the inhabitants* of America," [26] has, perhaps from a vain supposition that the people *here* were to be frightened at the pomp and description of a king, given (though very unwisely on his part) the real character of the present one. "But," says this writer, "if you are inclined to pay compliments to an administration which we do not complain of (meaning the Marquis of Rockingham's [27] at the repeal of the Stamp Act), it is very unfair in you to withhold them from that prince *by whose nod alone they were permitted to do anything*." This is toryism with a witness! Here is idolatry even without a mask, and he who can calmly hear and digest such doctrine has forfeited his claim to rationality—an apostate from the order of manhood—and ought to be considered as one who has not only given up the proper dignity of man, but sunk himself beneath the rank of animals, and contemptibly crawls through the world like a worm.

However, it matters very little now what the King of England either says or does; he has wickedly broken through every moral and human obligation, trampled nature and conscience beneath his feet, and by a steady and constitutional spirit of insolence and cruelty procured for himself a universal hatred. It is *now* the interest of America to provide for herself. She has already a large and young family, whom it is more her duty to take care of than to be granting away her property to support a power who is become a reproach to the names of men and Christians—ye whose office it is to watch over the morals of a nation, of whatsoever sect or denomination ye are of, as well as ye who are more immediately the guardians of the public liberty, if ye wish to preserve your native country uncontaminated by European corruption, ye must in secret wish a separation. But leaving the moral part to private reflection, I shall chiefly confine my farther remarks to the following heads:

First, that it is the interest of America to be separated from Britain.

Secondly, which is the easiest and most practicable plan, reconciliation or independence? with some occasional remarks.

In support of the first, I could, if I judged it proper, produce the opinion of some of the ablest and most experienced men on this continent, and whose sentiments on that head are not yet publicly known. It is in reality a self-evident position; for no nation in a state of foreign dependence, limited in its commerce and cramped and fettered in its legislative powers, can ever arrive at any material eminence. America does not yet know what opulence is; and although the progress which she has made stands unparalleled in the history of other nations, it is but childhood compared with what she would be capable of arriving at had she, as she ought to have, the legislative powers in her own hands. England is at this time proudly coveting what would do her no good were she to accomplish it, and the continent hesitating on a matter which will be her final ruin if neglected. It is the commerce and not the conquest of America by which England is to be benefited, and that would in a great measure continue were the countries as independent of each other as France and Spain, because in many articles neither can go to a better market. But it is the independence of this country of Britain, or any other, which is now the main and only object worthy of contention, and which, like all other truths discovered by necessity, will appear clear and stronger every day.

First, because it will come to that one time or other.

Secondly, because the longer it is delayed, the harder it will be to accomplish.

I have frequently amused myself, both in public and private companies, with silently remarking the specious errors of those who speak without reflecting. And among the many which I have heard, the following seems the most general, viz., that had this rupture happened forty or fifty years hence, instead of now, the continent would have been more able to have shaken off the dependence. To which I reply that our military ability, *at this time*, arises from the experience gained in the last war,[28] and which in forty or fifty years' time would have been totally extinct. The continent would not, by that time, have had a general or even a military officer left, and we, or those who may succeed us, would have been as ignorant of martial matters as the ancient Indians; and this single position, closely attended to, will unanswerably prove that the present time is preferable to all others. The argument turns thus: At the conclusion of the last war, we had experience but wanted numbers, and forty or fifty years hence we shall have numbers without experience; wherefore the proper point of time must be some particular point between the two extremes, in which a sufficiency of the former remains and a proper increase of the latter is obtained. And that point of time is the present time.

The reader will pardon this digression, as it does not properly come under the head I first set out with and to which I again return by the following position, viz.:

Should affairs be patched up with Britain and she to remain the governing and sovereign power of America (which, as matters are now circumstanced, is giving up the point entirely), we shall deprive ourselves of the very means of sinking the debt we have or may contract. The value of the back lands, which some of the provinces are clandestinely deprived of by the unjust extension of the limits of Canada,[29] valued only at five pounds sterling per hundred acres, amount to upward of twenty-five millions, Pennsylvania currency; and the quit-rents, at one penny sterling per acre, to two millions yearly.

It is by the sale of those lands that the debt may be sunk, without burden to any, and the quit-rent reserved thereon will always lessen and in time will wholly support the yearly expense of government. It matters not how long the debt is in paying, so that the lands when sold be applied to the discharge of it and for the execution of which the Congress for the time being will be the continental trustees.

I proceed now to the second head, viz., which is the easiest and most practicable plan, reconciliation or independence; with some occasional remarks.

He who takes nature for his guide is not easily beaten out of his argument, and on that ground I answer *generally that independence being a single simple line, contained within ourselves, and reconciliation a matter exceedingly perplexed and complicated, and in which a treacherous capricious court is to interfere, gives the answer without a doubt.*

The present state of America is truly alarming to every man who is capable of reflection. Without law, without government, without any other mode of power than what is founded on and granted by courtesy. Held together by an unexampled occurrence of sentiment, which is nevertheless subject to change and which every secret enemy is endeavoring to dissolve. Our present condition is legislation without law, wisdom without a plan, a constitution without a name, and, what is strangely astonishing, perfect independence contending for dependence. The instance is without a precedent, the case never existed before; and who can tell what may be the event? The property of no man is secure in the present unbraced system of things. The mind of the multitude is left at random, and seeing no fixed object before them, they pursue such as fancy or opinion presents. Nothing is criminal, there is no such thing as treason; wherefore, everyone thinks himself at liberty to act as he pleases. The Tories [30] dared not have assembled offensively had they known that their lives, by that act, were forfeited to the laws of the state. A line of distinction should be drawn between English soldiers taken in battle and inhabitants of America taken in arms. The first are prisoners, but the latter traitors. The one forfeits his liberty, the other his head.

Notwithstanding our wisdom, there is a visible feebleness in some of our proceedings which gives encouragement to dissensions. The continental belt is too loosely buckled, and if something is not done in time, it will be too late to do anything and we shall fall into a state in which neither reconciliation nor independence will be practicable. The king and his worthless adherents are got at their old game of dividing the continent, and there are not wanting among us printers who will be busy in spreading specious falsehoods. The artful and hypocritical letter [31] which appeared a few months ago in two of the New York papers, and likewise in two others, is an evidence that there are men who want either judgment [or] [1] honesty.

It is easy getting into holes and corners and talking of reconciliation; but do such men seriously consider how difficult the task is, and how dangerous it may prove should the continent divide thereon? Do they take within their view all the various orders of men whose situation and circumstances, as well as their own, are to be considered therein? Do they put themselves in the place of the sufferer whose *all* is *already* gone, and of the soldier who has quitted *all* for the defense of his country? If their ill-judged moderation be suited to their own private situations only, regardless of others, the event will convince them that "they are reckoning without their host."

Put us, says some, on the footing we were on in sixty-three,[32] to which I answer the request is not now in the power of Britain to comply with, neither will she propose it; but if it were and even should be granted I ask, as a reasonable question, By what means is such a corrupt and faithless court to be kept to its engagements?

[1] [The New Edition has "and."]

Another Parliament, nay, even the present, may hereafter repeal the obligation, on the pretense of its being violently obtained or unwisely granted, and in that case where is our redress? No going to law with nations; cannon are the barristers of crowns; and the sword, not of justice but of war, decides the suit. To be on the footing of sixty-three, it is not sufficient that the laws only be put in ʲ the same state but that our circumstances likewise be put in ʲ the same state; our burnt and destroyed towns repaired or built up, our private losses made good, our public debts (contracted for defense) discharged; otherwise we shall be millions worse than we were at that enviable period. Such a request, had it been complied with a year ago, would have won the heart and soul of the continent, but now it is too late. "The Rubicon is passed."

Besides, the taking up arms merely to enforce the repeal of a pecuniary law seems as unwarrantable by the divine law and as repugnant to human feelings as the taking up arms to enforce obedience thereto. The object, on either side, does not justify the means, for the lives of men are too valuable to be cast away on such trifles. It is the violence which is done and threatened to our persons, the destruction of our property by an armed force, the invasion of our country by fire and sword which conscientiously qualifies the use of arms; and the instant in which such a mode of defense became necessary all subjection to Britain ought to have ceased, and the independence of America should have been considered as dating its era from and published by *the first musket that was fired against her*. This line is a line of consistency, neither drawn by caprice nor extended by ambition, but produced by a chain of events of which the colonies were not the authors.

I shall conclude these remarks with the following timely and well-intended hints. We ought to reflect that there are three different ways by which an independence may hereafter be effected; and that *one* of those *three* will, one day or other, be the fate of America, viz., by the legal voice of the people in Congress, by a military power, or by a mob. It may not always happen that our soldiers are citizens and the multitude a body of reasonable men; virtue, as I have already remarked, is not hereditary, neither is it

ʲ [The New Edition has "on."]

perpetual. Should an independence be brought about by the first of those means, we have every opportunity and every encouragement before us to form the noblest, purest constitution on the face of the earth. We have it in our power to begin the world over again. A situation similar to the present has not happened since the days of Noah until now. The birthday of a new world is at hand, and a race of men, perhaps as numerous as all Europe contains, are to receive their portion of freedom from the event of a few months. The reflection is awful; and in this point of view how trifling, how ridiculous, do the little paltry cavilings of a few weak or interested men appear when weighed against the business of a world.

Should we neglect the present favorable and inviting period, and independence be hereafter effected by any other means, we must charge the consequence to ourselves, or to those rather whose narrow and prejudiced souls are habitually opposing the measure, without either inquiring or reflecting. There are reasons to be given in support of independence which men should rather privately think of than be publicly told of. We ought not now to be debating whether we shall be independent or not, but anxious to accomplish it on a firm, secure, and honorable basis, and uneasy rather that it is not yet begun [k] upon. Every day convinces us of its necessity. Even the Tories (if such beings yet remain among us) should, of all men, be the most solicitous to promote it; for as the appointment of committees at first protected them from popular rage, so a wise and well-established form of government will be the only certain means of continuing it securely to them. Wherefore, if they have not virtue enough to be Whigs, they ought to have prudence enough to wish for independence.

In short, independence is the only bond that can tie and keep us together. We shall then see our object, and our ears will be legally shut against the schemes of an intriguing as well as a cruel enemy. We shall then, too, be on a proper footing to treat with Britain; for there is reason to conclude that the pride of that court will be less hurt by treating with the American states for terms of peace than with those whom she denominates "rebellious subjects" for

k [The New Edition has "began."]

terms of accommodation. It is our delaying it that encourages her to hope for conquest, and our backwardness tends only to prolong the war. As we have, without any good effect therefrom, withheld our trade to obtain a redress of our grievances, let us now try the alternative, by independently redressing them ourselves and then offering to open the trade. The mercantile and reasonable part of England will be still with us, because peace with trade is preferable to war without it. And if this offer be not accepted, other courts may be applied to.

On these grounds I rest the matter. And as no offer has yet been made to refute the doctrine contained in the former editions of this pamphlet, it is a negative proof that either the doctrine cannot be refuted or that the party in favor of it are too numerous to be opposed. Wherefore, instead of gazing at each other with suspicious or doubtful curiosity, let each of us hold out to his neighbor the hearty hand of friendship and unite in drawing a line which, like an act of oblivion, shall bury in forgetfulness every former dissension. Let the names of Whig and Tory be extinct, and let none other be heard among us than those of *a good citizen, an open and resolute friend, and a virtuous supporter of the rights of mankind and of the free and independent states of America.*

THE AMERICAN CRISIS

[ONE AND THIRTEEN]

THE AMERICAN CRISIS: I

THESE ARE THE TIMES that try men's souls. The summer soldier and the sunshine patriot will, in this crisis, shrink from the service of their country, but he that stands it *now* deserves the love and thanks of man and woman. Tyranny, like hell, is not easily conquered; yet we have this consolation with us that, the harder the conflict, the more glorious the triumph. What we obtain too cheap, we esteem too lightly; it is dearness only that gives everything its value. Heaven knows how to put a proper price upon its goods, and it would be strange indeed if so celestial an article as freedom should not be highly rated. Britain, with an army to enforce her tyranny, has declared that she has a right (*not only to tax*) but *to bind us in all cases whatsoever;* [1] and if being *bound in that manner* is not slavery, then is there not such a thing as slavery upon earth. Even the expression is impious, for so unlimited a power can belong only to God.

Whether the independence of the continent was declared too soon or delayed too long I will not now enter into as an argument; my own simple opinion is that, had it been eight months earlier, it would have been much better. We did not make a proper use of last winter, neither could we while we were in a dependent state. However, the fault, if it were one, was all our own;[a] we have none to blame but ourselves. But no great deal is lost yet. All that Howe has been doing for this month past is rather a ravage than a conquest, which the spirit of the Jerseys,[2] a year ago, would have quickly repulsed, and which time and a little resolution will soon recover.

I have as little superstition in me as any man living, but my

[a] The present winter is worth an age if rightly employed, but if lost or neglected the whole continent will partake of the evil; and there is no punishment that man does not deserve, be he who or what or where he will, that may be the means of sacrificing a season so precious and useful. [From *Common Sense,* p. 25.]

secret opinion has ever been and still is that God Almighty will not give up a people to military destruction or leave them unsupportedly to perish who have so earnestly and so repeatedly sought to avoid the calamities of war by every decent method which wisdom could invent. Neither have I so much of the infidel in me as to suppose that He has relinquished the government of the world and given us up to the care of devils, and as I do not I cannot see on what grounds the King of Britain can look up to heaven for help against us; a common murderer, a highwayman, or a housebreaker has as good a pretense as he.

'Tis surprising to see how rapidly a panic will sometimes run through a country. All nations and ages have been subject to them. Britain has trembled like an ague at the report of a French fleet of flat-bottomed boats, and in the fourteenth [b] century the whole English army, after ravaging the kingdom of France, was driven back like men petrified with fear; and this brave exploit was performed by a few broken forces collected and headed by a woman, Joan of Arc. Would that heaven might inspire some Jersey maid to spirit up her countrymen and save her fair fellow sufferers from ravage and ravishment! Yet panics, in some cases, have their uses; they produce as much good as hurt. Their duration is always short; the mind soon grows through them and acquires a firmer habit than before. But their peculiar advantage is that they are the touchstones of sincerity and hypocrisy, and bring things and men to light which might otherwise have lain forever undiscovered. In fact, they have the same effect on secret traitors which an imaginary apparition would have upon a private murderer. They sift out the hidden thoughts of man and hold them up in public to the world. Many a disguised Tory has lately shown his head that shall penitentially solemnize with curses the day on which Howe arrived upon the Delaware.

As I was with the troops at Fort Lee,[3] and marched with them to the edge of Pennsylvania, I am well acquainted with many circumstances which those who live at a distance know but little or nothing of. Our situation there was exceedingly cramped, the place being a narrow neck of land between the North River [4] and the

[b] [The fifteenth century.]

Hackensack. Our force was inconsiderable, being not one fourth so great as Howe could bring against us. We had no army at hand to have relieved the garrison, had we shut ourselves up and stood on our defense. Our ammunition, light artillery, and the best part of our stores had been removed, on the apprehension that Howe would endeavor to penetrate the Jerseys, in which case Fort Lee could be of no use to us; for it must occur to every thinking man, whether in the army or not, that these kind of field forts are only for temporary purposes and last in use no longer than the enemy directs his force against the particular object which such forts are raised to defend. Such was our situation and condition at Fort Lee on the morning of the twentieth of November, when an officer arrived with information that the enemy, with two hundred boats, had landed about seven miles above; Major General Greene,[5] who commanded the garrison, immediately ordered them under arms and sent express to General Washington at the town of Hackensack, distant by the way of the ferry six miles. Our first object was to secure the bridge over the Hackensack, which laid up the river between the enemy and us, about six miles from us and three from them. General Washington arrived in about three quarters of an hour and marched at the head of the troops toward the bridge, which place I expected we should have a brush for; however, they did not choose to dispute it with us, and the greatest part of our troops went over the bridge, the rest over the ferry, except some which passed at a mill on a small creek, between the bridge and the ferry, and made their way through some marshy grounds up to the town of Hackensack and there passed the river. We brought off as much baggage as the wagons could contain; the rest was lost. The simple object was to bring off the garrison and march them on till they could be strengthened by the Jersey or Pennsylvania militia, so as to be enabled to make a stand. We stayed four days at Newark, collected our outposts with some of the Jersey militia, and marched out twice to meet the enemy, on being informed that they were advancing, though our numbers were greatly inferior to theirs. Howe, in my little opinion, committed a great error in generalship in not throwing a body of forces off from Staten Island through Amboy, by which means he might have seized all our stores at Brunswick and intercepted our march into Pennsylvania; but if we believe the power of hell to be limited, we must likewise believe that their agents are under some providential control.

I shall not now attempt to give all the particulars of our retreat to the Delaware; suffice it for the present to say that both officers and men, though greatly harassed and fatigued, frequently without rest, covering, or provision—the inevitable consequences of a long retreat—bore it with a manly and martial spirit. All their wishes centered in one, which was that the country would turn out and help them to drive the enemy back. Voltaire [6] has remarked that King William [7] never appeared to full advantage but in difficulties and in action; the same remark may be made on General Washington, for the character fits him. There is a natural firmness in some minds which cannot be unlocked by trifles, but which, when unlocked, discovers a cabinet of fortitude; and I reckon it among those kind of public blessings which we do not immediately see that God has blessed him with uninterrupted health and given him a mind that can even flourish upon care.

I shall conclude this paper with some miscellaneous remarks on the state of our affairs and shall begin with asking the following questions: Why is it that the enemy have left the New England provinces, and made these middle ones the seat of war? The answer is easy: New England is not infested with Tories, and we are. I have been tender in raising the cry against these men and used numberless arguments to show them their danger, but it will not do to sacrifice a world either to their folly or their baseness. The period is now arrived in which either they or we must change our sentiments, or one or both must fall. And what is a Tory? Good God! what is he? I should not be afraid to go with a hundred Whigs against a thousand Tories, were they to attempt to get into arms. Every Tory is a coward; for a servile, slavish, self-interested fear is the foundation of Toryism, and a man under such influence, though he may be cruel, never can be brave.

But before the line of irrecoverable separation be drawn between us, let us reason the matter together. Your conduct is an invitation to the enemy, yet not one in a thousand of you has heart enough to join him. Howe is as much deceived by you as the American cause is injured by you. He expects you will all take up arms and flock to his standard, with muskets on your shoulders. Your opinions are of no use to him unless you support him personally, for 'tis soldiers and not Tories that he wants.

I once felt all that kind of anger which a man ought to feel against the mean principles that are held by the Tories: a noted one, who kept a tavern at Amboy, was standing at his door with as pretty a child in his hand, about eight or nine years old, as I ever saw, and after speaking his mind as freely as he thought was prudent, finished with this unfatherly expression, "Well! give me peace in my day." [8] Not a man lives on the continent but fully believes that a separation must some time or other finally take place, and a generous parent should have said, "If there must be trouble, let it be in my day, that my child may have peace," and this single reflection, well applied, is sufficient to awaken every man to duty. Not a place upon earth might be so happy as America. Her situation is remote from all the wrangling world, and she has nothing to do but to trade with them. A man can distinguish himself between temper and principle, and I am as confident as I am that God governs the world that America will never be happy till she gets clear of foreign dominion. Wars without ceasing will break out till that period arrives, and the continent must in the end be conqueror; for though the flame of liberty may sometimes cease to shine, the coal can never expire.

America did not nor does not want force, but she wanted a proper application of that force. Wisdom is not the purchase of a day, and it is no wonder that we should err at the first setting off. From an excess of tenderness, we were unwilling to raise an army and trusted our cause to the temporary defense of a well-meaning militia. A summer's experience has now taught us better; yet with those troops, while they were collected, we were able to set bounds to the progress of the enemy, and, thank God! they are again assembling. I always considered militia as the best troops in the world for a sudden exertion, but they will not do for a long campaign. Howe, it is probable, will make an attempt on this city; should he fail on this side of the Delaware, he is ruined. If he succeeds, our cause is not ruined. He stakes all on his side against a part on ours; admitting he succeeds, the consequence will be that armies from both ends of the continent will march to assist their suffering friends in the middle states; for he cannot go everywhere, it is impossible. I consider Howe as the greatest enemy the Tories have; he is bringing a war into their country, which, had it not been for him and partly for themselves, they had been clear of. Should he now be expelled, I wish with all the devotion of a Christian that the names of Whig and Tory may never more be mentioned; but should the Tories give him encouragement to come or assistance if he come, I as sincerely wish that our next year's arms may expel them from the continent, and the Congress appropriate their possessions to the relief of those who have suffered in well-doing. A single successful battle next year will settle the whole. America could carry on a two years' war by the confiscation of the property of disaffected persons and be made happy by their expulsion. Say not that this is revenge; call it rather the soft resentment of a suffering people who, having no object in view but the *good* of *all*, have staked their *own all* upon a seemingly doubtful event. Yet it is folly to argue against determined hardness; eloquence may strike the ear and the language of sorrow draw forth the tear of compassion, but nothing can reach the heart that is steeled with prejudice.

Quitting this class of men, I turn with the warm ardor of a friend to those who have nobly stood and are yet determined to stand the matter out; I call not upon a few but upon all—not on *this* state or *that* state, but on *every* state—up and help us, lay your shoulders to the wheel, better have too much force than too little when so great an object is at stake. Let it be told to the future world that in the depth of winter, when nothing but hope and virtue could survive, that the city and the country, alarmed at one common danger, came forth to meet and to repulse it. Say not that thousands are gone, turn out your tens of thousands; throw not the burden of the day upon Providence, but "show your faith by your works," [9] that God may bless you. It matters not where you live or what rank of life you hold, the evil or the blessing will reach you all. The far and the near, the home counties and the back, the rich and the poor will suffer or rejoice alike. The heart that feels not now is dead; the blood of his children will curse his cowardice who shrinks back at a time when a little might have saved the whole and made *them* happy. I love the man that can smile in trouble, that can gather strength from distress and grow brave by reflection. 'Tis the business of little minds to shrink, but he whose heart is firm and whose conscience approves his conduct will pursue his principles unto death. My own line of reasoning is to myself as straight and clear as a ray of light. Not all the treasures of the world, so far as I believe, could have induced me to support an offensive war, for I think it murder; but if a thief breaks into my house, burns and destroys my property, and kills or threatens to kill me or those that are in it and to "bind me in all cases whatsoever" to his absolute will, am I to suffer it? What signifies it to me whether he who does it is a king or a common man, my countryman or not my countryman; whether it be done by an individual villain or an army of them? If we reason to the root of things, we shall find no difference; neither can any just cause be assigned why we should punish in the one case and pardon in the other. Let them call me rebel and welcome, I feel no concern from it; but I should suffer the misery of devils were I to make a whore of my soul by swearing allegiance to one whose character is that of a sottish, stupid, stubborn, worthless, brutish man. I conceive likewise a horrid idea in receiving mercy from a being who, at the last day, shall be shrieking to the rocks and mountains to cover him and fleeing with terror from the orphan, the widow, and the slain of America.

There are cases which cannot be overdone by language, and this is one. There are persons, too, who see not the full extent of the evil which threatens them; they solace themselves with hopes that the enemy, if he succeed, will be merciful. It is the madness of folly to expect mercy from those who have refused to do justice; and even mercy, where conquest is the object, is only a trick of war; the cunning of the fox is as murderous as the violence of the wolf, and we ought to guard equally against both. Howe's first object is, partly by threats and partly by promises, to terrify or seduce the people to deliver up their arms and receive mercy.

The ministry recommended the same plan to Gage,[10] and this is what the Tories call making their peace, "a peace which passeth all understanding" *indeed*![11] A peace which would be the immediate forerunner of a worse ruin than any we have yet thought of. Ye men of Pennsylvania, do reason upon these things! Were the back counties to give up their arms, they would fall an easy prey to the Indians, who are all armed: this perhaps is what some Tories would not be sorry for. Were the home counties to deliver up their arms, they would be exposed to the resentment of the back counties, who would then have it in their power to chastise their defection at pleasure. And were any one state to give up its arms, *that* state must be garrisoned by all Howe's army of Britons and Hessians to preserve it from the anger of the rest. Mutual fear is the principal link in the chain of mutual love, and woe be to that state that breaks the compact. Howe is mercifully inviting you to barbarous destruction, and men must be either rogues or fools that will not see it. I dwell not upon the vapors of imagination; I bring reason to your ears and, in language as plain as A, B, C, hold up truth to your eyes.

I thank God that I fear not. I see no real cause for fear. I know our situation well and can see the way out of it. While our army was collected Howe dared not risk a battle, and it is no credit to him that he decamped from the White Plains and waited a mean opportunity to ravage the defenseless Jerseys; but it is great credit to us that, with a handful of men, we sustained an orderly retreat for near a hundred miles, brought off our ammunition, all our field pieces, the greatest part of our stores, and had four rivers to pass. None can say that our retreat was precipitate, for we were near three weeks in performing it, that the country might have time to come in. Twice we marched back to meet the enemy and remained out till dark. The sign of fear was not seen in our camp; and had not some of the cowardly and disaffected inhabitants spread false alarms through the country, the Jerseys had never been ravaged. Once more we are again collected and collecting; our new army at both ends of the continent is recruiting fast, and we shall be able to open the next campaign with sixty thousand men, well armed and clothed. This is our situation, and who will may know it. By perseverance and fortitude we have the prospect of a glorious issue; by cowardice and submission, the sad choice of a variety of evils—a ravaged country, a depopulated city, habitations without safety and slavery without hope, our homes turned into barracks and bawdyhouses for Hessians,[12] and a future race to provide for whose fathers we shall doubt of. Look on this picture and weep over it! and if there yet remains one thoughtless wretch who believes it not, let him suffer it unlamented.

COMMON SENSE

December 23, 1776.[13]

THE AMERICAN CRISIS: XIII

THOUGHTS ON THE PEACE AND THE PROBABLE ADVANTAGES THEREOF

"THE TIMES that tried men's souls" [a] are over, and the greatest and completest revolution the world ever knew gloriously and happily accomplished.

But to pass from the extremes of danger to safety, from the tumult of war to the tranquillity of peace, though sweet in contemplation, requires a gradual composure of the senses to receive it. Even calmness has the power of stunning, when it opens too instantly upon us. The long and raging hurricane that should cease in a moment would leave us in a state rather of wonder than enjoyment, and some moments of recollection must pass before we could be capable of tasting the felicity of repose. There are but few instances in which the mind is fitted for sudden transitions; it takes in its pleasures by reflection and comparison, and those must have time to act before the relish for new scenes is complete.

In the present case, the mighty magnitude of the object, the various uncertainties of fate it has undergone, the numerous and complicated dangers we have suffered or escaped, the eminence we now stand on, and the vast prospect before us must all conspire to impress us with contemplation.

To see it in our power to make a world happy, to teach mankind the art of being so, to exhibit on the theater of the universe a character hitherto unknown, and to have, as it were, a new creation entrusted to our hands are honors that command reflection and can neither be too highly estimated nor too gratefully received.

In this pause then of recollection, while the storm is ceasing and the long-agitated mind vibrating to a rest, let us look back on the scenes we have passed and learn from experience what is yet to be done.

[a] "These are the times that try men's souls," *The Crisis No. I,* published December, 1776. [See p. 55.]

Never, I say, had a country so many openings to happiness as this. Her setting out in life, like the rising of a fair morning, was unclouded and promising. Her cause was good. Her principles just and liberal. Her temper serene and firm. Her conduct regulated by the nicest steps, and everything about her wore the mark of honor. It is not every country (perhaps there is not another in the world) that can boast so fair an origin. Even the first settlement of America corresponds with the character of the revolution. Rome, once the proud mistress of the universe, was originally a band of ruffians. Plunder and rapine made her rich, and her oppression of millions made her great. But America need never be ashamed to tell her birth, nor relate the stages by which she rose to empire.

The remembrance, then, of what is past, if it operates rightly, must inspire her with the most laudable of all ambition, that of adding to the fair fame she began with. The world has seen her great in adversity: struggling, without a thought of yielding, beneath accumulated difficulties, bravely, nay proudly, encountering distress; and rising in resolution as the storm increased. All this is justly due to her, for her fortitude has merited the character. Let then the world see that she can bear prosperity and that her honest virtue in time of peace is equal to the bravest virtue in time of war.

She is now descending to the scenes of quiet and domestic life. Not beneath the cypress shade of disappointment, but to enjoy in her own land and under her own vine the sweet of her labors and the reward of her toil. In this situation, may she never forget that a fair national reputation is of as much importance as independence. That it possesses a charm that wins upon the world and makes even enemies civil. That it gives a dignity which is often superior to power, and commands reverence where pomp and splendor fail.

It would be a circumstance ever to be lamented and never to be forgotten were a single blot, from any cause whatever, suffered to fall on a revolution which to the end of time must be an honor to the age that accomplished it, and which has contributed more to enlighten the world and diffuse a spirit of freedom and liberality among mankind than any human event (if this may be called one) that ever preceded it.

It is not among the least of the calamities of a long-continued war that it unhinges the mind from those nice sensations which at other times appear so amiable. The continual spectacle of woe blunts the finer feelings, and the necessity of bearing with the sight renders it familiar. In like manner are many of the moral obligations of society weakened, till the custom of acting by necessity becomes an apology where it is truly a crime. Yet let but a nation conceive rightly of its character, and it will be chastely just in protecting it. None ever began with a fairer than America, and none can be under a greater obligation to preserve it.

The debt which America has contracted, compared with the cause she has gained, and the advantages to flow from it, ought scarcely to be mentioned. She has it in her choice to do and to live as happily as she pleases The world is in her hands. She has no foreign power to monopolize her commerce, perplex her legislation, or control her prosperity. The struggle is over, which must one day have happened, and, perhaps, never could have happened at a better time.[b] And instead of a domineering master, she has gained an *ally* whose exemplary greatness and universal liberality have extorted a confession even from her enemies.

[b] That the revolution began at the exact period of time best fitted to the purpose is sufficiently proved by the event. But the great hinge on which the whole machine turned is the union of the states, and this union was naturally produced by the inability of any one state to support itself against any foreign enemy without the assistance of the rest.

Had the states severally been less able than they were when the war began, their united strength would not have been equal to the undertaking and they must, in all human probability, have failed. And, on the other hand, had they severally been more able they might not have seen or, what is more, might not have felt the necessity of uniting and, either by attempting to stand alone or in small confederacies, would have been separately conquered.

Now, as we cannot see a time (and many years must pass away before it can arrive) when the strength of any one state or several united can be equal to the whole of the present United States, and as we have seen the extreme difficulty of collectively prosecuting the war to a successful issue and preserving our national importance in the world, therefore, from the experience we have had and the knowledge we have gained, we must, unless we make a waste of

With the blessings of peace, independence, and a universal commerce, the states, individually and collectively, will have leisure and opportunity to regulate and establish their domestic concerns and to put it beyond the power of calumny to throw the least reflection on their honor. Character is much easier kept than recovered; and that man—if any such there be—who, from sinister views or littleness of soul, lends unseen his hand to injure it contrives a wound it will never be in his power to heal.

As we have established an inheritance for posterity, let that inheritance descend with every mark of an honorable conveyance. The little it will cost, compared with the worth of the states, the greatness of the object, and the value of the national character, will be a profitable exchange.

But that which must more forcibly strike a thoughtful, penetrating mind, and which includes and renders easy all inferior concerns, is the *union of the states*. On this our great national character depends. It is this which must give us importance abroad and security at home. It is through this only that we are or

---

wisdom, be strongly impressed with the advantage as well as the necessity of strengthening that happy union which had been our salvation and without which we should have been a ruined people.

While I was writing this note, I cast my eye on the pamphlet, *Common Sense*, from which I shall make an extract, as it exactly applies to the case. It is as follows:

"I have never met with a man, either in England or America, who has not confessed it as his opinion that a separation between the countries would take place one time or other; and there is no instance in which we have shown less judgment than in endeavoring to describe what we call the ripeness or fitness of the continent for independence.

"As all men allow the measure and differ only in their opinion of the time, let us, in order to remove mistakes, take a general survey of things and endeavor, if possible, to find out the *very time*. But we need not to go far; the inquiry ceases at once, for *the time has found us*. The general concurrence, the glorious union of all things prove the fact.

"It is not in numbers but in a union that our great strength lies. The continent is just arrived at that pitch of strength in which no single colony is able to support itself, and the whole, when united, can accomplish the matter; and either more or less than this might be fatal in its effects." [The discrepancies between this version and the text of *Common Sense* as given on pages 34 f. of this edition apparently represent Paine's improvement on this earlier work.]

can be nationally known in the world; it is the flag of the United States which renders our ships and commerce safe on the seas or in a foreign port. Our Mediterranean passes must be obtained under the same style. All our treaties, whether of alliance, peace, or commerce, are formed under the sovereignty of the United States, and Europe knows us by no other name or title.

The division of the empire into states is for our own convenience, but abroad this distinction ceases. The affairs of each state are local. They can go no further than to itself. And were the whole worth of even the richest of them expended in revenue, it would not be sufficient to support sovereignty against a foreign attack. In short, we have no other national sovereignty than as United States. It would even be fatal for us if we had—too expensive to be maintained and impossible to be supported. Individuals or individual states may call themselves what they please; but the world, and especially the world of enemies, is not to be held in awe by the whistling of a name. Sovereignty must have power to protect all the parts that compose and constitute it; and as *United States* we are equal to the importance of the title, but otherwise we are not. Our union, well and wisely regulated and cemented, is the cheapest way of being great, the easiest way of being powerful, and the happiest invention in government which the circumstances of America can admit of. Because it collects from each state that which, by being inadequate, can be of no use to it, and forms an aggregate that serves for all.

The states of Holland are an unfortunate instance of the effects of individual sovereignty. Their disjointed condition exposes them to numerous intrigues, losses, calamities, and enemies; and the almost impossibility of bringing their measures to a decision, and that decision into execution, is to them, and would be to us, a source of endless misfortune.

It is with confederated states as with individuals in society: something must be yielded up to make the whole secure. In this view of things we gain by what we give and draw an annual interest greater than the capital. I ever feel myself hurt when I hear the union, that great palladium of our liberty and safety, the least irreverently spoken of. It is the most sacred thing in the constitution of America and that which every man should be most proud and tender of. Our citizenship in the United States is our national character. Our citizenship in any particular state is only our local distinction. By the latter we are known at home, by the former to the world. Our great title is *Americans;* our inferior one varies with the place.

So far as my endeavors could go, they have all been directed to conciliate the affections, unite the interests, and draw and keep the mind of the country together; and the better to assist in this foundation work of the revolution, I have avoided all places of profit or office, either in the state I live in or in the United States,[1] kept myself at a distance from all parties and party connections, and even disregarded all private and inferior concerns; and when we take into view the great work which we have gone through and feel, as we ought to feel, the just importance of it, we shall then see that the little wranglings and indecent contentions of personal parley are as dishonorable to our characters as they are injurious to our repose.

It was the cause of America that made me an author. The force with which it struck my mind and the dangerous condition the country appeared to me in, by courting an impossible and an unnatural reconciliation with those who were determined to reduce her, instead of striking out into the only line that could cement and save her—*a declaration of independence*—made it impossible for me, feeling as I did, to be silent; and if, in the course of more than seven years, I have rendered her any service, I have likewise added something to the reputation of literature by freely and disinterestedly employing it in the great cause of mankind and showing that there may be genius without prostitution.

Independence always appeared to me practicable and probable, provided the sentiment of the country could be formed and held to the object; and there is no instance in the world where a people so extended and wedded to former habits of thinking, and under such a variety of circumstances, were so instantly and effectually pervaded by a turn in politics as in the case of independence, and who supported their opinion, undiminished, through such a succession of good and ill fortune till they crowned it with success.

But as the scenes of war are closed and every man preparing for home and happier times, I therefore take my leave of the subject. I have most sincerely followed it from beginning to end and through all its turns and windings; and whatever country I may hereafter be in, I shall always feel an honest pride at the part I have taken and acted, and a gratitude to nature and providence for putting it in my power to be of some use to mankind.

COMMON SENSE

Philadelphia, April 19, 1783 [2]

RIGHTS OF MAN

SELECTIONS FROM
PARTS ONE AND TWO

RIGHTS OF MAN

PART ONE

TO GEORGE WASHINGTON
PRESIDENT OF THE UNITED STATES OF AMERICA

S IR, I present you a small treatise in defense of those prin
ciples of freedom which your exemplary virtue has so emi
nently contributed to establish. That the rights of man may
become as universal as your benevolence can wish, and that you
may enjoy the happiness of seeing the New World regenerate the
Old, is the prayer of,

Sir,
Your much obliged and
obedient humble servant,
Thomas Paine

[Of the Limits of Constitutional Law]

AMONG THE INCIVILITIES by which nations or individuals provoke and irritate each other, Mr. Burke's pamphlet on the French Revolution is an extraordinary instance. Neither the people of France nor the National Assembly were troubling themselves about the affairs of England or the English Parliament; and that Mr. Burke should commence an unprovoked attack upon them, both in Parliament and in public, is a conduct that cannot be pardoned on the score of manners nor justified on that of policy. There is scarcely an epithet of abuse to be found in the English language with which Mr. Burke has not loaded the French nation and the National Assembly. Everything which rancor, prejudice, ignorance, or knowledge could suggest are poured forth in the copious fury of near four hundred pages. In the strain and on the plan Mr. Burke was writing, he might have written on to as many thousands. When the tongue or the pen is let loose in a frenzy of passion, it is the man and not the subject that becomes exhausted.

Hitherto Mr. Burke has not been mistaken and disappointed in the opinions he had formed of the affairs of France; but such is the ingenuity of his hope, or the malignancy of his despair, that it furnishes him with new pretenses to go on. There was a time when it was impossible to make Mr. Burke believe there would be any revolution in France. His opinion then was that the French had neither spirit to undertake it nor fortitude to support it, and now that there is one he seeks an escape by condemning it.

Not sufficiently content with abusing the National Assembly, a great part of his work is taken up with abusing Dr. Price [1] (one of the best-hearted men that lives) and the two societies in England known by the name of the Revolution Society and the Society for Constitutional Information.[2]

Dr. Price had preached a sermon on the fourth of November, 1789, being the anniversary of what is called in England the Revolution, which took place in 1688. Mr. Burke, speaking of this sermon, says,

The political divine proceeds dogmatically to assert that, by the principles of the Revolution, the people of England have acquired three fundamental rights:

1. To choose our own governors.
2. To cashier them for misconduct.
3. To frame a government for ourselves.

Dr. Price does not say that the right to do these things exists in this or in that person, or in this or in that description of persons, but that it exists in the *whole,* that it is a right resident in the nation. Mr. Burke, on the contrary, denies that such a right exists in the nation, either in whole or in part, or that it exists anywhere; and, what is still more strange and marvelous, he says, "that the people of England utterly disclaim such a right, ahd that they will resist the practical assertion of it with their lives and fortunes."

That men should take up arms and spend their lives and fortunes *not* to maintain their rights, but to maintain they have *not* rights, is an entirely new species of discovery and suited to the paradoxical genius of Mr. Burke.

The method which Mr. Burke takes to prove that the people of England had no such rights and that such rights do not now exist in the nation, either in whole or in part, or anywhere at all, is of the same marvelous and monstrous kind with what he has already said; for his arguments are that the persons or the generation of persons in whom they did exist are dead, and with them the right is dead also.

To prove this, he quotes a declaration made by Parliament about a hundred years ago to William and Mary, in these words: "The Lords Spiritual and Temporal, and Commons, do, in the name of the people aforesaid" (meaning the people of England then living), "most humbly and faithfully *submit* themselves, their *heirs* and *posterities, forever.*" He also quotes a clause of another act of Parliament made in the same reign, the terms of which, he says, "bind us" (meaning the people of that day), "our *heirs* and our *posterity,* to *them,* their *heirs* and *posterity,* to the end of time."

Mr. Burke conceives his point sufficiently established by producing these clauses, which he enforces by saying that they exclude the right of the nation *forever*. And not yet content with making such declarations, repeated over and over again, he further says "that if the people of England possessed such a right before the Revolution" (which he acknowledges to have been the case, not only in England but throughout Europe, at an early period), "yet that the *English nation* did, at the time of the Revolution, most solemnly renounce and abdicate it, for themselves, and for *all their posterity, forever*."

As Mr. Burke occasionally applies the poison drawn from his horrid principles, not only to the English nation, but to the French Revolution and the National Assembly, and charges that august, illuminated, and illuminating body of men with the epithet of "usurpers," I shall, *sans cérémonie*, place another system of principles in opposition to his.

The English Parliament of 1688 did a certain thing which, for themselves and their constituents, they had a right to do and which it appeared right should be done. But in addition to this right, which they possessed by delegation, *they set up another right by assumption*, that of binding and controlling posterity to the end of time.

The case, therefore, divides itself into two parts: the right which they possessed by delegation, and the right which they set up by assumption. The first is admitted, but with respect to the second, I reply:

There never did, there never will, and there never can exist a Parliament, or any description of men, or any generation of men, in any country, possessed of the right or the power of binding and controlling posterity to the "end of time," or of commanding forever how the world shall be governed or who shall govern it; and therefore all such clauses, acts, or declarations, by which the makers of them attempt to do what they have neither the right nor the power to do, nor the power to execute, are in themselves null and void.

Every age and generation must be as free to act for itself, *in all cases*, as the ages and generation which preceded it. The vanity and presumption of governing beyond the grave is the most ridiculous and insolent of all tyrannies.

Man has no property in man; neither has any generation a property in the generations which are to follow. The Parliament or the people of 1688, or of any other period, had no more right to dispose of the people of the present day, or to bind or to control them *in any shape whatever,* than the Parliament or the people of the present day have to dispose of, bind, or control those who are to live a hundred or a thousand years hence.

Every generation is and must be competent to all the purposes which its occasions require. It is the living, and not the dead, that are to be accommodated. When man ceases to be, his power and his wants cease with him; and having no longer any participation in the concerns of this world, he has no longer any authority in directing who shall be its governors, or how its government shall be organized or how administered.

I am not contending for nor against any form of government, nor for nor against any party here or elsewhere. That which a whole nation chooses to do it has a right to do. Mr. Burke says, No. Where then does the right exist? I am contending for the rights of the *living,* and against their being willed away and controlled and contracted for by the manuscript assumed authority of the dead; and Mr. Burke is contending for the authority of the dead over the rights and freedom of the living.

There was a time when kings disposed of their crowns by will upon their deathbeds and consigned the people, like beasts of the field, to whatever successor they appointed. This is now so exploded as scarcely to be remembered and so monstrous as hardly to be believed. But the parliamentary clauses upon which Mr. Burke builds his political church are of the same nature.

The laws of every country must be analogous to some common principle. In England, no parent or master, nor all the authority of Parliament, omnipotent as it has called itself, can bind or control the personal freedom even of an individual beyond the age of twenty-one years. On what ground of right, then, could the Parliament of 1688, or any other parliament, bind all posterity forever?

Those who have quitted the world and those who are not yet arrived in it are as remote from each other as the utmost stretch of moral imagination can conceive. What possible obligation, then, can exist between them; what rule or principle can be laid down that two nonentities, the one out of existence and the other not in, and who never can meet in this world, that the one should control the other to the end of time?

In England, it is said that money cannot be taken out of the pockets of the people without their consent. But who authorized, or who could authorize, the Parliament of 1688 to control and take away the freedom of posterity, and limit and confine their right of acting in certain cases forever, who were not in existence to give or to withhold their consent?

A greater absurdity cannot present itself to the understanding of man than what Mr. Burke offers to his readers. He tells them, and he tells the world to come, that a certain body of men, who existed a hundred years ago, made a law; and that there does not now exist in the nation, nor ever will, nor ever can, a power to alter it. Under how many subtilties or absurdities has the divine right to govern been imposed on the credulity of mankind! Mr. Burke has discovered a new one, and he has shortened his journey to Rome by appealing to the power of this infallible Parliament of former days; and he produces what it has done as of divine authority, for that power must certainly be more than human which no human power to the end of time can alter.

But Mr. Burke has done some service, not to his cause, but to his country, by bringing those clauses into public view. They serve to demonstrate how necessary it is at all times to watch against the attempted encroachment of power and to prevent its running to excess.

It is somewhat extraordinary that the offense for which James II [3] was expelled, that of setting up power by *assumption*, should be re-acted, under another shape and form, by the Parliament that expelled him. It shows that the rights of man were but imperfectly understood at the Revolution; for certain it is that the right which that Parliament set up by *assumption* (for by delegation it had it not, and could not have it because none could give it) over the persons and freedom of posterity forever was the same tyrannical, unfounded kind which James attempted to set up over the Parliament and the nation, and for which he was expelled.

The only differenee is (for in principle they differ not) that the one was a usurper over the living and the other over the unborn; and as the one has no better authority to stand upon than the other, both of them must be equally null and void, and of no effect.

From what, or from whence, does Mr. Burke prove the right of any human power to bind posterity forever? He has produced his clauses, but he must produce also his proofs that such a right existed and show how it existed. If it ever existed, it must now exist; for whatever appertains to the nature of man cannot be annihilated by man.

It is the nature of man to die, and he will continue to die as long as he continues to be born. But Mr. Burke has set up a sort of political Adam, in whom all posterity are bound forever; he must therefore prove that his Adam possessed such a power or such a right.

The weaker any cord is, the less it will bear to be stretched and the worse is the policy to stretch it, unless it is intended to break it. Had a person contemplated the overthrow of Mr. Burke's positions, he would have proceeded as Mr. Burke has done. He would have magnified the authorities on purpose to have called the *right* of them into question, and the instant the question of right was started the authorities must have been given up.

It requires but a very small glance of thought to perceive that, although laws made in one generation often continue in force through succeeding generations, yet they continue to derive their force from the consent of the living. A law not repealed continues in force, not because it cannot be repealed, but because it is not repealed; and the nonrepealing passes for consent.

But Mr. Burke's clauses have not even this qualification in their favor. They become null by attempting to become immortal. The nature of them precludes consent. They destroy the right which they *might* have by grounding it on a right which they *cannot* have. Immortal power is not a human right, and therefore cannot be a right of Parliament.

The Parliament of 1688 might as well have passed an act to have authorized themselves to live forever as to make their authority to live forever. All therefore that can be said of them is that they are a formality of words, of as much import as if those who used them had addressed a congratulation to themselves and, in the oriental style of antiquity, had said, O Parliament, live forever!

The circumstances of the world are continually changing, and the opinions of men change also; and as government is for the living, and not for the dead, it is the living only that has any right in it. That which may be thought right and found convenient in one age may be thought wrong and found inconvenient in another. In such cases, who is to decide, the living or the dead?

As almost one hundred pages of Mr. Burke's book are employed upon these clauses, it will consequently follow that if the clauses themselves, so far as they set up an *assumed, usurped* dominion over posterity forever, are unauthoritative and in their nature null and void, that all his voluminous inferences and declamation drawn therefrom or founded thereon are null and void also, and on this ground I rest the matter.

. . . .

[OF THE NATURAL AND CIVIL RIGHTS OF MAN]

I have now to follow Mr. Burke through a pathless wilderness of rhapsodies and a sort of descant upon governments, in which he asserts whatever he pleases, on the presumption of its being believed, without offering either evidence or reasons for so doing.

Before anything can be reasoned upon to a conclusion, certain facts, principles, or data to reason from must be established, admitted, or denied. Mr. Burke, with his usual outrage, abuses the Declaration of the Rights of Man,[a] published by the National Assembly of France, as the basis on which the Constitution of France is built. This he calls "paltry and blurred sheets of paper about the rights of man."

Does Mr. Burke mean to deny that *man* has any rights? If he

[a] [See pp. 96 ff.]

does, then he must mean that there are no such things as rights anywhere and that he has none himself, for who is there in the world but man? But if Mr. Burke means to admit that man has rights, the question then will be, what are those rights, and how came man by them originally?

The error of those who reason by precedents drawn from antiquity, respecting the rights of man, is that they do not go far enough into antiquity. They do not go the whole way. They stop in some of the intermediate stages of a hundred or a thousand years and produce what was then done as a rule for the present day. This is no authority at all.

If we travel still further into antiquity, we shall find a directly contrary opinion and practice prevailing; and if antiquity is to be authority, a thousand such authorities may be produced, successively contradicting each other; but if we proceed on, we shall at last come out right: we shall come to the time when man came from the hand of his Maker. What was he then? Man. Man was his high and only title, and a higher cannot be given him. But of titles I shall speak hereafter.

We have now arrived at the origin of man and at the origin of his rights. As to the manner in which the world has been governed from that day to this, it is no further any concern of ours than to make a proper use of the errors or the improvements which the history of it presents. Those who lived a hundred or a thousand years ago were then moderns as we are now. They had *their* ancients, and those ancients had others, and we also shall be ancients in our turn.

If the mere name of antiquity is to govern in the affairs of life, the people who are to live a hundred or a thousand years hence may as well take us for a precedent, as we make a precedent of those who lived a hundred or a thousand years ago.

The fact is that portions of antiquity, by proving everything, establish nothing. It is authority against authority all the way, till we come to the divine origin of the rights of man at the creation. Here our inquiries find a resting place and our reason finds a home.

If a dispute about the rights of man had arisen at a distance of a hundred years from the creation, it is to this source of authority they must have referred; and it is to the same source of authority that we must now refer.

Though I mean not to touch upon any sectarian principle of religion, yet it may be worth observing that the genealogy of Christ is traced to Adam. Why then not trace the rights of man to the creation of man? I will answer the question. Because there have been upstart governments thrusting themselves between and presumptuously working to *unmake* man.

If any generation of men ever possessed the right of dictating the mode by which the world should be governed forever, it was the first generation that existed; and if that generation did it not, no succeeding generation can show any authority for doing it, nor can set any up.

The illuminating and divine principle of the equal rights of man (for it has its origin from the Maker of man) relates not only to the living individuals, but to generations of men succeeding each other. Every generation is equal in rights to the generations which preceded it, by the same rule that every individual is born equal in rights with his contemporary.

Every history of the creation and every traditionary account, whether from the lettered or unlettered world, however they may vary in their opinion or belief of certain particulars, all agree in establishing one point, *the unity of man;* by which I mean that men are all of *one degree,* and consequently that all men are born equal and with equal natural rights, in the same manner as if posterity had been continued by *creation* instead of *generation,* the latter being only the mode by which the former is carried forward; and consequently every child born into the world must be considered as deriving its existence from God. The world is as new to him as it was to the first man that existed, and his natural right in it is of the same kind.

The Mosaic account of the creation, whether taken as divine authority or merely historical, is fully up to this point, *the unity or equality of man.* The expressions admit of no controversy. "And God said, let us make man in our own image. In the image of God created he him; male and female created he them." The distinction of sexes is pointed out, but no other distinction is even implied. If this be not divine authority, it is at least historical authority and shows that the equality of man, so far from being a modern doctrine, is the oldest upon record.

It is also to be observed that all the religions known in the world are founded, so far as they relate to man, on the *unity of man,* as being all of one degree. Whether in heaven or in hell, or in whatever state man may be supposed to exist hereafter, the good and the bad are the only distinctions. Nay, even the laws of governments are obliged to slide into this principle, by making degrees to consist in crimes and not in persons.

It is one of the greatest of all truths, and of the highest advantage to cultivate. By considering man in this light, and by instructing him to consider himself in this light, it places him in a close connection with all his duties, whether to his Creator or to the creation, of which he is a part; and it is only when he forgets his origin, or, to use a more fashionable phrase, his *birth and family,* that he becomes dissolute.

It is not among the least of the evils of the present existing governments in all parts of Europe, that man, considered as man, is thrown back to a vast distance from his Maker, and the artificial chasm filled up by a succession of barriers, or a sort of turnpike gates, through which he has to pass.

I will quote Mr. Burke's catalogue of barriers that he has set up between man and his Maker. Putting himself in the character of a herald, he says: "We fear God; we look with *awe* to kings, with affection to parliaments, with duty to magistrates, with reverence to priests, and with respect to nobility." Mr. Burke has forgotten to put in "chivalry." He has also forgotten to put in Peter.

The duty of man is not a wilderness of turnpike gates, through which he is to pass by tickets from one to the other. It is plain and simple and consists but of two points: his duty to God, which every man must feel; and with respect to his neighbor, to do as he would be done by. If those to whom power is delegated do well they will be respected, if not they will be despised; and with regard to those to whom no power is delegated, but who assume it, the rational world can know nothing of them.

Hitherto we have spoken only (and that but in part) of the natural rights of man. We have now to consider the civil rights of man and to show how the one originates from the other. Man did not enter into society to become *worse* than he was before, nor to have fewer rights than he had before, but to have those rights better secured. His natural rights are the foundation of all his civil rights. But in order to pursue this distinction with more precision, it is necessary to make the different qualities of natural and civil rights.

A few words will explain this. Natural rights are those which appertain to man in right of his existence. Of this kind are all the intellectual rights, or rights of the mind, and also all those rights of acting as an individual for his own comfort and happiness which are not injurious to the natural rights of others. Civil rights are those which appertain to man in right of his being a member of society.

Every civil right has for its foundation some natural right pre-existing in the individual, but to the enjoyment of which his individual power is not in all cases sufficiently competent. Of this kind are all those which relate to security and protection.

From this short review it will be easy to distinguish between that class of natural rights which man retains after entering into society and those which he throws into the common stock as a member of society.

The natural rights which he retains are all those in which the *power* to execute is as perfect in the individual as the right itself. Among this class, as is before mentioned, are all the intellectual rights, or rights of the mind; consequently religion is one of those rights.

The natural rights which are not retained are all those in which, though the right is perfect in the individual, the power to execute them is defective. They answer not his purpose. A man, by natural right, has a right to judge in his own cause, and so far as the right of the mind is concerned he never surrenders it; but what avails it him to judge if he has not power to redress? He therefore deposits his right in the common stock of society and takes the arm of society, of which he is a part, in preference and in addition to his own. Society *grants* him nothing. Every man is proprietor in society and draws on the capital as a matter of right.

From these premises, two or three certain conclusions will follow:

First, that every civil right grows out of a natural right; or, in other words, is a natural right exchanged.

Secondly, that civil power, properly considered as such, is made up of the aggregate of that class of the natural rights of man which becomes defective in the individual in point of power and answers not his purpose, but when collected to a focus becomes competent to the purpose of everyone.

Thirdly, that the power produced from the aggregate of natural rights, imperfect in power in the individual, cannot be applied to invade the natural rights which are retained in the individual and in which the power to execute is as perfect as the right itself.

We have now, in a few words, traced man from a natural individual to a member of society and shown, or endeavored to show, the quality of the natural rights retained and those which are exchanged for civil rights. Let us now apply those principles to governments.

[OF THE NATURE OF GOVERNMENT]

In casting our eyes over the world, it is extremely easy to distinguish the governments which have arisen out of society, or out of the social compact, from those which have not; but to place this in a clearer light than what a single glance may afford, it will be proper to take a review of the several sources from which the governments have arisen and on which they have been founded.

They may be all comprehended under three heads. *First,* superstition. *Secondly,* power. *Thirdly,* the common interests of society and the common rights of man.

The first was a government of priestcraft, the second, of conquerors, and the third, of reason.

When a set of artful men pretended, through the medium of oracles, to hold intercourse with the Deity, as familiarly as they now march up the backstairs in European courts, the world was completely under the government of superstition. The oracles were consulted, and whatever they were made to say became the law; and this sort of government lasted as long as this sort of superstition lasted.

After these a race of conquerors arose whose government, like that of William the Conqueror, was founded in power, and the sword assumed the name of a scepter. Governments thus established last as long as the power to support them lasts; but that they might avail themselves of every engine in their favor, they united fraud to force and set up an idol which they called "Divine Right," and which, in imitation of the Pope, who affects to be spiritual and temporal, and in contradiction to the founder of the Christian religion, twisted itself afterward into an idol of another shape, called "Church and State." The key of Saint Peter and the key of the treasury became quartered on one another, and the wondering, cheated multitude worshiped the invention.

When I contemplate the natural dignity of man, when I feel (for nature has not been kind enough to me to blunt my feelings) for the honor and happiness of its character, I become irritated at the attempt to govern mankind by force and fraud, as if they were all knaves and fools, and can scarcely avoid disgust at those who are thus imposed upon.

We have now to review the governments which arise out of society, in contradistinction to those which arose out of superstition and conquest.

It has been thought a considerable advance toward establishing the principles of freedom to say that government is a compact between those who govern and those who are governed, but this cannot be true, because it is putting the effect before the cause; for as a man must have existed before governments existed, there necessarily was a time when governments did not exist, and consequently there could originally exist no governors to form such a compact with.

The fact therefore must be that the *individuals themselves*, each in his own personal and sovereign right, *entered into a compact with each other* to produce a government; and this is the only mode in which governments have a right to arise and the only principle on which they have a right to exist.

To possess ourselves of a clear idea of what government is, or ought to be, we must trace it to its origin. In doing this, we shall easily discover that governments must have arisen either *out* of the people or *over* the people. Mr. Burke has made no distinction.

He investigates nothing to its source, and therefore he confounds everything; but he has signified his intention of undertaking at some future opportunity a comparison between the constitutions of England and France.

As he thus renders it a subject of controversy by throwing the gauntlet, I take him upon his own ground. It is in high challenges that high truths have the right of appearing; and I accept it with the more readiness because it affords me, at the same time, an opportunity of pursuing the subject with respect to governments arising out of society.

But it will be first necessary to define what is meant by a "constitution." It is not sufficient that we adopt the word; we must fix also a standard signification to it.

A constitution is not a thing in name only, but in fact. It has not an ideal, but a real existence; and wherever it cannot be produced in a visible form, there is none. A constitution is a thing *antecedent* to a government, and a government is only the creature of a constitution. The constitution of a country is not the act of its government, but of the people constituting a government.

It is the body of elements to which you can refer and quote article by article, and which contains the principles on which the government shall be established, the manner in which it shall be organized, the powers it shall have, the mode of elections, the duration of parliaments or by what other name such bodies may be called, the powers which the executive part of the government shall have, and, in fine, everything that relates to the complete organization of a civil government and the principles on which it shall act and by which it shall be bound.

A constitution, therefore, is to a government what the laws made afterward by that government are to a court of judicature. The court of judicature does not make the laws, neither can it alter them; it only acts in conformity to the laws made, and the government is in like manner governed by the constitution.

.   .   .   .

[OF ARISTOCRACY]

The French constitution says, "there shall be no titles," and of consequence all that class of equivocal generation which in some countries is called "aristocracy" and in others "nobility" is done away, and the "peer" is exalted into "man."

Titles are but nicknames, and every nickname is a title. The thing is perfectly harmless in itself, but it marks a sort of foppery in the human character which degrades it. It renders man diminutive in things which are great, and the counterfeit of woman in things which are little. It talks about its fine blue "riband" like a girl, and shows its new "garter" like a child. A certain writer, of some antiquity, says, "When I was a child, I thought as a child; but when I became a man, I put away childish things." [4]

It is, properly, from the elevated mind of France that the folly of titles has been abolished. It has outgrown the baby clothes of "count" and "duke," and breeched itself in manhood. France has not leveled, it has exalted. It has put down the dwarf to set up the man. The insignificance of a senseless word like "duke," "count," or "earl" has ceased to please. Even those who possessed them have disowned the gibberish and as they outgrew the rickets have despised the rattle.

The genuine mind of man, thirsting for its native home, society, contemns the gewgaws that separate him from it. Titles are like circles drawn by the magician's wand to contract the sphere of man's felicity. He lives immured within the Bastille of a word and surveys at a distance the envied life of man.

Is it then any wonder that titles should fall in France? Is it not a greater wonder they should be kept up anywhere? What are they? What is their worth and "what is their amount?" When we think or speak of a "judge" or a "general," we associate with it the ideas of office and character; we think of gravity in the one and bravery in the other; but when we use a word merely as a title, no ideas associate with it.

Through all the vocabulary of Adam, there is no such an animal as a duke or a count; neither can we connect any idea to the words. Whether they mean strength or weakness, wisdom or folly, a child or a man, or a rider or a horse, is all equivocal. What respect then can be paid to that which describes nothing and which means nothing? Imagination has given figure and character to centaurs, satyrs, and down to all the fairy tribe, but titles baffle even the powers of fancy and are a chimerical nondescript.

But this is not all. If a whole country is disposed to hold them in contempt, all their value is gone and none will own them. It is common opinion only that makes them anything or nothing, or worse than nothing. There is no occasion to take titles away, for they take themselves away when society concurs to ridicule them. This species of imaginary consequence has visibly declined in every part of Europe, and it hastens to its exit as the world of reason continues to rise.

There was a time when the lowest class of what are called nobility was more thought of than the highest is now, and when a man in armor riding through Christendom in search of adventure was more stared at than a modern duke. The world has seen this folly fall, and it has fallen by being laughed at, and the farce of titles will follow its fate.

The patriots of France have discovered in good time that rank and dignity in society must take a new ground. The old one has fallen through. It must now take the substantial ground of character, instead of the chimerical ground of titles; and they have brought their titles to the altar and made of them a burnt offering to reason.

If no mischief had annexed itself to the folly of titles, they would not have been worth a serious and formal destruction, such as the National Assembly have decreed them; and this makes it necessary to inquire further into the nature and character of aristocracy.

That, then, which is called aristocracy in some countries and nobility in others arose out of the governments founded upon conquest. It was originally a military order for the purpose of supporting military government (for such were all governments founded in conquest); and to keep up a succession of this order for the purpose for which it was established, all the younger branches of those families were disinherited and the law of *primogenitureship* set up.

The nature and character of aristocracy shows itself to us in this law. It is a law against every law of nature, and nature herself calls for its destruction. Establish family justice, and aristocracy falls. By the aristocratical law of primogenitureship, in a family of six children, five are exposed. Aristocracy has never more than one child. The rest are begotten to be devoured. They are thrown to the cannibal for prey, and the natural parent prepares the unnatural repast.

As everything which is out of nature in man affects, more or less, the interest of society, so does this. All the children which the aristocracy disowns (which are all except the eldest) are, in general, cast like orphans on a parish, to be provided for by the public, but at a greater charge. Unnecessary offices and places in governments and courts are created at the expense of the public to maintain them.

With what kind of parental reflections can the father or mother contemplate their younger offspring? By nature they are children and by marriage they are heirs, but by aristocracy they are bastards and orphans. They are the flesh and blood of their parents in one line, and nothing akin to them in the other. To restore, therefore, parents to their children and children to their parents—relations to each other and man to society—and to exterminate the monster aristocracy, root and branch, the French constitution has destroyed the law of primogenitureship. Here then lies the monster; and Mr. Burke, if he pleases, may write its epitaph.

Hitherto we have considered aristocracy chiefly in one point of view. We have now to consider it in another. But whether we view it before or behind, or sideways, or anyway else, domestically or publicly, it is still a monster.

In France, aristocracy has one feature less in its countenance than what it has in some other countries. It did not compose a body of hereditary legislators. It was not "a corporation of aristocracy," for such I have heard M. de Lafayette [5] describe an English House of Peers. Let us then examine the grounds upon which the French constitution has resolved against having such a House in France:

Because, *in the first place,* as is already mentioned, aristocracy is kept up by family tyranny and injustice.

Secondly, because there is an unusual unfitness in an aristocracy to be legislators for a nation. Their ideas of "distributive justice" are corrupted at the very source. They begin life by trampling on all their younger brothers and sisters and relations of every kind, and are taught and educated so to do. With what ideas of justice or honor can that man enter a house of legislation who absorbs in his own person the inheritance of a whole family of children or doles out to them some pitiful portion with the insolence of a gift?

Thirdly, because the idea of hereditary legislators is as inconsistent as that of hereditary judges or hereditary juries, and as absurd as a hereditary mathematician or a hereditary wise man, and as ridiculous as a hereditary poet-laureate.

Fourthly, because a body of men holding themselves accountable to nobody ought not to be trusted by anybody.

Fifthly, because it is continuing the uncivilized principles of the governments founded in conquest and the base idea of man having property in man and governing him by personal right.

Sixthly, because aristocracy has a tendency to degenerate the human species. By the universal economy of nature it is known, and by the instance of the Jews it is proved, that the human species has a tendency to degenerate, in any small number of persons, when separated from the general stock of society and intermarrying constantly with each other.

It defeats even its pretended end and becomes in time the opposite of what is noble in man. Mr. Burke talks of nobility; let him show what it is. The greatest characters the world has known have risen on the democratic floor. Aristocracy has not been able to keep a proportionate pace with democracy.

The artificial noble shrinks into a dwarf before the noble of nature; and in the few instances of those (for there are some in all countries) in whom nature, as by a miracle, has survived in aristocracy, *those men despise it.*

. . . .

[OF RELIGIOUS FREEDOM]

The French constitution has abolished or renounced *toleration,* and *intolerance* also, and has established *universal right of conscience.*

Toleration is not the *opposite* of intoleration, but is the *counterfeit* of it. Both are despotisms. The one assumes to itself the right of withholding liberty of conscience, and the other of granting it. The one is the Pope armed with fire and faggot, and the other is the Pope selling or granting indulgences. The former is church and state, and the latter is church and traffic.

But toleration may be viewed in a much stronger light. Man worships not himself but his Maker; and the liberty of conscience which he claims is not for the service of himself but of his God. In this case, therefore, we must necessarily have the associated idea of two beings: the *mortal* who renders the worship, and the *immortal being* who is worshiped.

Toleration therefore, places itself not between man and man, nor between church and church, nor between one denomination of religion and another, but between God and man—between the being who worships and the *being* who is worshiped; and by the same act of assumed authority by which it tolerates man to pay his worship, it presumptuously and blasphemously sets up itself to tolerate the Almighty to receive it.

Were a bill brought into Parliament entitled, "An *act* to tolerate or grant liberty to the Almighty to receive the worship of a Jew or a Turk" or "to prohibit the Almighty from receiving it," all men would startle and call it blasphemy. There would be an uproar. The presumption of toleration in religious matters would then present itself unmasked; but the presumption is not the less because the name of man only appears to those laws, for the associated idea of the *worshiper* and the *worshiped* cannot be separated.

Who, then, art thou, vain dust and ashes! by whatever name thou art called, whether a king, a bishop, a church or a state, a parliament or anything else, that obtrudest thine insignificance between the soul of man and his Maker? Mind thine own concerns. If he believes not as thou believest, it is a proof that thou believest not as he believeth, and there is no earthly power can determine between you.

With respect to what are called denominations of religion, if everyone is left to judge of his own religion, there is no such thing as a religion that is wrong; but if they are to judge of each other's religion, there is no such thing as a religion that is right, and therefore all the world is right or all the world is wrong.

But with respect to religion itself, without regard to names and as directing itself from the universal family of mankind to the divine object of all adoration, *it is man bringing to his Maker the fruits of his heart;* and though these fruits may differ from each other like the fruits of the earth, the grateful tribute of everyone is accepted.

A bishop of Durham, or a bishop of Winchester, or the archbishop who heads the dukes will not refuse a tithe sheaf of wheat because it is not a cock of hay, nor a cock of hay because it is not a sheaf of wheat, nor a pig because it is neither the one nor the other; but these same persons, under the figure of an established church, will not permit their Maker to receive the various tithes of man's devotion.

One of the continual choruses of Mr. Burke's book is "church and state." He does not mean some one particular church or some one particular state, but any church and state; and he uses the term as a general figure to hold forth the political doctrine of always uniting the church with the state in every country, and he censures the National Assembly for not having done this in France. Let us bestow a few thoughts on this subject.

All religions are in their nature mild and benign and united with principles of morality. They could not have made proselytes at first by professing anything that was vicious, cruel, persecuting, or immoral. Like everything else, they had their beginning; and they proceeded by persuasion, exhortation, and example. How, then, is it that they lose their native mildness and become morose and intolerant?

It proceeds from the connection which Mr. Burke recommends. By engendering the church with the state, a sort of mule animal, capable only of destroying, and not of breeding up, is produced, called, "the church established by law." It is a stranger, even from its birth, to any parent mother on which it is begotten and whom in time it kicks out and destroys.

The Inquisition in Spain does not proceed from the religion originally professed, but from this mule animal engendered between the church and the state. The burnings in Smithfield[6] proceeded from the same heterogeneous production; and it was the regeneration of this strange animal in England afterward that renewed rancor and irreligion among the inhabitants and that drove the people called Quakers and Dissenters to America.[7]

Persecution is not an original feature in *any* religion, but it is always the strongly marked feature of all law religions, or religions established by law. Take away the law establishment, and every religion reassumes its original benignity. In America, a Catholic priest is a good citizen, a good character, and a good neighbor; an Episcopal minister is of the same description; and this proceeds, independently of the men, from there being no law establishment in America.

If, also, we view this matter in a temporal sense, we shall see the ill effects it has had on the prosperity of nations. The union of church and state has impoverished Spain. The revoking the Edict of Nantes[8] drove the silk manufacture from France into England, and church and state are now driving the cotton manufacture from England to America and France.

Let then Mr. Burke continue to preach his antipolitical doctrine of church and state. It will do some good. The National Assembly will not follow his advice, but will benefit by his folly. It was by observing the ill effects of it in England that America has been warned against it; and it is by experiencing them in France that the National Assembly have abolished it and, like America, have established *universal right of conscience and universal right of citizenship.*[b]

. . . .

The conspiracy being thus dispersed, one of the first works of the National Assembly, instead of vindictive proclamations, as has been the case with other governments, published a Declaration of the Rights of Man, as the basis on which the new constitution was to be built, and which is here subjoined.

[b] When in any country we see extraordinary circumstances taking place, they naturally lead any man who has a talent for observation and investigation to inquire into the causes. The manufactures of Manchester, Birmingham, and Sheffield are the principal manufactures in England. From whence did this arise? A little observation will explain the case.

The principal and the generality of the inhabitants of those places are not of what is called in England "the church established by law"; and they or their fathers (for it is within but a few years) withdrew from the persecution of the chartered towns, where test laws more particularly operate, and established a sort of asylum for themselves in those places. It was the only asylum that then offered, for the rest of Europe was worse.

But the case is now changing. France and America bid all comers welcome, and initiate them into all the rights of citizenship. Policy and interest, therefore, will, but perhaps too late, dictate in England what reason and justice could not. Those manufactures are withdrawing and are arising in other places. There is now [1791] erecting at Passy, three miles from Paris, a large cotton mill, and several are already erected in America. Soon after the rejecting the bill for repealing the test law, one of the richest manufacturers in England said in my hearing, "England, Sir, is not a country for a Dissenter to live in— we must go to France."

These are truths, and it is doing justice to both parties to tell them. It is chiefly the Dissenters who have carried English manufactures to the height they are now at, and the same men have it in their power to carry them away; and though those manufactures would afterward continue to be made in those places, the foreign market would be lost. There are frequently appearing in the London *Gazette* extracts from certain acts to prevent machines and, as far as it can extend to, persons from going out of the country.

It appears from these that the ill effects of the test laws and church establishment begin to be much suspected, but the remedy of force can never supply the remedy of reason. In the progress of less than a century, all the unrepresented part of England, of all denominations, which is at least a hundred times the most numerous, may begin to feel the necessity of a constitution, and then all those matters will come regularly before them.

DECLARATION OF THE RIGHTS OF MAN
AND OF CITIZENS

BY THE NATIONAL ASSEMBLY OF FRANCE

The representatives of the people of France, formed into a National Assembly, considering that ignorance, neglect, or contempt of human rights are the sole causes of public misfortunes and corruptions of government, have resolved to set forth in a solemn declaration these natural, imprescriptible, and unalienable rights; that, this declaration being constantly present to the minds of the members of the body social, they may be ever kept attentive to their rights and their duties; that the acts of the legislative and executive powers of government, being capable of being every moment compared with the end of political institutions, may be more respected; and also that the future claims of the citizens, being directed by simple and incontestible principles, may always tend to the maintenance of the constitution and the general happiness.

For these reasons the National Assembly does recognize and declare, in the presence of the Supreme Being, and with the hope of His blessing and favor, the following *sacred* rights of men and of citizens:

I. *Men are born, and always continue, free and equal in respect of their rights. Civil distinctions, therefore, can be founded only on public utility.*

II. *The end of all political associations is the preservation of the natural and imprescriptible rights of man; and these rights are liberty, property, security, and resistance of oppression.*

III. *The nation is essentially the source of all sovereignty; nor can any individual or any body of men be entitled to any authority which is not expressly derived from it.*

IV. Political liberty consists in the power of doing whatever does not injure another. The exercise of the natural rights of every man has no other limits than those which are necessary to secure to every *other* man the free exercise of the same rights, and these limits are determinable only by the law.

V. The law ought to prohibit only actions hurtful to society.

What is not prohibited by the law should not be hindered; nor should anyone be compelled to that which the law does not require.

VI. The law is an expression of the will of the community. All citizens have a right to concur, either personally or by their representatives, in its formation. It should be the same to all, whether it protects or punishes; and *all being equal in its sight are equally eligible to all honors, places, and employments, according to their different abilities, without any other distinction than that created by their virtues and talents.*

VII. No man should be accused, arrested, or held in confinement, except in cases determined by the law and according to the forms which it has prescribed. All who promote, solicit, execute, or cause to be executed arbitrary orders ought to be punished, and every citizen called upon or apprehended by virtue of the law ought immediately to obey and renders himself culpable by resistance.

VIII. The law ought to impose no other penalties but such as are absolutely and evidently necessary, and no one ought to be punished but in virtue of a law promulgated before the offense and legally applied.

IX. Every man being presumed innocent till he has been convicted, whenever his detention becomes indispensable, all rigor to him—more than is necessary to secure his person—ought to be provided against by the law.

X. No man ought to be molested on account of his opinions, not even on account of his *religious* opinions, provided his avowal of them does not disturb the public order established by the law.

XI. The unrestrained communication of thoughts and opinions being one of the most precious rights of man, every citizen may speak, write, and publish freely, provided he is responsible for the abuse of this liberty in cases determined by the law.

XII. A public force being necessary to give security to the rights of men and of citizens, that force is instituted for the benefit of the community, and not for the particular benefit of the persons with whom it is entrusted.

XIII. A common contribution being necessary for the support of the public force and for defraying the other expenses of the government, it ought to be divided equally among the members of the community, according to their abilities.

XIV. Every citizen has a right, either by himself or his representative, to a free voice in determining the necessity of public contributions, the appropriation of them, and their amount, mode of assessment, and duration.

XV. Every community has a right to demand of all its agents an account of their conduct.

XVI. Every community in which a separation of powers and a security of rights is not provided for wants a constitution.

XVII. The rights to property being inviolable and sacred, no one ought to be deprived of it, except in cases of evident public necessity, legally ascertained, and on condition of a previous just indemnity.

OBSERVATIONS ON THE DECLARATION
OF RIGHTS

The three first articles comprehend in general terms the whole of a Declaration of Rights; all the succeeding articles either originate from them or follow as elucidations. The fourth, fifth, and sixth define more particularly what is only generally expressed in the first, second, and third.

The seventh, eighth, ninth, tenth, and eleventh articles are declaratory of *principles* upon which laws shall be constructed conformable to *rights* already declared. But it is questioned by some very good people in France, as well as in other countries, whether the tenth article sufficiently guarantees the right it is intended to accord with; besides which, it takes off from the divine dignity of religion and weakens its operative force upon the mind to make it a subject of human laws. It then presents itself to man like light intercepted by a cloudy medium, in which the source of it is obscured from his sight, and he sees nothing to reverence in the dusky ray.[c]

[c] There is a single idea which, if it strikes rightly upon the mind either in a legal or a religious sense, will prevent any man or any body of men or any government from going wrong on the subject of religion, which is that before any human institutions of government were known in the world there existed, if I may so express it, a compact between God and man from the beginning of time; and that, as the relation and condition which man in his *individual person* stands in toward his Maker cannot be changed or any ways altered by any human laws or human authority, that religious devotion which is a part of this

The remaining articles, beginning with the twelfth, are substantially contained in the principles of the preceding articles; but in the particular situation in which France then was, having to undo what was wrong as well as to set up what was right, it was proper to be more particular than what in another condition of things would be necessary.

While the Declaration of Rights was before the National Assembly, some of its members remarked that, if a Declaration of Rights was published, it should be accompanied by a Declaration of Duties. The observation discovered a mind that reflected, and it only erred by not reflecting far enough. A Declaration of Rights is, by reciprocity, a Declaration of Duties also. Whatever is my right as a man is also the right of another, and it becomes my duty to guarantee as well as to possess.

The three first articles are the basis of liberty, as well individual as national; nor can any country be called free whose government does not take its beginning from the principles they contain and continue to preserve them pure; and the whole of the Declaration of Rights is of more value to the world and will do more good than all the laws and statutes that have yet been promulgated.

In the declaratory exordium which prefaces the Declaration of Rights, we see the solemn and majestic spectacle of a nation opening its commission, under the auspices of its Creator, to establish a government; a scene so new and so transcendently unequaled by anything in the European world that the name of a revolution is diminutive of its character, and it rises into a regeneration of man.

What are the present governments of Europe but a scene of iniquity and oppression? What is that of England? Do not its own inhabitants say it is a market where every man has his price,

---

compact cannot so much as be made a subject of human laws and that all laws must conform themselves to this prior existing compact and not assume to make the compact conform to the laws, which, besides being human, are subsequent thereto. The first act of man, when he looked around and saw himself a creature which he did not make and a world furnished for his reception, must have been devotion; and devotion must ever continue sacred to every individual man *as it appears right to him,* and governments do mischief by interfering.

and where corruption is common traffic, at the expense of a deluded people? No wonder, then, that the French Revolution is traduced.

Had it confined itself merely to the destruction of flagrant despotism, perhaps Mr. Burke and some others had been silent. Their cry now is, "It is gone too far"—that is, it has gone too far for them. It stares corruption in the face, and the venal tribe are all alarmed. Their fear discovers itself in their outrage, and they are but publishing the groans of a wounded vice.

But from such opposition the French Revolution, instead of suffering, receives a homage. The more it is struck, the more sparks it will emit; and the fear is it will not be struck enough. It has nothing to dread from attacks; truth has given it an establishment, and time will record it with a name as lasting as his own.

Having now traced the progress of the French Revolution through most of its principal stages, from its commencement to the taking of the Bastille and its establishment by the Declaration of Rights, I will close the subject with the energetic apostrophe of M. de Lafayette: "May this great monument raised to Liberty [9] serve as a lesson to the oppressor and an example to the oppressed!" [d]

. . . .

[OF HEREDITARY GOVERNMENT] [e]

Notwithstanding the nonsense—for it deserves no better name —that Mr. Burke has asserted about hereditary rights and hereditary succession, and that a nation has not a right to form a government for itself, it happened to fall in his way to give some account of what Government is. "Government," says he, "is a contrivance of human wisdom."

[d] See page [182] of this work.—N.B. Since the taking of the Bastille, the occurrences have been published; but the matters recorded in this narrative are prior to that period, and some of them, as may be easily seen, can be but very little known.

[e] [From "Miscellaneous Chapter," Part I.]

Admitting that government is a contrivance of human *wisdom*, it must necessarily follow that hereditary succession and hereditary rights (as they are called) can make no part of it, because it is impossible to make wisdom hereditary; and on the other hand, *that* cannot be a wise contrivance which in its operation may commit the government of a nation to the wisdom of an idiot. The ground which Mr. Burke now takes is fatal to every part of his cause.

The argument changes from hereditary rights to hereditary wisdom; and the question is, Who is the wisest man? He must now show that everyone in the line of hereditary succession was a Solomon, or his title is not good to be a king. What a stroke has Mr. Burke now made! To use a sailor's phrase, he has "swabbed the deck" and scarcely left a name legible in the list of kings, and he has mowed down and thinned the House of Peers with a scythe as formidable as death and time. But Mr. Burke appears to have been aware of this retort, and he has taken care to guard against it by making government to be not only a *contrivance* of human wisdom but a *monopoly* of wisdom. He puts the nation as fools on one side and places his government of wisdom, all wise men of Gotham, on the other side; and he then proclaims and says that "men have a *right* that their *wants* should be provided for by this wisdom."

Having thus made proclamation, he next proceeds to explain to them what their *wants* are, and also what their *rights* are.

In this he has succeeded dexterously, for he makes their wants to be a *want* of wisdom; but as this is but cold comfort, he then informs them that they have a *right* (not to any of the wisdom) but to be governed by it; and in order to impress them with a solemn reverence for this monopoly government of wisdom and of its vast capacity for all purposes, possible or impossible, right or wrong, he proceeds with astrological, mysterious importance to tell them its powers in these words:

The rights of man in government are their advantages; and these are often in balances between differences of good; and in compromises sometimes between *good* and *evil,* and sometimes between *evil* and *evil*. Political reason is a *computing principle;* adding, subtracting, multiplying, and dividing, morally and not metaphysically or mathematically, true moral demonstrations.

As the wondering audience whom Mr. Burke supposes himself talking to may not understand all this learned jargon, I will undertake to be its interpreter. The meaning then, good people, of all this is *that government is governed by no principle whatever; that it can make evil good, or good evil, just as it pleases. In short, that government is arbitrary power.*

But there are some things which Mr. Burke has forgotten. First, he has not shown where the wisdom originally came from; and, secondly, he has not shown by what authority it first began to act. In the manner he introduces the matter, it is either government stealing wisdom or wisdom stealing government. It is without an origin, and its powers without authority. In short, it is usurpation.

.   .   .   .

But, to arrange this matter in a clearer view than what general expressions can convey, it will be necessary to state the distinct heads under which (what is called) a hereditary crown or, more properly speaking, a hereditary succession to the government of a nation can be considered,[f] which are:

First, the right of a particular family to establish itself.
Secondly, the right of a nation to establish a particular family.

With respect to the *first* of these heads, that of a family establishing itself with hereditary powers on its own authority and independent of the consent of a nation, all men will concur in calling it despotism; and it would be trespassing on their understanding to attempt to prove it.

But the *second* head, that of a nation establishing a particular family with *hereditary powers,* does not present itself as despotism on the first reflection; but if men will permit a second reflection to take place and carry that reflection forward but one remove out of their own persons to that of their offspring, they will then see that hereditary succession becomes in its consequences the same despotism to others which they reprobated for themselves. It op-

[f] [See p. 161.]

erates to preclude the consent of the succeeding generations, and the preclusion of consent is despotism.

When the person who at any time shall be in possession of a government, or those who stand in succession to him, shall say to a nation, I hold this power in "contempt" of you, it signifies not on what authority he pretends to say it. It is no relief but an aggravation to a person in slavery to reflect that he was sold by his parent; and as that which heightens the criminality of an act cannot be produced to prove the legality of it, hereditary succession cannot be established as a legal thing.

In order to arrive to a more perfect decision on this head, it will be proper to consider the generation which undertakes to establish a family with *hereditary powers,* apart and separate from the generations which are to follow; and also to consider the character in which the *first* generation acts with respect to succeeding generations.

The generation which first selects a person and puts him at the head of its government, either with the title of king or any other distinction, acts its *own choice,* be it wise or foolish, as a free agent for itself. The person so set up is not hereditary, but selected and appointed; and the generation who sets him up does not live under a hereditary government, but under a government of its own choice and establishment. Were the generation who sets him up and the person so set up to live forever, it never could become hereditary succession; and, of consequence, hereditary succession can only follow on the death of the first parties.

As therefore hereditary succession is out of the question with respect to the *first* generation, we have now to consider the character in which *that* generation acts with respect to the commencing generation and to all succeeding ones.

It assumes a character to which it has neither right nor title. It changes itself from a *legislator* to a *testator* and affects to make its will, which is to have operation after the demise of the makers, to bequeath the government; and it not only attempts to bequeath but to establish on the succeeding generation a new and different form of government under which itself lived.

Itself, as is already observed, lived not under a hereditary government but under a government of its own choice and establishment; and it now attempts, by virtue of a will and testament (which it has not authority to make), to take from the commencing generation and all future ones the rights and free agency by which itself acted.

But, exclusive of the right which any generation has to act collectively as a testator, the objects to which it applies itself in this case are not within the compass of any law or of any will or testament.

The rights of men in society are neither devisable nor transferable nor annihilable, but are descendible only; and it is not in the power of any generation to intercept finally and cut off the descent. If the present generation, or any other, are disposed to be slaves, it does not lessen the right of the succeeding generation to be free; wrongs cannot have a legal descent. When Mr. Burke attempts to maintain that the *English nation did at the Revolution of 1688 most solemnly renounce and abdicate their right for themselves and for all their posterity forever,* he speaks a language that merits not reply and which can only excite contempt for his prostitute principles or pity for his ignorance.

In whatever light hereditary succession, as growing out of the will and testament of some former generation, presents itself, it is an absurdity. A cannot make a will to take from B the property of B and give it to C; yet this is the manner in which (what is called) hereditary succession by law operates.

A certain former generation made a will to take away the rights of the commencing generation and all future ones, and to convey those rights to a third person, who afterward comes forward and tells them, in Mr. Burke's language, that they have *no rights,* that their rights are already bequeathed to him, and that he will govern in *contempt* of them. From such principles and such ignorance, good Lord, deliver the world!

. . . .

CONCLUSION

Reason and ignorance, the opposites of each other, influence the great bulk of mankind. If either of these can be rendered sufficiently extensive in a country, the machinery of government goes easily on. Reason shows itself, and ignorance submits to whatever is dictated to it.

The two modes of government which prevail in the world are, first, government by election and representation; secondly, government by hereditary succession. The former is generally known by the name of republic; the latter by that of monarchy and aristocracy.

Those two distinct and opposite forms erect themselves on the two distinct and opposite bases of reason and ignorance. As the exercise of government requires talents and abilities, and as talents and abilities cannot have hereditary descent, it is evident that hereditary succession requires a belief from man to which his reason cannot subscribe and which can only be established upon his ignorance; and the more ignorant any country is, the better it is fitted for this species of government.

On the contrary, government in a well-constituted republic requires no belief from man beyond what his reason can give. He sees the rationale of the whole system, its origin and its operation; and as it is best supported when best understood, the human faculties act with boldness and acquire, under this form of government, a gigantic manliness.

As, therefore, each of those forms acts on a different base—the one moving freely by the aid of reason, the other by ignorance— we have next to consider what it is that gives motion to that species of government which is called mixed government, or, as it is sometimes ludicrously styled, a government of *this, that,* and *t'other*.

The moving power of this species of government is, of necessity, corruption. However imperfect election and representation may be in mixed governments, they still give exercise to a greater portion of reason than is convenient to the hereditary part, and therefore it becomes necessary to buy the reason up. A mixed government is an imperfect everything, cementing and soldering the discordant parts together by corruption to act as a whole. Mr. Burke appears highly disgusted that France, since she had resolved on a revolution, did not adopt what he calls "a British constitution"; and the regretful manner in which he expresses himself on this occasion implies a suspicion that the British constitution needed something to keep its defects in countenance.

In mixed governments, there is no responsibility; the parts cover each other till responsibility is lost, and the corruption which moves the machine contrives at the same time its own escape. When it is laid down as a maxim that *a king can do no wrong*, it places him in a state of similar security with that of idiots and persons insane, and responsibility is out of the question with respect to himself. It then descends upon the minister, who shelters himself under a majority in Parliament, which, by places, pensions, and corruption, he can always command; and that majority justifies itself by the same authority with which it protects the minister. In this rotary motion, responsibility is thrown off from the parts and from the whole.

When there is a part in a government which can do no wrong, it implies that it does nothing and is only the machine of another power, by whose advice and direction it acts. What is supposed to be the king in mixed governments is the cabinet; and as the cabinet is always a part of the Parliament and the members justifying in one character what they advise and act in another, a mixed government becomes a continual enigma, entailing upon a country, by the quantity of corruption necessary to solder the parts, the expense of supporting all the forms of government at once and finally resolving itself into a government by committee, in which the advisers, the actors, the approvers, the justifiers, the persons responsible, and the persons not responsible are the same persons.

By this pantomimical contrivance and change of scene and character, the parts help each other out in matters which neither of them singly would assume to act. When money is to be obtained, the mass of variety apparently dissolves, and a profusion of parliamentary praises passes between the parts. Each admires with astonishment the wisdom, the liberality, the disinterestedness of the other; and all of them breathe a pitying sigh at the burdens of the nation.

But in a well-constituted republic, nothing of this soldering, praising, and pitying can take place; the representation being equal throughout the country and complete in itself, however it may be arranged into legislative and executive, they have all one and the same natural source. The parts are not foreigners to each other, like democracy, aristocracy, and monarchy. As there are no discordant distinctions, there is nothing to corrupt by compromise nor confound by contrivance.

Public measures appeal of themselves to the understanding of the nation, and, resting on their own merits, disown any flattering application to vanity. The continual whine of lamenting the burden of taxes, however successfully it may be practiced in mixed governments, is inconsistent with the sense and spirit of a republic. If taxes are necessary, they are of course advantageous; but if they require an apology, the apology itself implies an impeachment. Why then is man thus imposed upon, or why does he impose upon himself?

When men are spoken of as kings and subjects, or when government is mentioned under the distinct or combined heads of monarchy, aristocracy, and democracy, what is it that reasoning man is to understand by the terms? If there really existed in the world two or more distinct and separate elements of human power, we should then see the several origins to which those terms would descriptively apply; but as there is but one species of man, there can be but one element of human power, and that element is man himself. Monarchy, aristocracy, and democracy are but creatures of imagination; and a thousand such may be contrived, as well as three.

From the revolutions of America and France and the symptoms that have appeared in other countries, it is evident that the opinion of the world is changed with respect to systems of government, and that revolutions are not within the compass of political calculations. The progress of time and circumstances, which men assign to the accomplishment of great changes, is too mechanical to measure the force of the mind and the rapidity of reflection by which revolutions are generated. All the old governments have received a shock from those that already appear and which were once more improbable, and are a greater subject of wonder than a general revolution in Europe would be now.

When we survey the wretched condition of man under the monarchical and hereditary systems of government, dragged from his home by one power or driven by another, and impoverished by taxes more than by enemies, it becomes evident that those systems are bad, and that a general revolution in the principle and construction of governments is necessary.

What is government more than the management of the affairs of a nation? It is not and from its nature cannot be the property of any particular man or family, but of the whole community, at whose expense it is supported; and though by force or contrivance it has been usurped into an inheritance, the usurpation cannot alter the right of things. Sovereignty, as a matter of right appertains to the nation only, and not to any individual, and a nation has at all times an inherent indefeasible right to abolish any form of government it finds inconvenient and establish such as accords with its interest, disposition, and happiness. The romantic and barbarous distinction of men into kings and subjects, though it may suit the condition of courtiers, cannot that of citizens, and is exploded by the principle upon which governments are now founded. Every citizen is a member of the sovereignty and as such can acknowledge no personal subjection, and his obedience can be only to the laws.

When men think of what government is, they must necessarily suppose it to possess a knowledge of all the objects and matters upon which its authority is to be exercised. In this view of government, the republican system, as established by America and France, operates to embrace the whole of a nation; and the knowledge necessary to the interest of all the parts is to be found in the center which the parts by representation form. But the old governments are on a construction that excludes knowledge as well as happiness; government by monks, who know nothing of the world beyond the walls of a convent, is as consistent as government by kings.

What were formerly called revolutions were little more than a change of persons or an alteration of local circumstances. They rose and fell like things of course and had nothing in their existence or their fate that could influence beyond the spot that produced them. But what we now see in the world, from the revolutions of America and France, is a renovation of the natural order of things, a system of principles as universal as truth and the existence of man, and combining moral with political happiness and national prosperity:

I. Men are born and always continue free and equal in respect to their rights. Civil distinctions, therefore, can be founded only on public utility.

II. The end of all political associations is the preservation of the natural and imprescriptible rights of man; and these rights are liberty, property, security, and resistance of oppression.

III. The nation is essentially the source of all sovereignty; nor can any individual or any body of men be entitled to any authority which is not expressly derived from it.

In these principles there is nothing to throw a nation into confusion by inflaming ambition. They are calculated to call forth wisdom and abilities and to exercise them for the public good and not for the emolument or aggrandizement of particular descriptions of men or families. Monarchial sovereignty, the enemy of mankind and the source of misery, is abolished; and sovereignty itself is restored to its natural and original place, the nation. Were this the case throughout Europe, the cause of wars would be taken away.

It is attributed to Henry IV of France,[10] a man of an enlarged and benevolent heart, that he proposed, about the year 1610, a plan of abolishing war in Europe. The plan consisted in constituting a European congress or, as the French authors style it, a pacific republic, by appointing delegates from the several nations, who were to act as a court of arbitration in any disputes that might arise between nation and nation. Had such a plan been adopted at the time it was proposed, the taxes of England and France, as two of the parties, would have been at least ten millions sterling annually to each nation less than they were at the commencement of the French Revolution.

To conceive a cause why such a plan has not been adopted (and that, instead of a congress for the purpose of *preventing* war, it has been called only to *terminate* a war after fruitless expense of several years), it will be necessary to consider the interest of governments as a distinct interest to that of nations.

Whatever is the cause of taxes to a nation becomes also the means of revenue to a government. Every war terminates with an addition of taxes, and consequently with an addition of revenue; and in any event of war, in the manner they are now commenced and concluded, the power and interest of governments are increased. War, therefore, from its productiveness, as it easily furnishes the pretense of necessity for taxes and appointments to places and offices, becomes a principal part of the system of old governments; and to establish any mode to abolish war, however advantageous it might be to nations, would be to take from such government the most lucrative of its branches. The frivolous matters upon which war is made show the disposition and avidity of governments to uphold the system of war and betray the motives upon which they act.

Why are not republics plunged into war but because the nature of their government does not admit of an interest distinct from that of the nation? Even Holland, though an ill-constructed republic, and with a commerce extending over the world, existed nearly a century without war; and the instant the form of government was changed in France, the republican principles of peace and domestic prosperity and economy arose with the new government; and the same consequence would follow the same causes in other nations.

As war is the system of government on the old construction, the animosity which nations reciprocally entertain is nothing more than what the policy of their governments excites to keep up the spirit of the system. Each government accuses the other of perfidy, intrigue, and ambition as a means of heating the imagination of their respective nations and increasing them to hostilities. Man is not the enemy of man, but through the medium of a false system of government. Instead, therefore, of exclaiming against the ambition of kings, the exclamation should be directed against the principle of such governments; and instead of seeking to reform the individual, the wisdom of a nation should apply itself to reform the system.

Whether the forms and maxims of governments which are still in practice were adapted to the condition of the world at the period they were established is not in this case the question. The older they are, the less correspondence can they have with the present state of things. Time and change of circumstances and opinions have the same progressive effect in rendering modes of government obsolete as they have upon customs and manners. Agriculture, commerce, manufactures, and the tranquil arts, by which the prosperity of nations is best promoted, require a different system of government and a different species of knowledge to direct its operations than what might have been required in the former condition of the world.

As it is not difficult to perceive, from the enlightened state of mankind, that hereditary governments are verging to their decline and that revolutions on the broad basis of national sovereignty and government by representation are making their way in Europe, it would be an act of wisdom to anticipate their approach and produce revolutions by reason and accommodation, rather than commit them to the issue of convulsions.

From what we now see, nothing of reform on the political world ought to be held improbable. It is an age of revolutions, in which everything may be looked for. The intrigue of courts, by which the system of war is kept up, may provoke a confederation of nations to abolish it; and a European congress to patronize the progress of free government and promote the civilization of nations with each other is an event nearer in probability than once were the revolutions and alliance of France and America.

RIGHTS OF MAN
PART TWO

INTRODUCTION

WHAT ARCHIMEDES said of the mechanical powers may be applied to reason and liberty: "Had we," said he, "a place to stand upon, we might raise the world." The Revolution of America presented in politics what was only theory in mechanics. So deeply rooted were all the governments of the Old World, and so effectually had the tyranny and the antiquity of habit established itself over the mind that no beginning could be made in Asia, Africa, or Europe to reform the political condition of man. Freedom had been hunted round the globe; reason was considered as rebellion; and the slavery of fear had made men afraid to think.

But such is the irresistible nature of truth that all it asks and all it wants is the liberty of appearing. The sun needs no inscription to distinguish him from darkness, and no sooner did the American governments display themselves to the world than despotism felt a shock and man began to contemplate redress.

The independence of America, considered merely as a separation from England, would have been a matter but of little importance, had it not been accompanied by a revolution in the principles and practice of governments. She made a stand, not for herself only, but for the world, and looked beyond the advantages herself could receive. Even the Hessian, though hired to fight against her, may live to bless his defeat; and England, condemning the viciousness of its government, rejoice in its miscarriage.

As America was the only spot in the political world where the principles of universal reformation could begin, so also was it the best in the natural world. An assemblage of circumstances conspired, not only to give birth, but to add gigantic maturity to its principles.

The scene which that country presents to the eye of a spectator has something in it which generates and encourages great ideas. Nature appears to him in magnitude. The mighty objects he beholds act upon his mind by enlarging it, and he partakes of the greatness he contemplates. Its first settlers were emigrants from different European nations and of diversified professions of religion, retiring from the governmental persecutions of the Old World and meeting in the New, not as enemies but as brothers. The wants which necessarily accompany the cultivation of a wilderness produced among them a state of society, which countries long harassed by the quarrels and intrigues of governments had neglected to cherish. In such a situation man becomes what he ought. He sees his species, not with the inhuman idea of a natural enemy, but as kindred; and the example shows to the artificial world that man must go back to nature for information.

From the rapid progress which America makes in every species of improvement, it is rational to conclude that if the governments of Asia, Africa, and Europe had begun on a principle similar to that of America, or had not been very early corrupted therefrom, that those countries must, by this time, have been in a far superior condition to what they are. Age after age has passed away for no other purpose than to behold their wretchedness. Could we suppose a spectator who knew nothing of the world and who was put into it merely to make his observations, he would take a great part of the Old World to be new, just struggling with the difficulties and hardships of an infant settlement. He could not suppose that the hordes of miserable poor, with which old countries abound, could be any other than those who had not yet had time to provide for themselves. Little would he think they were the consequence of what in such countries is called government.

If, from the more wretched parts of the Old World, we look at those which are in an advanced stage of improvement, we still find the greedy hand of government thrusting itself into every corner and crevice of industry and grasping the spoil of the multitude. Invention is continually exercised to furnish new pretenses for revenue and taxation. It watches prosperity as its prey and permits none to escape without tribute.

As revolutions have begun (and the probability is always greater against a thing beginning than of proceeding after it has begun), it is natural to expect that other revolutions will follow. The amazing and still increasing expenses with which old governments are conducted, the numerous wars they engage in or provoke, the embarrassment they throw in the way of universal civilization and commerce, and the oppression and usurpation they practice at home, have wearied out the patience and exhausted the property of the world. In such a situation, and with the examples already existing, revolutions are to be looked for. They are become subjects of universal conversation and may be considered as the *order of the day*.

If systems of government can be introduced less expensive and more productive of general happiness than those which have existed, all attempts to oppose their progress will in the end be fruitless. Reason, like time, will make its own way, and prejudice will fall in a combat with interest. If universal peace, civilization, and commerce are ever to be the happy lot of man, it cannot be accomplished but by a revolution in the system of governments. All the monarchical governments are military. War is their trade, plunder and revenue their objects. While such governments continue, peace has not the absolute security of a day.

What is the history of all monarchical governments but a disgustful picture of human wretchedness and the accidental respite of a few years' repose? Wearied with war and tired with human butchery, they sat down to rest and called it peace. This certainly is not the condition that heaven intended for man; and if *this be monarchy*, well might monarchy be reckoned among the sins of the Jews.

The revolutions which formerly took place in the world had nothing in them that interested the bulk of mankind. They extended only to a change of persons and measures, but not of principles, and rose or fell among the common transactions of the moment. What we now behold may not improperly be called a "counterrevolution."

Conquest and tyranny, at some early period, dispossessed man of his rights, and he is now recovering them. And as the tide of all human affairs has its ebb and flow in directions contrary to each other, so also is it in this. Government founded on a *moral theory, on a system of universal peace, on the indefeasible, hereditary rights of man,* is now revolving from West to East by a stronger impulse than the government of the sword revolved from East to West. It interests not particular individuals but nations in its progress and promises a new era to the human race.

The danger to which the success of revolutions is most exposed is that of attempting them before the principles on which they proceed, and the advantages to result from them, are sufficiently seen and understood. Almost everything appertaining to the circumstances of a nation has been absorbed and confounded under the general and mysterious word government. Though it avoids taking to its account the errors it commits, and the mischiefs it occasions, it fails not to arrogate to itself whatever has the appearance of prosperity. It robs industry of its honors by pedantically making itself the cause of its effects, and purloins from the general character of man the merits that appertain to him as a social being.

It may therefore be of use in this day of revolutions to discriminate between those things which are the effect of government and those which are not. This will best be done by taking a review of society and civilization and the consequences resulting therefrom as things distinct from what are called governments. By beginning with this investigation, we shall be able to assign effects to their proper cause and analyze the mass of common errors.

OF SOCIETY AND CIVILIZATION [a]

Great part of that order which reigns among mankind is not the effect of government. It had its origin in the principles of society and the natural constitution of man. It existed prior to government, and would exist if the formality of government was abolished. The mutual dependence and reciprocal interest which man has upon man and all parts of a civilized community upon

[a] [Chapter I, Part II.]

each other create that great chain of connection which holds it together. The landholder, the farmer, the manufacturer, the merchant, the tradesman, and every occupation, prospers by the aid which each receives from the other and from the whole. Common interest regulates their concerns and forms their laws; and the laws which common usage ordains have a greater influence than the laws of government. In fine, society performs for itself almost everything which is ascribed to government.

To understand the nature and quantity of government proper for man, it is necessary to attend to his character. As nature created him for social life, she fitted him for the station she intended. In all cases she made his natural wants greater than his individual powers. No one man is capable, without the aid of society, of supplying his own wants; and those wants acting upon every individual impel the whole of them into society, as naturally as gravitation acts to a center.

But she has gone further. She has not only forced man into society by a diversity of wants, which the reciprocal aid of each other can supply, but she has implanted in him a system of social affections which, though not necessary to his existence, are essential to his happiness. There is no period in life when this love for society ceases to act. It begins and ends with our being.

If we examine with attention into the composition and constitution of man, the diversity of his wants, and the diversity of talents in different men for reciprocally accommodating the wants of each other, his propensity to society, and consequently to preserve the advantages resulting from it, we shall easily discover that a great part of what is called government is mere imposition.

Government is no farther necessary than to supply the few cases to which society and civilization are not conveniently competent; and instances are not wanting to show that everything which government can usefully add thereto has been performed by the common consent of society without government.

For upward of two years from the commencement of the American war, and to a longer period in several of the American states, there were no established forms of government. The old governments had been abolished, and the country was too much occupied in defense to employ its attention in establishing new governments; yet during this interval order and harmony were preserved as inviolate as in any country in Europe.

There is a natural aptness in man, and more so in society, because it embraces a greater variety of abilities and resources, to accommodate itself to whatever situation it is in. The instant formal government is abolished, society begins to act. A general association takes place, and common interest produces common security.

So far is it from being true, as has been pretended, that the abolition of any formal government is the dissolution of society, that it acts by a contrary impulse and brings the latter the closer together. All that part of its organization which it had committed to its government devolves again upon itself and acts through its medium.

When men, as well from natural instinct as from reciprocal benefits, have habituated themselves to social and civilized life, there is always enough of its principles in practice to carry them through any changes they may find necessary or convenient to make in their government. In short, man is so naturally a creature of society that it is almost impossible to put him out of it.

Formal government makes but a small part of civilized life; and when even the best that human wisdom can devise is established, it is a thing more in name and idea than in fact. It is to the great and fundamental principles of society and civilization—to the common usage universally consented to, and mutually and reciprocally maintained—to the unceasing circulation of interest, which, passing through its million channels, invigorates the whole mass of civilized man—it is to these things, infinitely more than to anything which even the best instituted government can perform, that the safety and prosperity of the individual and of the whole depends.

The more perfect civilization is, the less occasion has it for government, because the more does it regulate its own affairs and govern itself; but so contrary is the practice of old governments to the reason of the case that the expenses of them increase in the proportion they ought to diminish. It is but few general laws that civilized life requires, and those of such common use-fulness that whether they are enforced by the forms of govern-ment or not the effect will be nearly the same. If we consider what the principles are that first condense men into society and what the motives that regulate their mutual intercourse afterward, we shall find, by the time we arrive at what is called government, that nearly the whole of the business is performed by the natural opera-tion of the parts upon each other.

Man, with respect to all those matters, is more a creature of consistency than he is aware or that governments would wish him to believe. All the great laws of society are laws of nature. Those of trade and commerce, whether with respect to the intercourse of individuals or of nations, are laws of mutual and reciprocal in-terest. They are followed and obeyed because it is the interest of the parties so to do, and not on account of any formal laws their governments may impose or interpose.

But how often is the natural propensity to society disturbed or destroyed by the operations of government. When the latter, in-stead of being ingrafted on the principles of the former, assumes to exist for itself and acts by partialities of favor and oppression, it becomes the cause of the mischiefs it ought to prevent.

If we look back to the riots and tumults which at various times have happened in England, we shall find that they did not proceed from the want of a government, but that government was itself the generating cause; instead of consolidating society, it divided it; it deprived it of its natural cohesion, and engendered discon-tents and disorders which otherwise would not have existed.

In those associations which men promiscuously form for the purpose of trade, or of any concern in which government is totally out of the question and in which they act merely on the principles of society, we see how naturally the various parties unite; and this shows by comparison that governments, so far from being always the cause or means of order, are often the destruction of it. The riots of 1780 [1] had no other source than the remains of those prejudices which the government itself had encouraged. But with respect to England there are also other causes.

Excess and inequality of taxation, however disguised in the

means, never fail to appear in their effects. As a great mass of the community are thrown thereby into poverty and discontent, they are constantly on the brink of commotion and, deprived as they unfortunately are of the means of information, are easily heated to outrage. Whatever the apparent cause of any riots may be, the real one is always want of happiness. It shows that something is wrong in the system of government that injures the felicity by which society is to be preserved.

But as fact is superior to reasoning, the instance of America presents itself to confirm these observations. If there is a country in the world where concord, according to common calculation, would be least expected, it is America. Made up as it is of people from different nations,[b] accustomed to different forms and habits of government, speaking different languages, and more different in their modes of worship, it would appear that the union of such a people was impracticable; but by the simple operation of constructing government on the principles of society and the rights of man, every difficulty retires and all the parts are brought into cordial unison. There the poor are not oppressed, the rich are not privileged. Industry is not mortified by the splendid extravagance of a court rioting at its expense. Their taxes are few because their government is just; and as there is nothing to render them wretched, there is nothing to engender riots and tumults.

A metaphysical man like Mr. Burke would have tortured his invention to discover how such a people could be governed. He would have supposed that some must be managed by fraud, others

[b] That part of America which is generally called New England, including New Hampshire, Massachusetts, Rhode Island, and Connecticut, is peopled chiefly by English descendants. In the State of New York, about half are Dutch, the rest English, Scotch, and Irish. In New Jersey, a mixture of English and Dutch, with some Scotch and Irish. In Pennsylvania, about one third are English, another Germans, and the remainder Scotch and Irish, with some Swedes. The states to the southward have a greater proportion of English than the middle states, but in all of them there is a mixture; and besides those enumerated, there are a considerable number of French and some few of all the European nations lying on the coast. The most numerous religious denomination is the Presbyterian; but no one sect is established above another, and all men are equally citizens.

by force, and all by some contrivance; that genius must be hired to impose upon ignorance, and show and parade to fascinate the vulgar. Lost in the abundance of his researches, he would have resolved and re-resolved, and finally overlooked the plain and easy road that lay directly before him.

One of the great advantages of the American Revolution has been that it led to a discovery of the principles and laid open the imposition of governments. All the revolutions till then had been worked within the atmosphere of a court, and never on the great floor of a nation. The parties were always of the class of courtiers; and whatever was their rage for reformation, they carefully preserved that fraud of the profession.

In all cases they took care to represent government as a thing made up of mysteries, which only themselves understood; and they hid from the understanding of the nation the only thing that was beneficial to know, namely, *that government is nothing more than a national association acting on the principles of society.*

Having thus endeavored to show that the social and civilized state of man is capable of performing within itself almost everything necessary to its protection and government, it will be proper, on the other hand, to take a review of the present old governments and examine whether their principles and practice are correspondent thereto.

OF THE OLD AND NEW SYSTEMS OF GOVERNMENT [c]

Nothing can appear more contradictory than the principles on which the old governments began and the condition to which society, civilization, and commerce are capable of carrying mankind. Government on the old system is an assumption of power for the aggrandizement of itself; on the new, a delegation of power for the common benefit of society. The former supports itself by keeping up a system of war; the latter promotes a system of peace as the true means of enriching a nation. The one encourages national prejudices; the other promotes universal so-

[c] [Part II, Chapter III.]

ciety as the means of universal commerce. The one measures its prosperity by the quantity of revenue it extorts; the other proves its excellence by the small quantity of taxes it requires.

Mr. Burke has talked of "old and new Whigs." If he can amuse himself with childish names and distinctions, I shall not interrupt his pleasure. It is not to him, but to Abbé Sieyès,[2] that I address this chapter. I am already engaged to the latter gentleman to discuss the subject of monarchical government; and as it naturally occurs in comparing the old and new systems, I make this the opportunity of presenting to him my observations. I shall occasionally take Mr. Burke in my way.

Though it might be proved that the system of government now called the "new" is the most ancient in principle of all that have existed, being founded on the original inherent rights of man, yet, as tyranny and the sword have suspended the exercise of those rights for many centuries past, it serves better the purpose of distinction to call it a "new" than to claim the right of calling it the old.

The first general distinction between those two systems is that the one now called the old is *hereditary*, either in whole or in part; and the new is entirely *representative*. It rejects all hereditary government:

First, as being an imposition on mankind.

Secondly, as being inadequate to the purposes for which government is necessary.

With respect to the first of these heads. It cannot be proved by what right hereditary government could begin; neither does there exist within the compass of mortal power a right to establish it. Man has no authority over posterity in matters of personal right, and therefore no man or body of men had or can have a right to set up hereditary government. Were even ourselves to come again into existence, instead of being succeeded by posterity, we have not now the right of taking from ourselves the rights which would then be ours. On what ground, then, do we pretend to take them from others?

All hereditary government is in its nature tyranny. A heritable crown or a heritable throne, or by what other fanciful name such things may be called, have no other significant explanation than that mankind are heritable property. To inherit a government is to inherit the people, as if they were flocks and herds.

With respect to the second head, that of being inadequate to the purposes for which government is necessary, we have only to consider what government essentially is and compare it with the circumstances to which hereditary succession is subject. Government ought to be a thing always in maturity. It ought to be so constructed as to be superior to all the accidents to which individual man is subject, and therefore hereditary succession, by being *subject to them all,* is the most irregular and imperfect of all the systems of government.

We have heard the rights of man called a *leveling* system, but the only system to which the word "leveling" is truly applicable is the hereditary monarchical system. It is a system of *mental leveling.* It indiscriminately admits every species of character to the same authority. Vice and virtue, ignorance and wisdom, in short, every quality, good or bad, is put on the same level. Kings succeed each other, not as rationals, but as animals. It signifies not what their mental or moral characters are.

Can we then be surprised at the abject state of the human mind in monarchical countries when the government itself is formed on such an abject leveling system? It has no fixed character. Today it is one thing; tomorrow it is something else. It changes with the temper of every succeeding individual and is subject to all the varieties of each. It is government through the medium of passions and accidents.

It appears under all the various characters of childhood, decrepitude, dotage, a thing at nurse, in leading strings, or on crutches. It reverses the wholesome order of nature. It occasionally puts children over men, and the conceits of nonage over wisdom and experience. In short, we cannot conceive a more ridiculous figure of government than hereditary succession, in all its cases, presents.

Could it be made a decree in nature or an edict registered in heaven, and man could know it, that virtue and wisdom should invariably appertain to hereditary succession, the objections to it would be removed; but when we see that nature acts as if she disowned and sported with the hereditary system, that the mental characters of successors in all countries are below the average of human understanding, that one is a tyrant, another an idiot, a third insane, and some all three together, it is impossible to attach confidence to it when reason in man has power to act.

It is not to the Abbé Sieyès that I need apply this reasoning; he has already saved me that trouble by giving his own opinion upon the case. "If it be asked," says he, "what is my opinion with respect to hereditary right, I answer without hesitation that, in good theory, a hereditary transmission of any power or office can never accord with the laws of a true representation. Hereditaryship is, in this sense, as much an attaint upon principle as an outrage upon society. But let us," continues he, "refer to the history of all elective monarchies and principalities; is there one in which the elective mode is not worse than the hereditary succession?"

As to debating on which is the worse of the two is admitting both to be bad, and herein we are agreed. The preference which the Abbé has given is a condemnation of the thing he prefers. Such a mode of reasoning on such a subject is inadmissible, because it finally amounts to an accusation upon Providence, as if she had left to man no other choice with respect to government than between two evils, the best of which he admits to be "an attaint upon principle and an outrage upon society."

Passing over, for the present, all the evils and mischiefs which monarchy has occasioned in the world, nothing can more effectually prove its uselessness in a state of *civil government* than making it hereditary. Would we make any office hereditary that required wisdom and abilities to fill it? And where wisdom and abilities are not necessary, such an office, whatever it may be, is superfluous or insignificant.

Hereditary succession is a burlesque upon monarchy. It puts it in the most ridiculous light by presenting it as an office which any child or idiot may fill. It requires some talents to be a common mechanic, but to be a king requires only the animal figure of a man—a sort of breathing automaton. This sort of superstition may last a few years more, but it cannot long resist the awakened reason and interest of man.

As to Mr. Burke, he is a stickler for monarchy, not altogether as a pensioner—if he is one, which I believe—but as a political man. He has taken up a contemptible opinion of mankind, who in their turn are taking up the same of him. He considers them as a herd of beings that must be governed by fraud, effigy, and show; and an idol would be as good a figure of monarchy with him as a man. I will, however, do him the justice to say that, with respect to America, he has been very complimentary. He always contended, at least in my hearing, that the people of America are more enlightened than those of England or of any other country in Europe, and that therefore the imposition of show was not necessary in their government.

Though the comparison between hereditary and elective monarchy which the Abbé has made is unnecessary to the case, because the representative system rejects both, yet, were I to make the comparison, I should decide contrary to what he has done.

The civil wars which have originated from contested hereditary claims are numerous, and have been more dreadful and of longer continuance than those which have been occasioned by election. All the civil wars in France arose from the hereditary system; they were either produced by hereditary claims or by the imperfection of the hereditary form, which admits of regencies or monarchies at nurse.

With respect to England, its history is full of the same misfortunes. The contests for succession between the houses of York and Lancaster lasted a whole century, and others of a similar nature have renewed themselves since that period. Those of 1715 and 1745[3] were of the same kind. The succession war for the crown of Spain embroiled almost half of Europe. The disturbances in Holland are generated from the hereditaryship of the stadtholder. A government calling itself free, with a hereditary office, is like a thorn in the flesh that produces a fermentation which endeavors to discharge it.

But I might go further and place also foreign wars, of whatever kind, to the same cause. It is by adding the evil of hereditary succession to that of monarchy that a permanent family interest is created whose constant objects are dominion and revenue. Poland, though an elective monarchy, has had fewer wars than those which are hereditary; and it is the only government that has made a voluntary essay, though but a small one, to reform the condition of the country.

Having thus glanced at a few of the defects of the old or hereditary system of government, let us compare it with the new or representative system.

The representative system takes society and civilization for its basis; nature, reason, and experience for its guide.

Experience, in all ages, and in all countries, has demonstrated that it is impossible to control nature in her distribution of mental powers. She gives them as she pleases. Whatever is the rule by which she, apparently to us, scatters them among mankind, that rule remains a secret to man. It would be as ridiculous to attempt to fix the hereditaryship of human beauty as of wisdom.

Whatever wisdom constituently is, it is like a seedless plant; it may be reared when it appears, but it cannot be voluntarily produced. There is always a sufficiency somewhere in the general mass of society for all purposes; but with respect to the parts of society, it is continually changing its place. It rises in one today, in another tomorrow, and has most probably visited in rotation every family of the earth and again withdrawn.

As this is the order of nature, the order of government must necessarily follow it, or government will, as we see it does, degenerate into ignorance. The hereditary system, therefore, is as repugnant to human wisdom as to human rights and is as absurd as it is unjust.

As the republic of letters brings forward the best literary productions by giving to genius a fair and universal chance, so the representative system of government is calculated to produce the wisest laws by collecting wisdom where it can be found. I smile to myself when I contemplate the ridiculous insignificance into which literature and all the sciences would sink were they made hereditary, and I carry the same idea into governments. A hereditary governor is as inconsistent as a hereditary author. I know not whether Homer or Euclid had sons, but I will venture an opinion that if they had, and had left their works unfinished, those sons could not have completed them.

Do we need a stronger evidence of the absurdity of hereditary government than is seen in the descendants of those men, in any line of life, who once were famous? Is there scarcely an instance in which there is not a total reverse of character? It appears as if the tide of mental faculties flowed as far as it could in certain channels, and then forsook its course and arose in others. How irrational then is the hereditary system which establishes channels of power, in company with which wisdom refuses to flow! By continuing this absurdity, man is perpetually in contradiction with himself; he accepts for a king or a chief magistrate or a legislator a person whom he would not elect for a constable.

It appears to general observation that revolutions create genius and talents, but those events do no more than bring them forward. There is existing in man a mass of sense lying in a dormant state and which, unless something excites it to action, will descend with him, in that condition, to the grave. As it is to the advantage of society that the whole of its faculties should be employed, the construction of government ought to be such as to bring forward, by a quiet and regular operation, all that extent of capacity which never fails to appear in revolutions.

This cannot take place in the insipid state of hereditary government, not only because it prevents, but because it operates to benumb. When the mind of a nation is bowed down by any political superstition in its government, such as hereditary succession is, it loses a considerable portion of its powers on all other subjects and objects.

Hereditary succession requires the same obedience to ignorance as to wisdom; and when once the mind can bring itself to pay this indiscriminate reverence, it descends below the stature of mental manhood. It is fit to be great only in little things. It acts a treachery upon itself and suffocates the sensations that urge to detection.

Though the ancient governments present to us a miserable picture of the condition of man, there is one which, above all others, exempts itself from the general description. I mean the democracy of the Athenians. We see more to admire and less to condemn in that great, extraordinary people than in anything which history affords.

Mr. Burke is so little acquainted with constituent principles of government that he confounds democracy and representation together. Representation was a thing unknown in the ancient democracies. In those the mass of the people met and enacted laws (grammatically speaking) in the first person.

Simple democracy was no other than the common hall of the ancients. It signifies the *form* as well as the public principle of the government. As these democracies increased in population and the territory extended, the simple democratical form became unwieldy and impracticable; and as the system of representation was not known, the consequence was they either degenerated convulsively into monarchies or became absorbed into such as then existed.

Had the system of representation been then understood as it now is, there is no reason to believe that those forms of government now called monarchical and aristocratical would ever have taken place. It was the want of some method to consolidate the parts of society, after it became too populous and too extensive for the simple democratical form, and also the lax and solitary condition of shepherds and herdsmen in other parts of the world, that afforded opportunities to those unnatural modes of government to begin.

As it is necessary to clear away the rubbish of errors into which the subject of government has been thrown, I shall proceed to remark on some others.

It has always been the political craft of courtiers and court governments to abuse something which they called "republicanism," but what republicanism was or is they never attempt to explain. Let us examine a little into this case.

The only forms of government are the democratical, the aristocratical, the monarchical, and what is now called the representative.

What is called a "republic" is not any *particular form* of government. It is wholly characteristical of the purport, matter, or object for which a government ought to be instituted and on which it is to be employed: *res publica*, "the public affairs," or "the public good"; or, literally translated, the "public thing."

It is a word of a good original, referring to what ought to be the character and business of government; and in this sense it is naturally opposed to the word "monarchy," which has a base original signification. It means arbitrary power in an individual person, in the exercise of which *himself*, and not the *res publica*, is the object.

Every government that does not act on the principle of a *republic*, or in other words that does not make the *res publica* its whole and sole object, is not a good government. Republican government is no other than government established and conducted for the interest of the public, as well individually as collectively. It is not necessarily connected with any particular form, but it most naturally associates with the representative form, as being best calculated to secure the end for which a nation is at the expense of supporting it.

Various forms of government have affected to style themselves a republic. Poland calls itself a republic, which is a hereditary aristocracy with what is called an elective monarchy. Holland calls itself a republic which is chiefly aristocratical with a hereditary stadtholdership.

But the government of America, which is wholly on the system of representation, is the only real republic in character and practice that now exists. Its government has no other object than the public business of the nation, and therefore it is properly a republic; and the Americans have taken care that *this*, and no other, shall always be the object of the government, by their rejecting everything hereditary and establishing government on the system of representation only.

Those who have said that a republic is not a *form* of government calculated for countries of great extent mistook, in the first place, the *business* of a government for a *form* of government; for the *res publica* equally appertains to every extent of territory and population. And, in the second place, if they meant anything with respect to *form*, it was the simple democratical form, such as was the mode of government in the ancient democracies, in which there was no representation. The case, therefore, is not that a republic cannot be extensive, but that it cannot be extensive on the simple democratical form; and the question naturally presents itself, "What is the best form of government for conducting the *res publica*, or the public business of a nation, after it becomes too extensive and populous for the simple democratical form?"

It cannot be monarchy, because monarchy is subject to an objection of the same amount to which the simple democratical form was subject.

It is possible that an individual may lay down a system of principles on which government shall be constitutionally established to any extent of territory. This is no more than an operation of the mind acting by its own powers. But the practice upon those principles, as applying to the various and numerous circumstances of a nation, its agriculture, manufacture, trade, commerce, etc., requires a knowledge of a different kind and which can be had only from the various parts of society.

It is an assemblage of practical knowledge which no one individual can possess, and therefore the monarchical form is as much limited in useful practice from the incompetency of knowledge as was the democratical form from the multiplying of population. The one degenerates, by extension, into confusion; the other, into ignorance and incapacity, of which all the great monarchies are in evidence. The monarchical form, therefore, could not be a substitute for the democratical, because it has equal inconveniences.

Much less could it when made hereditary. This is the most effectual of all forms to preclude knowledge. Neither could the high democratical mind have voluntarily yielded itself to be governed by children and idiots, and all the motley insignificance of character which attends such a mere animal system, the disgrace and the reproach of reason and of man.

As to the aristocratical form, it has the same vices and defects with the monarchical, except that the chance of abilities is better from the proportion of numbers, but there is still no security for the right use and application of them.[d]

Referring, then, to the original simple democracy, it affords the true data from which government on a large scale can begin. It is incapable of extension, not from its principle, but from the inconvenience of its form; and monarchy and aristocracy, from their incapacity. Retaining then democracy as the ground, and rejecting the corrupt systems of monarchy and aristocracy, the representative system naturally presents itself, remedying at once the defects of the simple democracy as to form and the incapacity of the other two with respect to knowledge.

Simple democracy was society governing itself without the aid of secondary means. By ingrafting representation upon democracy, we arrive at a system of government capable of embracing and confederating all the various interests, and every extent of territory and population; and that also with advantages as much superior to hereditary government as the republic of letters is to hereditary literature.

It is on this system that the American government is founded. It is representation ingrafted upon democracy. It has fixed the form by a scale parallel in all cases to the extent of the principle. What Athens was in miniature, America will be in magnitude. The one was the wonder of the ancient world; the other is becoming the admiration and model of the present. It is the easiest of all the forms of government to be understood and the most eligible in practice, and excludes at once the ignorance and insecurity of the hereditary mode and the inconvenience of the simple democracy.

It is impossible to conceive a system of government capable of acting over such an extent of territory and such a circle of interests as is immediately produced by the operation of representation. France, great and popular as it is, is but a spot in the capaciousness of the system. It adapts itself to all possible cases. It is preferable to simple democracy, even in small territories. Athens, by representation, would have outrivaled her own democracy.

[d] For a character of aristocracy, the reader is referred to *Rights of Man*, Part I, page [88].

That which is called government, or rather that which we ought to conceive government to be, is no more than some common center in which all the parts of society unite. This cannot be accomplished by any method so conducive to the various interests of the community as by the representative system.

It concentrates the knowledge necessary to the interests of the parts and of the whole. It places government in a state of constant maturity. It is, as has been already observed, never young, never old. It is subject neither to nonage nor dotage. It is never in the cradle nor on crutches. It admits not of a separation between knowledge and power, and is superior, as government always ought to be, to all the accidents of individual man, and is therefore superior to what is called monarchy.

A nation is not a body the figure of which is to be represented by the human body, but is like a body contained within a circle, having a common center in which every radius meets, and that center is formed by representation. To connect representation with what is called monarchy is eccentric government. Representation is of itself the delegated monarchy of a nation and cannot debase itself by dividing it with another.

Mr. Burke has two or three times, in his parliamentary speeches and in his publications, made use of a jingle of words that convey no ideas. Speaking of government, he says, "it is better to have monarchy for its basis and republicanism for its corrective than republicanism for its basis and monarchy for its corrective." If he means that it is better to correct folly with wisdom than wisdom with folly, I will not otherwise contend with him than that it would be much better to reject the folly entirely.

But what is this thing that Mr. Burke calls monarchy? Will he explain it? All men can understand what representation is, and that it must necessarily include a variety of knowledge and talents. But what security is there for the same qualities on the part of monarchy? Or, when this monarchy is a child, where then is the wisdom? What does it know about government? Who then is the monarch, or where is the monarchy? If it is to be performed by regency, it proves to be a farce.

A regency is a mock species of republic, and the whole of monarchy deserves no better description. It is a thing as various as imagination can paint. It has none of the stable character that government ought to possess. Every succession is a revolution, and every regency a counterrevolution. The whole of it is a scene of perpetual court cabal and intrigue, of which Mr. Burke is himself an instance.

To render monarchy consistent with government, the next in succession should not be born a child, but a man at once, and that man a Solomon. It is ridiculous that nations are to wait and government be interrupted till boys grow to be men.

Whether I have too little sense to see or too much to be imposed upon, whether I have too much or too little pride or of anything else, I leave out of the question; but certain it is that what is called monarchy always appears to me a silly, contemptible thing. I compare it to something kept behind a curtain, about which there is a great deal of bustle and fuss and a wonderful air of seeming solemnity; but when, by any accident, the curtain happens to open and the company see what it is, they burst into laughter.

In the representative system of government, nothing of this can happen. Like the nation itself, it possesses a perpetual stamina, as well of body as of mind, and presents itself on the open theater of the world in a fair and manly manner. Whatever are its excellences or its defects, they are visible to all. It exists not by fraud and mystery, it deals not in cant and sophistry, but inspires a language that, passing from heart to heart, is felt and understood.

We must shut our eyes against reason, we must basely degrade our understanding, not to see the folly of what is called monarchy. Nature is orderly in all her works, but this is a mode of government that counteracts nature. It turns the progress of the human faculties upside down. It subjects age to be governed by children and wisdom by folly. On the contrary, the representative system is always parallel with the order and immutable laws of nature and meets the reason of man in every part. For example:

In the American Federal Government, more power is delegated to the President of the United States than to any other individual member of Congress.[4] He cannot, therefore, be elected to this office under the age of thirty-five years. By this time the judgment of man becomes matured, and he has lived long enough to be acquainted with men and things, and the country with him.

But on the monarchial plan (exclusive of the numerous chances there are against every man born into the world of drawing a prize in the lottery of human faculties) the next in succession, whatever he may be, is put at the head of a nation and of a government at the age of eighteen years.

Does this appear like an act of wisdom? Is it consistent with the proper dignity and the manly character of a nation? Where is the propriety of calling such a lad the father of the people? In all other cases a person is a minor until the age of twenty-one years. Before this period he is not trusted with the management of an acre of land, or with the heritable property of a flock of sheep or a herd of swine; but, wonderful to tell! he may, at the age of eighteen years, be trusted with a nation.

That monarchy is all a bubble, a mere court artifice to procure money, is evident (at least to me) in every character in which it can be viewed. It would be impossible, on the rational system of representative government, to make out a bill of expenses to such an enormous amount as this deception admits. Government is not of itself a very chargeable institution. The whole expense of the Federal Government of America, founded, as I have already said, on the system of representation and extending over a country nearly ten times as large as England, is but six hundred thousand dollars, or one hundred and thirty thousand pounds sterling.

I presume that no man in his sober senses will compare the character of any of the kings of Europe with that of General Washington. Yet in France, and also in England, the expense of the civil list only for the support of one man is eight times greater than the whole expense of the Federal Government in America. To assign a reason for this appears almost impossible. The generality of people in America, especially the poor, are more able to pay taxes than the generality of people either in France or England. But the case is that the representative system diffuses such a body of knowledge throughout a nation on the subject of government as to explode ignorance and preclude imposition. The craft of courts cannot be acted on that ground. There is no place for mystery, nowhere for it to begin. Those who are not in the representation know as much of the nature of business as those who are. An affectation of mysterious importance would there be scouted. Nations can have no secrets; and the secrets of courts, like those of individuals, are always their defects.

In the representative system, the reason for everything must publicly appear. Every man is a proprietor in government and considers it a necessary part of his business to understand. It concerns his interest, because it affects his property. He examines the cost and compares it with the advantages; and above all, he does not adopt the slavish custom of following what in other governments are called leaders.

It can only be by blinding the understanding of man, and making him believe that government is some wonderful mysterious thing, that excessive revenues are obtained. Monarchy is well calculated to ensure this end. It is the popery of government, a thing kept up to amuse the ignorant and quiet them into paying taxes.

The government of a free country, properly speaking, is not in the persons but in the laws. The enacting of those requires no great expense; and when they are administered, the whole of civil government is performed—the rest is all court contrivance.

OF CONSTITUTIONS [e]

That men mean distinct and separate things when they speak of constitutions and of government is evident, or why are those terms distinctly and separately used? A constitution is not the act of a government, but of a people constituting a government; and government without a constitution is power without a right.

All power exercised over a nation must have some beginning. It must be either delegated or assumed. There are no other sources. All delegated power is trust, and all assumed power is usurpation. Time does not alter the nature and quality of either.

In viewing this subject, the case and circumstances of America present themselves as in the beginning of the world, and our inquiry into the origin of government is shortened by referring to

[e] [Chapter IV, Part II.]

the facts that have arisen in our own day. We have no occasion to roam for information into the obscure field of antiquity, nor hazard ourselves upon conjecture. We are brought at once to the point of seeing government begin, as if we had lived in the beginning of time. The real volume, not of history but of facts, is directly before us, unmutilated by contrivance or the errors of tradition.

I will here concisely state the commencement of the American constitutions, by which the difference between constitutions and government will sufficiently appear.

It may not be improper to remind the reader that the United States of America consist of thirteen separate states, each of which established a government for itself after the Declaration of Independence, done the fourth of July, 1776. Each state acted independently of the rest in forming its government, but the same general principle pervades the whole. When the several state governments were formed, they proceeded to form the Federal Government, that acts over the whole in all matters which concern the interest of the whole or which relate to the intercourse of the several states with each other or with foreign nations. I will begin with giving an instance from one of the state governments (that of Pennsylvania) and then proceed to the Federal Government.

The state of Pennsylvania, though nearly of the same extent of territory as England, was then divided into only twelve counties. Each of those counties had elected a committee at the commencement of the dispute with the English government; and as the city of Philadelphia, which also had its committee, was the most central for intelligence, it became the center of communication to the several county committees. When it became necessary to proceed to the formation of a government, the committee of Philadelphia proposed a conference of all the county committees, to be held in that city, and which met the latter end of July, 1776.

Though these committees had been elected by the people, they were not elected expressly for the purpose, nor invested with the authority of forming a constitution; and as they could not, consistently with the American idea of rights, assume such a power, they could only confer upon the matter and put it into a train of operation. The conferees, therefore, did no more than state the case and recommend to the several counties to elect six representatives for each county, to meet in convention at Philadelphia, with powers to form a constitution and propose it for public consideration.

This convention, of which Benjamin Franklin [5] was president, having met and deliberated and agreed upon a constitution, they next ordered it to be published, not as a thing established but for the consideration of the whole people, their approbation or rejection, and then adjourned to a stated time.

When the time of the adjournment was expired, the convention re-assembled; and as the general opinion of the people in approbation of it was then known, the constitution was signed, sealed, and proclaimed on the *authority of the people*, and the original instrument deposited as a public record.

The convention then appointed a day for the general election of the representatives who were to compose the Government, and the time it should commence; and having done this, they dissolved and returned to their several homes and occupations.

In this constitution were laid down, first, a declaration of rights. Then followed the form which the government should have and the powers it should possess: the authority of the courts of judicature and of juries; the manner in which elections should be conducted and the proportion of representatives to the number of electors; the time which each succeeeding assembly should continue, which was one year; the mode of levying and of accounting for the expenditure of public money, of appointing public officers, etc.

No article of this constitution could be altered or infringed at the discretion of the government that was to ensue. It was to that government a law. But as it would have been unwise to preclude the benefit of experience, and in order also to prevent the accumulation of errors, if any should be found, and to preserve a unison of government with the circumstances of the state at all times, the constitution provided that, at the expiration of every seven years, a convention should be elected for the express purpose of revising the constitution and making alterations, additions, or abolitions therein, if any such should be found necessary.

Here we see a regular process—a government issuing out of a constitution, formed by the people in their original character; and that constitution serving, not only as an authority, but as a law of control to the government. It was the political bible of the state. Scarcely a family was without it. Every member of the government had a copy; and nothing was more common when any debate arose on the principle of a bill, or on the extent of any species of authority, than for the members to take the printed constitution out of their pocket and read the chapter with which such a matter in debate was connected.

Having thus given an instance from one of the states, I will show the proceedings by which the Federal Constitution of the United States arose and was formed.

Congress, at its two first meetings in September 1774 and May 1775, was nothing more than a deputation from the legislatures of the several provinces, afterward states, and had no other authority than what arose from common consent and the necessity of its acting as a public body. In everything which related to the internal affairs of America, Congress went no farther than to issue recommendations to the several provincial assemblies, who at discretion adopted them or not.

Nothing on the part of Congress was compulsive; yet, in this situation, it was more faithfully and affectionately obeyed than was any government in Europe. This instance, like that of the National Assembly of France, sufficiently shows that the strength of government does not consist in anything *within* itself, but in the attachment of a nation and the interest which the people feel in supporting it. When this is lost, government is but a child in power; and though, like the old government of France, it may harass individuals for a while, it but facilitates its own fall.

After the Declaration of Independence, it became consistent with the principle on which representative government is founded that the authority of Congress should be defined and established. Whether that authority should be more or less than Congress then discretionally exercised was not the question. It was merely the rectitude of the measure.

For this purpose, the act called the Act of Confederation (which was a sort of imperfect federal constitution) was proposed and, after long deliberation, was concluded in the year 1781. It was not the act of Congress, because it is repugnant to the principles of representative government that a body should give power to itself. Congress first informed the several states of the powers which it conceived were necessary to be invested in the union, to enable it to perform the duties and services required from it; and the states severally agreed with each other and concentrated in Congress those powers.

It may not be improper to observe that in both those instances (the one of Pennsylvania and the other of the United States) there is no such thing as the idea of a compact between the people on one side and the government on the other. The compact was that of the people with each other, to produce and constitute a government.

To suppose that any government can be a party in a compact with the whole people is to suppose it to have existence before it can have a right to exist. The only instance in which a compact can take place between the people and those who exercise the government is that the people shall pay them while they choose to employ them.

Government is not a trade which any man or body of men has a right to set up and exercise for his own emolument, but is altogether a trust, in right of those by whom that trust is delegated and by whom it is always resumable. It has of itself no rights; they are altogether duties.

Having thus given two instances of the original formation of a constitution, I will show the manner in which both have been changed since their first establishment.

The powers vested in the governments of the several states by the state constitutions were found, upon experience, to be too great; and those vested in the Federal Government by the Act of Confederation too little. The defect was not in the principle, but in the distribution of power.

Numerous publications, in pamphlets and in the newspapers, appeared on the propriety and necessity of new modeling the Federal Government. After some time of public discussion, carried on through the channel of the press and in conversations, the state of Virginia, experiencing some inconvenience with respect to commerce, proposed holding a continental conference, in consequence of which a deputation from five or six of the state assemblies met at Annapolis in Maryland in 1786.

This meeting, not conceiving itself sufficiently authorized to go into the business of reform, did no more than state their general opinions of the propriety of the measure, and recommended that a convention of all the states should be held the year following.

This convention met at Philadelphia in May, 1787, of which General Washington was elected President. He was not at that time connected with any of the state governments or with Congress. He delivered up his commission when the war ended and since then had lived a private citizen. The convention went deeply into all the subjects, and having, after a variety of debate and investigation, agreed among themselves upon the several parts of a Federal Constitution, the next question was the manner of giving it authority and practice.

For this purpose, they did not, like a cabal of courtiers, send for a Dutch stadtholder or a German elector,[6] but they referred the whole matter to the sense and interest of the country.

They first directed that the proposed Constitution should be published. Secondly, that each state should elect a convention expressly for the purpose of taking it into consideration and of ratifying or rejecting it; and that as soon as the approbation and ratification of any nine states should be given, that those states should proceed to the election of their proportion of members to the new Federal Government; and that the operation of it should then begin and the former Federal Government cease.

The several states proceeded accordingly to elect their conventions. Some of those conventions ratified the Constitution by very large majorities, and two or three unanimously. In others there were much debate and division of opinion. In the Massachusetts Convention, which met at Boston, the majority was not above nineteen or twenty in about three hundred members, but such is the nature of representative government that it quietly decides all matters by majority.

After the debate in the Massachusetts Convention was closed, and the vote taken, the objecting members rose and declared:

That though they had argued and voted against it, because certain parts appeared to them in a different light to what they appeared to other members: yet, as the vote had decided in favor of the Constitution as proposed, they should give it the same practical support as if they had voted for it.

As soon as nine states [7] had concurred (and the rest followed in the order their conventions were elected), the old fabric of the Federal Government was taken down and the new one elected, of which General Washington is President. In this place I cannot help remarking that the character and services of this gentleman are sufficient to put all those men called kings to shame.

While they are receiving from the sweat and labors of mankind a prodigality of pay, to which neither their abilities nor their services can entitle them, he is rendering every service in his power and refusing every pecuniary reward. He accepted no pay as Commander-in-Chief; he accepts none as President of the United States.

After the new Federal Constitution was established, the state of Pennsylvania, conceiving that some parts of its own constitution required to be altered, elected a convention for that purpose. The proposed alterations were published, and the people concurring therein, they were established.

In forming those constitutions or in altering them, little or no inconvenience took place. The ordinary course of things was not interrupted, and the advantages have been much. It is always the interest of a far greater number of people in a nation to have things right than to let them remain wrong; and when public matters are open to debate, and the public judgment freè, it will not decide wrong, unless it decides too hastily.

In the two instances of changing the constitutions, the governments then in being were not actors either way. Government has no right to make itself a party in any debates respecting the principles or mode of forming or of changing constitutions.

It is not for the benefit of those who exercise the powers of government that constitutions and the governments issuing from them are established. In all those matters the right of judging and acting are in those who pay, and not in those who receive.

A constitution is the property of a nation, and not of those who exercise the government. All the constitutions of America are declared to be established on the authority of the people. In France, the word "nation" is used instead of "the people," but in both cases a constitution is a thing antecedent to the government and always distinct therefrom.

In England, it is not difficult to perceive that everything has a constitution except the nation. Every society and association that is established first agreed upon a number of original articles, digested into form, which are its constitution. It then appointed its officers, whose powers and authorities are described in that constitution, and the government of that society then commenced. Those officers, by whatever name they are called, have no authority to add to, alter, or abridge the original articles. It is only to the constituting power that this right belongs.

.   .   .   .

[GOVERNMENT BY REPRESENTATION VERSUS GOVERNMENT BY PRECEDENT]

From the want of a constitution in England to restrain and regulate the wild impulse of power, many of the laws are irrational and tyrannical, and the administration of them vague and problematical.

The attention of the government of England (for I rather choose to call it by this name than the English government) appears, since its political connection with Germany,[8] to have been so completely engrossed and absorbed by foreign affairs and the means of raising taxes that it seems to exist for no other purposes. Domestic concerns are neglected; and with respect to regular law, there is scarcely such a thing.

Almost every case must now be determined by some precedent, be that precedent good or bad, or whether it properly applies or not; and the practice has become so general as to suggest a suspicion that it proceeds from a deeper policy than at first sight appears.

Since the revolution of America, and more so since that of France, this preaching up the doctrine of precedents, drawn from times and circumstances antecedent to those events, has been the studied practice of the English government. The generality of those precedents are founded on principles and opinions, the reverse of what they ought to be; and the greater distance of time they are drawn from, the more they are to be suspected.

But by associating those precedents with a superstitious reverence for ancient things, as monks show relics and call them holy, the generality of mankind are deceived into the design. Governments now act as if they were afraid to awaken a single reflection in man. They are softly leading him to the sepulcher of precedents, to deaden his faculties and call his attention from the scene of revolutions.

They feel that he is arriving at knowledge faster than they wish, and their policy of precedents is the barometer of their fears. This political popery, like the ecclesiastical popery of old, has had its day and is hastening to its exit. The ragged relic and the antiquated precedent, the monk and the monarch, will molder together.

Government by precedent, without any regard to the principle of the precedent, is one of the vilest systems that can be set up. In numerous instances the precedent ought to operate as a warning and not as an example, and requires to be shunned instead of imitated; but instead of this, precedents are taken in the lump and put at once for constitution and for law.

Either the doctrine of precedents is policy to keep a man in a state of ignorance, or it is a practical confession that wisdom degenerates in governments as governments increase in age and can only hobble along by the stilts and crutches of precedents.

How is it that the same persons who would proudly be thought wiser than their predecessors appear at the same time only as the ghosts of departed wisdom? How strangely is antiquity treated! To answer some purposes, it is spoken of as the times of darkness and ignorance; and to answer others, it is put for the light of the world.

If the doctrine of precedents is to be followed, the expenses of government need not continue the same. Why pay men extravagantly who have but little to do? If everything that can happen is already in precedent, legislation is at an end, and precedent, like a dictionary, determines every case. Either, therefore, government has arrived at its dotage and requires to be renovated, or all the occasions for exercising its wisdom have occurred.

We now see all over Europe, and particularly in England, the curious phenomenon of a nation looking one way and the government the other—the one forward and the other backward. If governments are to go on by precedent while nations go on by improvement, they must at last come to a final separation; and the sooner and the more civilly they determine this point, the better it will be for them.[f]

Having thus spoken of constitutions generally as things distinct from actual governments, let us proceed to consider the parts of which a constitution is composed.

Opinions differ more on this subject than with respect to the whole. That a nation ought to have a constitution, as a rule for the conduct of its government, is a simple question to which all men, not directly courtiers, will agree. It is only on the component parts that questions and opinions multiply.

But this difficulty, like every other, will diminish when put into

[f] In England, the improvements in agriculture, useful arts, manufactures, and commerce have been made in opposition to the genius of its government, which is that of following precedents. It is from the enterprise and industry of the individuals and their numerous associations, in which, tritely speaking, government is neither pillow nor bolster, that these improvements have proceeded.

No man thought about the government, or who was *in* or who was *out,* when he was planning or executing those things, and all he had to hope with respect to government was that it would let him alone. Three or four very silly ministerial newspapers are continually offending against the spirit of national improvement by ascribing it to a minister. They may with as much truth ascribe this book to a minister.

a train of being rightly understood. The first thing is that a nation has a right to establish a constitution.

Whether it exercises this right in the most judicious manner at first, it is quite another case. It exercises it agreeably to the judgment it possesses; and by continuing to do so, all errors will at last be exploded.

When this right is established in a nation, there is no fear that it will be employed to its own injury. A nation can have no interest in being wrong.

Though all the constitutions of America are on one general principle, yet no two of them are exactly alike in their component parts or in the distribution of the powers which they give to the actual governments. Some are more and others less complex.

In forming a constitution, it is first necessary to consider what are the ends for which government is necessary; secondly, what are the best means, and the least expensive, for accomplishing those ends.

Government is nothing more than a national association; and the object of this association is the good of all, as well individually as collectively. Every man wishes to pursue his occupation and enjoy the fruits of his labors and the produce of his property, in peace and safety, and with the least possible expense. When these things are accomplished, all the objects for which government ought to be established are answered.

It has been customary to consider government under three distinct general heads: the legislative, the executive, and the judicial.

But if we permit our judgment to act unencumbered by the habit of multiplied terms, we can perceive no more than two divisions of power of which civil government is composed, namely, that of legislating or enacting laws, and that of executing or administering them. Everything, therefore, appertaining to civil government classes itself under one or other of these two divisions.

So far as regards the execution of the laws, that which is called the judicial power is strictly and properly the executive power of every country. It is that power to which every individual has an appeal and which causes the laws to be executed; neither have we any other clear idea with respect to the official execution of the laws. In England, and also in America and France, this power begins with the magistrate and proceeds up through all the courts of judicature.

I leave to courtiers to explain what is meant by calling monarchy the executive power. It is merely a name in which acts of government are done; and any other, or none at all, would answer the same purpose.

Laws have neither more nor less authority on this account. It must be from the justness of their principles and the interest which a nation feels therein that they derive support; if they require any other than this, it is a sign that something in the system of government is imperfect. Laws difficult to be executed cannot be generally good.

With respect to the organization of the *legislative power,* different modes have been adopted in different countries. In America, it is generally composed of two houses. In France, it consists of but one; but in both countries, it is wholly by representation.

The case is that mankind (from the long tyranny of assumed power) have had so few opportunities of making the necessary trials on modes and principles of government, in order to discover the best, *that government is but now beginning to be known,* and experience is yet wanting to determine many particulars.

The objections against two houses are, *first,* that there is an inconsistency in any part of a whole legislature coming to a final determination by vote on any matter, whilst *that matter,* with respect to *that whole,* is yet only in a train of deliberation, and consequently open to new illustrations.

Secondly, that by taking the vote on each, as a separate body, it always admits of the possibility, and is often the case in practice, that the minority governs the majority, and that, in some instances, to a great degree of inconsistency.

Thirdly, that two houses arbitrarily checking or controlling each other is inconsistent, because it cannot be proved, on the principles of just representation, that either should be wiser or better than the other. They may check in the wrong as well as in the right; and therefore to give the power where we cannot give the wisdom to use it, nor be assured of its being rightly used, renders the hazard at least equal to the precaution.[g]

The objection against a single house is that it is always in a condition of committing itself too soon. But it should at the same time be remembered that when there is a constitution which defines the power and establishes the principles within which a legislature shall act, there is already a more effectual check provided and more powerfully operating than any other check can be. For example:

Were a bill brought into any of the American legislatures similar to that which was passed into an act of the English Parliament, at the commencement of the reign of George I, to extend the duration of the assemblies to a longer period than they now sit, the check is in the constitution, which in effect says, *thus far shalt thou go and no further*.

But in order to remove the objection against a single house (that of acting with too quick an impulse) and at the same time

[g] With respect to the two houses of which the English Parliament is composed, they appear to be effectually influenced into one and, as a legislature, to have no temper of its own. The minister, whoever he at any time may be, touches it as with an opium wand, and it sleeps obedience.

But if we look at the distinct abilities of the two houses, the difference will appear so great as to show the inconsistency of placing power where there can be no certainty of the judgment to use it. Wretched as the state of representation is in England, it is manhood compared with what is called the House of Lords; and so little is this nicknamed house regarded that the people scarcely inquire at any time what it is doing. It appears also to be most under influence and the furthest removed from the general interest of the nation. In the debate on engaging in the Russian and Turkish War, the majority in the House of Peers in favor of it was upward of ninety, when in the other house, which was more than double its numbers, the majority was sixty-three.

The proceedings on Mr. Fox's bill,[9] respecting the rights of juries, merits also to be noticed. The persons called the peers were not the objects of that bill. They are already in possession of more privileges than that bill gave to others. They are their own jury; and if anyone of that house were prosecuted for a libel, he would not suffer, even upon conviction, for the first offense. Such inequality in laws ought not to exist in any country. The French Constitution says that *the law is the same to every individual, whether to protect or to punish. All are equal in its sight.*

to avoid the inconsistencies, in some cases absurdities, arising from the two houses, the following method has been proposed as an improvement on both:

First, to have but one representation.

Secondly, to divide that representation by lot into two or three parts.

Thirdly, that every proposed bill shall first be debated in those parts, by succession, that they may become hearers of each other, but without taking any vote. After which the whole representation to assemble for a general debate and determination by vote.

To this proposed improvement has been added another for the purpose of keeping the representation in a state of constant renovation, which is that one third of the representation of each county shall go out at the expiration of one year, and the number be replaced by new elections. Another third at the expiration of the second year, replaced in like manner, and every third year to be a general election.[h]

But in whatever manner the separate parts of a constitution may be arranged, there is one general principle that distinguishes freedom from slavery, which is that all *hereditary government over a people is to them a species of slavery, and representative government is freedom.*

.   .   .   .

The presidency in America (or, as it is sometimes called, the executive) is the only office from which a foreigner is excluded, and in England it is the only one to which he is admitted. A foreigner cannot be a member of Parliament, but he may be what is called a "king." If there is any reason for excluding foreigners, it ought to be from those offices where most mischief can be acted and where, by uniting every bias of interest and attachment, the trust is best secured.

[h] As to the state of representation in England, it is too absurd to be reasoned upon. Almost all the represented parts are decreasing in population, and the unrepresented parts are increasing. A general convention of the nation is necessary to take the whole state of its government into consideration.

But as nations proceed in the great business of forming constitutions, they will examine with more precision into the nature and business of that department which is called the "executive." What the legislative and judicial departments are everyone can see; but with respect to what, in Europe, is called the "executive," as distinct from those two, it is either a political superfluity or a chaos of unknown things. Some kind of official department, to which reports shall be made from different parts of the nation or from abroad, to be laid before the national representatives, is all that is necessary; but there is no consistency in calling this the executive; neither can it be considered in any other light than as inferior to the legislature. The sovereign authority in any country is the power of making laws, and everything else is an official department.

Next to the arrangement of the principles and the organization of the several parts of a constitution is the provision to be made for the support of the persons to whom the nation shall confide the administration of the constitutional powers.

A nation can have no right to the time and services of any person at his own expense whom it may choose to employ or entrust in any department whatever; neither can any reason be given for making provision for the support of any one part of the government and not for the other.

But, admitting that the honor of being entrusted with any part of a government is to be considered a sufficient reward, it ought to be so to every person alike. If the members of the legislature of any country are to serve at their own expense, that which is called the executive, whether monarchial or by any other name, ought to serve in like manner. It is inconsistent to pay the one and accept the service of the other gratis.

In America every department in the government is decently provided for, but no one is extravagantly paid. Every member of Congress and of the state assemblies is allowed a sufficiency for his expenses. Whereas in England a most prodigal provision is made for the support of one part of the government and none for the other, the consequence of which is that the one is furnished with the means of corruption and the other is put into the condition of being corrupted. Less than a fourth part of such expense, applied as it is in America, would remedy a great part of the corruption.

Another reform in the American Constitution is the exploding all oaths of personality. The oath of allegiance is to the nation only. The putting any individual as a figure for a nation is improper. The happiness of a nation is the first object, and therefore the intention of an oath of allegiance ought not to be obscured by being figuratively taken to or in the name of any person. The oath, called the civic oath, in France, viz., the "nation, the law, and the king," is improper. If taken at all, it ought to be as in America, to the nation only.

The law may or may not be good; but, in this place, it can have no other meaning than as being conducive to the happiness of the nation, and therefore is included in it. The remainder of the oath is improper, on the ground that all person oaths ought to be abolished. They are the remains of tyranny on one part and slavery on the other, and the name of the Creator ought not to be introduced to witness the degradation of his creation; or if taken, as is already mentioned, as figurative of the nation, it is in this place redundant.

But whatever apology may be made for oaths at the first establishment of a government, they ought not to be permitted afterward. If a government requires the support of oaths, it is a sign that it is not worth supporting and ought not to be supported. Make government what it ought to be, and it will support itself.

To conclude this part of the subject: One of the greatest improvements that has been made for the perpetual security and progress of constitutional liberty is the provision which the new constitutions make for occasionally revising, altering and amending them.

The principle upon which Mr. Burke formed his political creed, that "of binding and controlling posterity to the end of time, and renouncing and abdicating the rights of all posterity forever," is now become too detestable to be made a subject for debate; and, therefore, I pass it over with no other notice than exposing it.

Government is but now beginning to be known. Hitherto it has been the mere exercise of power, which forbade all effectual inquiry into rights and grounded itself wholly on possession. While the enemy of liberty was its judge, the progress of its principles must have been small indeed.

The constitutions of America, and also that of France, have either fixed a period for their revision or laid down the mode by which improvements shall be made.

It is perhaps impossible to establish anything that combines principles with opinions and practice which the progress of circumstances, through a length of years, will not in some measure derange or render inconsistent; and therefore, to prevent inconveniences accumulating till they discourage reformations or provoke revolutions, it is best to regulate them as they occur.

The rights of man are the rights of all generations of men and cannot be monopolized by any. That which is worth following will be followed for the sake of its worth; and it is in this that its security lies, and not in any conditions with which it may be encumbered. When a man leaves property to his heirs, he does not connect it with an obligation that they shall accept it. Why, then, should we do otherwise with respect to constitutions?

The best constitution that could now be devised, consistent with the condition of the present moment, may be far short of that excellence which a few years may afford. There is a morning of reason rising upon man, on the subject of government, that has not appeared before. As the barbarism of the present old governments expires, the moral condition of the nations with respect to each other will be changed.

Man will not be brought up with the savage idea of considering his species as enemies because the accident of birth gave the individuals existence in countries distinguished by different names; and as constitutions have always some relation to external as well as domestic circumstances, the means of benefiting by every change, foreign or domestic, should be a part of every constitution.

We already see an alteration in the national disposition of England and France toward each other, which, when we look back only a few years, is itself a revolution. Who could have foreseen, or who would have believed, that a French National Assembly would ever have been a popular toast in England or that a friendly alliance of the two nations should become the wish of either?

It shows that man, were he not corrupted by governments, is naturally the friend of man and that human nature is not of itself vicious. The spirit of jealousy and ferocity which the governments of the two countries inspired, and which they rendered subservient to the purpose of taxation, is now yielding to the dictates of reason, interest, and humanity.

The trade of courts is beginning to be understood, and the affectation of mystery, with all the artificial sorcery by which they imposed upon mankind, is on the decline. It has received its death wound; and though it may linger, it will expire.

Government ought to be as much open to improvement as anything which appertains to man, instead of which it has been monopolized from age to age by the most ignorant and vicious of the human race. Need we any other proof of their wretched management than the excess of debt and taxes with which every nation groans and the quarrels into which they have precipitated the world?

Just emerging from such a barbarous condition, it is too soon to determine to what extent of improvement government may yet be carried. For what we can foresee, all Europe may form but one great republic, and man be free of the whole.

DISSERTATION ON FIRST
PRINCIPLES OF GOVERNMENT

DISSERTATION ON FIRST PRINCIPLES
OF GOVERNMENT

THERE IS NO SUBJECT more interesting to every man than the subject of government. His security, be he rich or poor, and in a great measure his prosperity are connected therewith; it is therefore his interest as well as his duty to make himself acquainted with its principles and what the practice ought to be.

Every art and science, however imperfectly known at first, has been studied, improved, and brought to what we call perfection by the progressive labors of succeeding generations; but the science of government has stood still. No improvement has been made in the principle and scarcely any in the practice till the American Revolution began. In all the countries of Europe (except in France) the same forms and systems that were erected in the remote ages of ignorance still continue, and their antiquity is put in the place of principle; it is forbidden to investigate their origin or by what right they exist. If it be asked how has this happened, the answer is easy: they are established on a principle that is false, and they employ their power to prevent detection.

Notwithstanding the mystery with which the science of government has been enveloped, for the purpose of enslaving, plundering, and imposing upon mankind, it is of all things the least mysterious and the most easy to be understood. The meanest capacity cannot be at a loss if it begins its inquiries at the right point. Every art and science has some point or alphabet at which the study of that art or science begins and by the assistance of which the progress is facilitated. The same method ought to be observed with respect to the science of government.

Instead, then, of embarrassing the subject in the outset with the numerous subdivisions under which different forms of government have been classed, such as aristocracy, democracy, oligarchy, monarchy, etc., the better method will be to begin with what may be called primary divisions, or those under which all the several subdivisions will be comprehended.

The primary divisions are but two:

First, government by election and representation.
Secondly, government by hereditary succession.

All the several forms and systems of government, however numerous or diversified, class themselves under one or other of those primary divisions; for either they are on the system of representation or on that of hereditary succession. As to that equivocal thing called "mixed government," [1] such as the late government of Holland and the present government of England, it does not make an exception to the general rule because the parts separately considered are either representative or hereditary.

Beginning then our inquiries at this point, we have first to examine into the nature of those two primary divisions. If they are equally right in principle, it is mere matter of opinion which we prefer. If the one be demonstratively better than the other, that difference directs our choice; but if one of them should be so absolutely false as not to have a right of existence, the matter settles itself at once, because a negative proved on one thing, where two only are offered and one must be accepted, amounts to an affirmative on the other.

The revolutions that are now spreading themselves in the world have their origin in this state of the case, and the present war [2] is a conflict between the representative system founded on the rights of the people and the hereditary system founded in usurpation. As to what are called monarchy, royalty, and aristocracy, they do not, either as things or as terms, sufficiently describe the hereditary system; they are but secondary things or signs of the hereditary system and which fall of themselves if that system has not a right to exist.

Were there no such terms as "monarchy," "royalty," and "aristocracy," or were other terms substituted in their place, the hereditary system, if it continued, would not be altered thereby. It would be the same system under any other titulary name as it is now.

The character therefore of the revolutions of the present day distinguishes itself most definitely by grounding itself on the system of representative government, in opposition to the hereditary. No other distinction reaches the whole of the principle.

Having thus opened the case generally, I proceed, in the first place, to examine the hereditary system because it has the priority in point of time. The representative system is the invention of the modern world; and that no doubt may arise as to my own opinion, I declare it beforehand, which is *that there is not a problem in Euclid more mathematically true than that hereditary government has not a right to exist. When therefore we take from any man the exercise of hereditary power, we take away that which he never had the right to possess and which no law or custom could or ever can give him a title to.*

The arguments that have hitherto been employed against the hereditary system have been chiefly founded upon the absurdity of it and its incompetence to the purpose of good government. Nothing can present to our judgment or to our imagination a figure of greater absurdity than that of seeing the government of a nation fall, as it frequently does, into the hands of a lad necessarily destitute of experience and often little better than a fool. It is an insult to every man of years, of character, and of talents in a country.

The moment we begin to reason upon the hereditary system, it falls into derision; let but a single idea begin, and a thousand will soon follow. Insignificance, imbecility, childhood, dotage, want of moral character—in fine, every defect, serious or laughable— unite to hold up the hereditary system as a figure of ridicule. Leaving, however, the ridiculousness of the thing to the reflections of the reader, I proceed to the more important part of the question, namely, whether such a system has a right to exist.

To be satisfied of the right of a thing to exist, we must be satisfied that it had a right to begin. If it had not a right to begin, it has not the right to continue. By what right, then, did the hereditary system begin? Let a man but ask himself this question, and he will find that he cannot satisfy himself with an answer.

The right which any man or any family had to set itself up at first to govern a nation and to establish itself hereditarily was no other than the right which Robespierre [3] had to do the same thing in France. If he had none, they had none. If they had any, he had as much; for it is impossible to discover superiority of right in any family, by virtue of which hereditary government could begin. The Capets, the Guelphs, the Robespierres, the Marats,[4] are all on the same standing as to the question of right. It belongs exclusively to none.

It is one step toward liberty to perceive that hereditary government could not begin as an exclusive right in any family. The next point will be whether, having once begun, it could grow into a right by the influence of time.

This would be supposing an absurdity; for either it is putting time in the place of principle or making it superior to principle, whereas time has no more connection with or influence upon principle than principle has upon time. The wrong which began a thousand years ago is as much a wrong as if it began today, and the right which originates today is as much a right as if it had the sanction of a thousand years.

Time with respect to principles is an eternal *now;* it has no operation upon them, it changes nothing of their nature and qualities. But what have we to do with a thousand years? Our lifetime is but a short portion of that period; and if we find the wrong in existence as soon as we begin to live, that is the point of time at which it begins to us, and our right to resist it is the same as if it never existed before.

As hereditary government could not begin as a natural right in any family, nor derive after its commencement any right from time, we have only to examine whether there exist in a nation a right to set it up and establish it by what is called law, as has been done in England. I answer "No," and that any law or any constitution made for that purpose is an act of treason against the right of every minor in the nation at the time it is made and against the rights of all succeeding generations.

I shall speak upon each of those cases. First, of the minor at the time such law is made. Secondly, of the generations that are to follow.

A nation, in a collective sense, comprehends all the individuals of whatever age, from just born to just dying. Of these, one part will be minors and the other aged. The average of life is not exactly the same in every climate and country, but in general the minority in years are the majority in numbers; that is, the number of persons under twenty-one years is greater than the number of persons above that age.

This difference in number is not necessary to the establishment of the principle I mean to lay down, but it serves to show the justice of it more strongly. The principle would be equally as good if the majority in years were also the majority in numbers.

The rights of minors are as sacred as the rights of the aged. The difference is altogether in the different age of the two parties, and nothing in the nature of the rights; the rights are the same rights and are to be preserved inviolate for the inheritance of the minors when they shall come of age. During the minority of minors, their rights are under the sacred guardianship of the aged.

The minor cannot surrender them, the guardian cannot dispossess him; consequently the aged part of a nation, who are the lawmakers for the *time being* and who, in the march of life, are but a few years ahead of those who are yet minors and to whom they must shortly give place, have not and cannot have the right to make a law to set up and establish hereditary government, or, to speak more distinctly, *a hereditary succession of governors,* because it is an attempt to deprive every minor in the nation, at the time such a law is made, of his inheritance of rights when he shall come of age and to subjugate him to a system of government to which, during his minority, he could neither consent nor object.

If a person who is a minor at the time such a law is proposed had happened to have been born a few years sooner, so as to be of the age of twenty-one years at the time of proposing it, his right to have objected against it, to have exposed the injustice and tyrannical principles of it and to have voted against it, will be admitted on all sides.

If, therefore, the law operates to prevent his exercising the same rights after he comes of age as he would have had a right to exercise had he been of age at the time, it is undeniably a law to take away and annul the rights of every person in the nation who shall be a minor at the time of making such a law, and consequently the right to make it cannot exist.

I come now to speak of government by hereditary succession, as it applies to succeeding generations, and to show that in this case, as in the case of minors, there does not exist in a nation a right to set it up.

A nation, though continually existing, is continually in a state of renewal and succession. It is never stationary. Every day produces new births, carries minors forward to maturity and old persons from the stage. In this ever-running flood of generations there is no part superior in authority to another. Could we conceive an idea of superiority in any, at what point of time, or in what century of the world, are we to fix it? To what cause are we to ascribe it? By what evidence are we to prove it? By what criterion are we to know it?

A single reflection will teach us that our ancestors, like ourselves, were but tenants for life in the great freehold of rights. The fee absolute was not in them, it is not in us; it belongs to the whole family of man through all ages. If we think otherwise than this, we think either as slaves or as tyrants. As slaves, if we think that any former generation had a right to bind us; as tyrants, if we think that we have authority to bind the generations that are to follow.

It may not be inapplicable to the subject to endeavor to define what is to be understood by a "generation" in the sense the word is here used.

As a natural term, its meaning is sufficiently clear. The father, the son, the grandson are so many distinct generations. But when we speak of a generation as describing the persons in whom legal authority resides, as distinct from another generation of the same description who are to succeed them, it comprehends all those who are above the age of twenty-one years at the time that we count from; and a generation of this kind will continue in authority between fourteen and twenty-one years, that is, until the number of minors, who shall have arrived at age, shall be greater than the number of persons remaining of the former stock.

For example, if France at this or any other moment contains twenty-four millions of souls, twelve millions will be males and twelve females. Of the twelve millions of males, six millions will be of the age of twenty-one years and six will be under, and the authority to govern will reside in the first six.

But every day will make some alteration, and in twenty-one years every one of those minors who survives will have arrived at age, and the greater part of the former stock will be gone; the majority of persons then living, in whom the legal authority resides, will be composed of those who, twenty-one years before, had no legal existence. Those will be fathers and grandfathers in their turn; and, in the next twenty-one years (or less), another race of minors arrived at age will succeed them, and so on.

As this is ever the case, and as every generation is equal in rights to another, it consequently follows that there cannot be a right in any to establish government by hereditary succession, because it would be supposing itself possessed of a right superior to the rest, namely, that of commanding by its own authority how the world shall be hereafter governed and who shall govern it.

Every age and generation is and must be (as a matter of right) as free to act for itself in all cases as the age and generation that preceded it. The vanity and presumption of governing beyond the grave is the most ridiculous and insolent of all tyrannies. Man has no property in man; neither has one generation a property in the generations that are to follow.

In the first part of the *Rights of Man* I have spoken of government by hereditary succession, and I will here close the subject with an extract from that work, which states it under the two following heads.[a]

The history of the English Parliament furnishes an example of this kind, and which merits to be recorded as being the greatest instance of legislative ignorance and want of principle that is to be found in any country. The case is as follows:

[a] [The quotation from *Rights of Man* omitted from this text of the "Dissertation" appears on pages 102-104 of the present work. The passage begins, "*First,* the right of a particular family . . ." and closes (with some necessary differences in phrasing), "good Lord, deliver the world."]

The English Parliament of 1688 imported a man and his wife from Holland, *William* and *Mary,* and made them King and Queen of England. Having done this, the said Parliament made a law to convey the government of the country to the heirs of William and Mary, in the following words: "We, the Lords Spiritual and Temporal, and Commons, do, in the name of the people of England, most humbly and faithfully submit *ourselves, our heirs and posterities,* to William and Mary, *their heirs and posterities,* forever." And in a subsequent law, as quoted by Edmund Burke, the said Parliament, in the name of the people of England then living, *binds the said people, their heirs and posterities, to William and Mary, their heirs and posterities, to the end of time.*

It is not sufficient that we laugh at the ignorance of such lawmakers; it is necessary that we reprobate their want of principle. The Constituent Assembly of France, 1789, fell into the same vice as the Parliament of England had done, and assumed to establish a hereditary succession in the family of the Capets as an act of the constitution of that year.

That every nation, *for the time being,* has a right to govern itself as it pleases must always be admitted; but government by hereditary succession is government for another race of people, and not for itself; and as those on whom it is to operate are not yet in existence, or are minors, so neither is the right in existence to set it up for them, and to assume such a right is treason against the right of posterity.

I here close the arguments on the first head, that of government by hereditary succession, and proceed to the second, that of government by election and representation, or, as it may be concisely expressed, *representative government,* in contradistinction to *hereditary government.*

Reasoning by exclusion, if *hereditary government* has not a right to exist, and that it has not is provable, *representative government* is admitted of course.

In contemplating government by election and representation, we amuse not ourselves in inquiring when or how, or by what right, it began. Its origin is ever in view. Man is himself the origin and the evidence of the right. It appertains to him in right of his existence, and his person is the title deed.

The true and only true basis of representative government is equality of rights. Every man has a right to one vote and no more in the choice of representatives. The rich have no more right to exclude the poor from the right of voting or of electing and being elected than the poor have to exclude the rich, and wherever it is attempted or proposed on either side it is a question of force and not of right. Who is he that would exclude another? That other has a right to exclude him.

That which is now called aristocracy implies an inequality of rights, but who are the persons that have a right to establish this inequality? Will the rich exclude themselves? No. Will the poor exclude themselves? No. By what right then can any be excluded? It would be a question if any man or class of men have a right to exclude themselves, but be this as it may, they cannot have the right to exclude another. The poor will not delegate such a right to the rich nor the rich to the poor, and to assume it is not only to assume arbitrary power but to assume a right to commit robbery.

Personal rights, of which the right of voting for representatives is one, are a species of property of the most sacred kind; and he that would employ his pecuniary property or presume upon the influence it gives him to dispossess or rob another of his property or rights uses that pecuniary property as he would use firearms and merits to have it taken from him.

Inequality of rights is created by a combination in one part of the community to exclude another part from its rights. Whenever it be made an article of a constitution or a law that the right of voting or of electing and being elected shall appertain exclusively to persons possessing a certain quantity of property, be it little or much, it is a combination of the persons possessing that quantity to exclude those who do not possess the same quantity. It is investing themselves with powers as a self-created part of society, to the exclusion of the rest.

It is always to be taken for granted that those who oppose an equality of rights never mean the exclusion should take place on themselves; and in this view of the case, pardoning the vanity of the thing, aristocracy is a subject of laughter. This self-soothing vanity is encouraged by another idea not less selfish, which is that the opposers conceive they are playing a safe game, in which there is a chance to gain and none to lose; that, at any rate, the doctrine of equality includes them and that, if they cannot get more rights than those whom they oppose and would exclude, they shall not have less.

This opinion has already been fatal to thousands who, not contented with *equal rights,* have sought more till they lost all, and experienced in themselves the degrading *inequality* they endeavored to fix upon others.

In any view of the case, it is dangerous and impolitic, sometimes ridiculous and always unjust, to make property the criterion of the right of voting. If the sum or value of the property upon which the right is to take place be considerable, it will exclude a majority of the people and unite them in a common interest against the government and against those who support it; and as the power is always with the majority, they can overturn such a government and its supporters whenever they please.

If, in order to avoid this danger, a small quantity of property be fixed as the criterion of the right, it exhibits liberty in disgrace by putting it in competition with accident and insignificance. When a broodmare shall fortunately produce a foal or a mule that, by being worth the sum in question, shall convey to its owner the right of voting or by its death take it from him, in whom does the origin of such a right exist? Is it in the man or in the mule? When we consider how many ways property may be acquired without merit and lost without crime, we ought to spurn the idea of making it a criterion of rights.

But the offensive part of the case is that this exclusion from the right of voting implies a stigma on the moral character of the persons excluded, and this is what no part of the community has a right to pronounce upon another part. No external circumstance can justify it; wealth is no proof of moral character, nor poverty of the want of it.

On the contrary, wealth is often the presumptive evidence of dishonesty and poverty the negative evidence of innocence. If therefore property, whether little or much, be made a criterion, the means by which that property has been acquired ought to be made a criterion also.

The only ground upon which exclusion from the right of voting is consistent with justice would be to inflict it as a punishment for a certain time upon those who should propose to take away that right from others. The right of voting for representatives is the primary right by which other rights are protected.

To take away this right is to reduce a man to slavery, for slavery consists in being subject to the will of another, and he that has not a vote in the election of representatives is in this case. The proposal, therefore, to disfranchise any class of men is as criminal as the proposal to take away property.

When we speak of right, we ought always to unite with it the idea of duties: rights become duties by reciprocity. The right which I enjoy becomes my duty to guarantee it to another, and he to me; and those who violate the duty justly incur a forfeiture of the right.

In a political view of the case, the strength and permanent security of government is in proportion to the number of people interested in supporting it. The true policy, therefore, is to interest the whole by an equality of rights, for the danger arises from exclusions. It is possible to exclude men from the right of voting, but it is impossible to exclude them from the right of rebelling against that exclusion; and when all other rights are taken away, the right of rebellion is made perfect.

While men could be persuaded they had no rights, or that rights appertained only to a certain class of men, or that government was a thing existing in right of itself, it was not difficult to govern them authoritatively. The ignorance in which they were held and the superstition in which they were instructed furnished the means of doing it.

But when the ignorance is gone and the superstition with it, when they perceive the imposition that has been acted upon them, when they reflect that the cultivator and the manufacturer are the primary means of all the wealth that exists in the world beyond what nature spontaneously produces, when they begin to feel their consequences by their usefulness and their right as members of society, it is then no longer possible to govern them as before. The fraud once detected cannot be reacted. To attempt it is to provoke derision or invite destruction.

That property will ever be unequal is certain. Industry, superiority of talents, dexterity of management, extreme frugality, fortunate opportunities or the opposite, or the means of those things, will ever produce that effect, without having recourse to the harsh, ill-sounding names of avarice and oppression; and besides this there are some men who, though they do not despise wealth, will not stoop to the drudgery or the means of acquiring it nor will be troubled with it beyond their wants or their independence, while in others there is an avidity to obtain it by every means not punishable—it makes the sole business of their lives, and they follow it as a religion. All that is required with respect to property is to obtain it honestly and not employ it criminally, but it is always criminally employed when it is made a criterion for exclusive rights.

In institutions that are purely pecuniary, such as that of a bank or a commercial company, the rights of the members composing that company are wholly created by the property they invest therein, and no other rights are represented in the government of that company than what arise out of that property; neither has that government cognizance of *anything but property*.

But the case is totally different with respect to the institution of civil government, organized on the system of representation. Such a government has cognizance of *everything* and of *every man* as a member of the national society, whether he has property or not; and therefore the principle requires that *every man* and *every kind of right* be represented, of which the right to acquire and to hold property is but one, and that not of the most essential kind.

The protection of a man's person is more sacred than the protection of property, and besides this the faculty of performing any kind of work or services by which he acquires a livelihood or maintaining his family is of the nature of property. It is property to him; he has acquired it, and it is as much the object of his protection as exterior property, possessed without that faculty, can be the object of protection in another person.

I have always believed that the best security for property, be it much or little, is to remove from every part of the community, as far as can possibly be done, every cause of complaint and every motive to violence, and this can only be done by an equality of rights. When rights are secure, property is secure in consequence. But when property is made a pretense for unequal or exclusive rights, it weakens the right to hold the property, and provokes indignation and tumult; for it is unnatural to believe that property can be secure under the guarantee of a society injured in its rights by the influence of that property.

Next to the injustice and ill-policy of making property a pretense for exclusive right is the unaccountable absurdity of giving to mere *sound* the idea of property and annexing to it certain rights, for what else is a *title* but sound? Nature is often giving to the world some extraordinary men who arrive at fame by merit and universal consent, such as Aristotle, Socrates, Plato, etc. They were truly great or noble. But when government sets up a manufactory of nobles, it is as absurd as if she undertook to manufacture wise men. Her nobles are all counterfeits.

This wax-work order has assumed the name of aristocracy, and the disgrace of it would be lessened if it could be considered only as childish imbecility. We pardon foppery because of its insignificance, and on the same ground we might pardon the foppery of titles. But the origin of aristocracy was worse than foppery. It was robbery. The first aristocrats in all countries were brigands. Those of later times, sycophants.

It is very well known that in England (and the same will be found in other countries), the great landed estates now held in descent were plundered from the quiet inhabitants at the Conquest. The possibility did not exist of acquiring such estates honestly. If it be asked how they could have been acquired, no answer but that of robbery can be given. That they were not acquired by trade, by commerce, by manufactures, by agriculture, or by any reputable employment is certain.

How then were they acquired? Blush, aristocracy, to hear your origin, for your progenitors were thieves. They were the Robespierres and the Jacobins of that day. When they had committed the robbery, they endeavored to lose the disgrace of it by sinking their real names under fictitious ones, which they called titles. It is ever the practice of felons to act in this manner. They never pass by their real names.

As property, honestly obtained, is best secured by an equality of rights, so ill-gotten property depends for protection on a monopoly of rights. He who has robbed another of his property will next endeavor to disarm him of his rights to secure that property; for when the robber becomes the legislator, he believes himself secure. That part of the government of England that is called the House of Lords was originally composed of persons who had committed the robberies of which I have been speaking. It was an association for the protection of the property they had stolen.

But besides the criminality of the origin of aristocracy, it has an injurious effect on the moral and physical character of man. Like slavery, it debilitates the human faculties; for as the mind bowed down by slavery loses in silence its elastic powers, so, in the contrary extreme, when it is buoyed up by folly it becomes incapable of exerting them and dwindles into imbecility. It is impossible that a mind employed upon ribands and titles can ever be great. The childishness of the objects consumes the man.

It is at all times necessary, and more particularly so during the progress of a revolution and until right ideas confirm themselves by habit, that we frequently refresh our patriotism by reference to first principles. It is by tracing things to their origin that we learn to understand them, and it is by keeping that line and that origin always in view that we never forget them.

An inquiry into the origin of rights will demonstrate to us that *rights* are not *gifts* from one man to another, nor from one class of men to another; for who is he who could be the first giver, or by what principle or on what authority could he possess the right of giving?

A declaration of rights is not a creation of them nor a donation of them. It is a manifest of the principle by which they exist, followed by a detail of what the rights are; for every civil right has a natural right for its foundation, and it includes the principle of a reciprocal guarantee of those rights from man to man. As, therefore, it is impossible to discover any origin of rights otherwise than in the origin of man, it consequently follows that rights appertain to man in right of his existence only, and must therefore be equal to every man.

The principle of an *equality of rights* is clear and simple. Every man can understand it, and it is by understanding his rights that he learns his duties; for where the rights of men are equal, every man must finally see the necessity of protecting the rights of others as the most effectual security for his own.

But if, in the formation of a constitution, we depart from the principle of equal rights or attempt any modification of it, we plunge into a labyrinth of difficulties from which there is no way out but by retreating. Where are we to stop? Or by what principle are we to find out the point to stop at that shall discriminate between men of the same country, part of whom shall be free and the rest not?

If property is to be made the criterion, it is a total departure from every moral principle of liberty, because it is attaching rights to mere matter and making man the agent of that matter. It is, moreover, holding up property as an apple of discord, and not only exciting but justifying war against it; for I maintain the principle that when property is used as an instrument to take away the rights of those who may happen not to possess property, it is used to an unlawful purpose, as firearms would be in a similar case.

In a state of nature all men are equal in rights, but they are not equal in power; the weak cannot protect themselves against the strong. This being the case, the institution of civil society is for the purpose of making an equalization of powers that shall be parallel to and a guarantee of the equality of rights. The laws of a country, when properly constructed, apply to this purpose.

Every man takes the arm of the law for his protection as more effectual than his own, and therefore every man has an equal right in the formation of the government and of the laws by which he is to be governed and judged. In extensive countries and societies, such as America and France, this right in the individual can only be exercised by delegation, that is, by election and representation; and hence it is that the institution of representative government arises.

Hitherto I have confined myself to matters of principle only. First, that hereditary government has not a right to exist, that it cannot be established on any principle of right, and that it is a violation of all principle. Secondly, that government by election and representation has its origin in the natural and eternal rights of man; for whether a man be his own lawgiver, as he would be in a state of nature, or whether he exercises his portion of legislative sovereignty in his own person, as might be the case in small democracies where all could assemble for the formation of the laws by which they were to be governed, or whether he exercises it in the choice of persons to represent him in a national assembly of representatives, the origin of the right is the same in all cases. The first, as is before observed, is defective in power; the second is practicable only in democracies of small extent; the third is the greatest scale upon which human government can be instituted.

Next to matters of *principle* are matters of *opinion*, and it is necessary to distinguish between the two. Whether the rights of men shall be equal is not a matter of opinion but of right, and consequently of principle; for men do not hold their rights as grants from each other, but each one in right of himself. Society is the guardian but not the giver. And as in extensive societies, such as America and France, the right of the individual in matters of government cannot be exercised but by election and representation, it consequently follows that the only system of government consistent with principle, where simple democracy is impracticable, is the representative system.

But as to the organical part, or the manner in which the several parts of government shall be arranged and composed, it is altogether *matter of opinion*. It is necessary that all the parts be conformable with the *principle of equal rights;* and so long as this principle be religiously adhered to no very material error can take place, neither can any error continue long in that part which falls within the province of opinion.

In all matters of opinion, the social compact, or the principle by which society is held together, requires that the majority of opinions becomes the rule for the whole and that the minority yields practical obedience thereto. This is perfectly conformable to the principle of equal rights; for, in the first place, every man has *a right to give an opinion,* but no man has a right that his opinion should *govern the rest.* In the second place, it is not supposed to be known beforehand on which side of any question, whether for or against, any man's opinion will fall. He may happen to be in a majority upon some questions and in a minority upon others, and by the same rule that he expects obedience in the one case he must yield it in the other.

All the disorders that have arisen in France during the progress of the Revolution have had their origin, not in the *principle of equal rights,* but in the violation of that principle. The principle of equal rights has been repeatedly violated, and that not by the majority but by the minority, and *that minority has been composed of men possessing property, as well as of men without property; property, therefore, even upon the experience already had, is no more a criterion of character than it is of rights.*

It will sometimes happen that the minority are right and the majority are wrong, but as soon as experience proves this to be the case, the minority will increase to a majority, and the error will reform itself by the tranquil operation of freedom of opinion and equality of rights. Nothing, therefore, can justify an insurrection; neither can it ever be necessary where rights are equal and opinions free.

Taking then the principle of equal rights as the foundation of the Revolution, and consequently of the constitution, the organical part, or the manner in which the several parts of the government shall be arranged in the constitution, will, as is already said, fall within the province of opinion.

Various methods will present themselves upon a question of this kind; and though experience is yet wanting to determine which is the best, it has, I think, sufficiently decided which is the worst. That is the worst which, in its deliberations and decisions, is subject to the precipitance and passion of an individual; and when the whole legislature is crowded into one body, it is an individual in mass. In all cases of deliberation, it is necessary to have a corps of reserve; and it would be better to divide the representation by lot into two parts, and let them revise and correct each other, than that the whole should sit together and debate at once.

Representative government is not necessarily confined to any one particular form. The principle is the same in all the forms under which it can be arranged. The equal rights of the people is the root from which the whole springs, and the branches may be arranged as present opinion or future experience shall best direct. As to that *hospital of incurables* (as Chesterfield [5] calls it), the British House of Peers, it is an excrescence growing out of corruption; and there is no more affinity or resemblance between any of the branches of a legislative body originating from the right of the people and the aforesaid House of Peers than between a regular member of the human body and an ulcerated wen.

As to that part of government that is called the "executive," it is necessary in the first place to fix a precise meaning to the word.

There are but two divisions into which power can be arranged. First, that of willing or decreeing the laws; secondly, that of executing or putting them in practice. The former corresponds to the intellectual faculties of the human mind, which reasons and determines what shall be done; the second, to the mechanical powers of the human body that puts that determination into practice.

If the former decides and the latter does not perform, it is a state of imbecility; and if the latter acts without the predetermination of the former, it is a state of lunacy. The executive department therefore is official and is subordinate to the legislative, as the body is to the mind in a state of health; for it is impossible to conceive the idea of two sovereignties, a sovereignty to *will* and a sovereignty to *act*.

The executive is not invested with the power of deliberating whether it shall act or not; it has no discretionary authority in the case, for it can *act no other thing* than what the laws decree and it is *obliged* to act conformably thereto; and in this view of the case the executive is made up of all the official departments that execute the laws, of which that which is called the "judiciary" is the chief.

But mankind have conceived an idea that *some kind of authority* is necessary to *superintend* the execution of the laws and to see that they are faithfully performed; and it is by confounding this superintending, authority with the official execution that we get embarrassed about the term "executive power." All the parts in the governments of the United States of America that are called the "executive" are no other than authorities to superintend the execution of the laws, and they are so far independent of the legislative that they know the legislative only through the laws and cannot be controlled or directed by it through any other medium.

In what manner this superintending authority shall be appointed or composed is a matter that falls within the province of opinion. Some may prefer one method and some another, and in all cases where opinion only and not principle is concerned the majority of opinions forms the rule for all.

There are however some things deducible from reason and evidenced by experience that serve to guide our decision upon the case. The one is never to invest any individual with extraordinary power; for besides his being tempted to misuse it, it will excite contention and commotion in the nation for the office. Secondly, never to invest power long in the hands of any number of individuals. The inconveniences that may be supposed to accompany frequent changes are less to be feared than the danger that arises from long continuance.

I shall conclude this discourse with offering some observations on the means of *preserving liberty;* for it is not only necessary that we establish it, but that we preserve it.

It is, in the first place, necessary that we distinguish between the means made use of to overthrow despotism, in order to prepare the way for the establishment of liberty, and the means to be used after the despotism is overthrown.

The means made use of in the first case are justified by necessity. Those means are, in general, insurrections; for while the established government of despotism continues in any country, it is scarcely possible that any other means can be used. It is also certain that, in the commencement of a revolution, the revolutionary party permit to themselves a *discretionary exercise of power* regulated more by circumstances than by principle, which, were the practice to continue, liberty would never be established, or if established would soon be overthrown. It is never to be expected in a revolution that every man is to change his opinion at the same moment.

There never yet was any truth or any principle so irresistibly obvious that all men believed it at once. Time and reason must cooperate with each other to the final establishment of any principle, and therefore those who may happen to be first convinced have not a right to persecute others on whom conviction operates more slowly. The moral principle of revolutions is to instruct, not to destroy.

Had a constitution been established two years ago (as ought to have been done), the violences that have since desolated France and injured the character of the Revolution would, in my opinion, have been prevented. The nation would then have had a bond of union, and every individual would have known the line of conduct he was to follow. But instead of this, a revolutionary government, a thing without either principle or authority, was substituted in its place; virtue and crime depended upon accident, and that which was patriotism one day became treason the next.

All these things have followed from the want of a constitution: for it is the nature and intention of a constitution to *prevent governing by party* by establishing a common principle that shall limit and control the power and impulse of party, and that says to all parties, *thus far shalt thou go and no further*. But in the absence of a constitution, men look entirely to party; and instead of principle governing party, party governs principle.

An avidity to punish is always dangerous to liberty. It leads men to stretch, to misinterpret, and to misapply even the best of laws. He that would make his own liberty secure must guard even his enemy from oppression; for if he violates this duty, he establishes a precedent that will reach to himself.

THOMAS PAINE

Paris, July, 1795

NOTES

COMMON SENSE

[1] Charles I, who became King of England in 1625, was condemned as a traitor and enemy of the nation and was beheaded in 1649.

[2] The words of Jesus as reported in Matthew 22:21. Tory politicians and pamphleteers of the period frequently used this injunction as Biblical authority for the submission of the individual to the state.

[3] Gideon delivered the Israelites from the Midianites, as described in Judges 6:1-27; 8:1-23.

[4] Samuel's yielding to the people's clamor for a king is related in I Samuel:8.

[5] William I, King of England, was the illegitimate son of Robert "Le Diable," Duke of Normandy. He invaded England in 1066, and acquired the throne as a result of his victory in the battle of Hastings.

[6] York and Lancaster were the two noble families whose rivalry for the throne of England brought on the Wars of the Roses, so called because the emblem of the House of York was a white rose and that of Lancaster a red rose. The contesting monarchs mentioned in this paragraph are Henry VI (reigned 1422-1461) and Edward IV (reigned 1461-1483).

[7] Henry VII reigned from 1485 to 1509.

[8] Sir William Meredith, who died in 1790, was a lord of the admiralty under Rockingham's first ministry (1765). He was also the author of several political works.

[9] This reference is too vague for positive identification. Paine probably has in mind one of two brothers, Henry Pelham (1695?-1754) or Thomas Pelham-Holles (1693-1768), both of whom, at various times, held ministerial positions in the English government. See *Dictionary of National Biography*.

[10] On April 19, 1775, the battles of Lexington and Concord were fought. These battles marked the opening hostilities of the American Revolution.

[11] The reference is to the Seven Years' War, carried on from 1756 to 1763 by Frederick II of Prussia against Austria, Russia, and France. During this war Hanover suffered materially from the ravages of the French.

[12] As a result of the destruction by the inhabitants of Boston of large quantities of tea sent from England (an event known as the "Boston Tea Party"), the English government passed in 1774 a series of acts greatly curtailing the freedom of the colony and causing much hardship.

[13] A quotation from *Paradise Lost*, iv. 98-99.

[14] In 1765 the British Parliament passed a Stamp Act, which required that all American newspapers, pamphlets, legal documents, etc., bear a revenue stamp. This act, which greatly angered the American colonies, was repealed the following year.

[15] Lord Frederick North was the British prime minister throughout most of the American Revolution. Many Americans naturally felt that the removal of North, who was a tool of the King, might alleviate the oppression which the colonists were suffering at the hand of the British government.

[16] The battle of Bunker Hill, fought in Boston on June 17, 1775, resulted in a victory for the British.

[17] George III, who reigned from 1760 to 1820.

[18] The Magna Charta, or Great Charter, was granted by King John of England in 1215 to the barons. This famous document is usually regarded as the basis of English liberties.

[19] Giacinto (Hyacinthe), Marquis de Dragonetti, was born in Lower Abruzzia in 1738. After entering the legal profession, he was named to a chair of public law at the University of Naples. In recognition of his legal talents, he was at various times a member of the Sicilian Council, president of the tribunal of commerce (whether in Sicily or Naples is not clear), president of the commission on titles (similarly not clear), and finally president of the Royal Court of Naples. His best-known work in his own day was the treatise, *Della Virtù e de' Premi,* published in Italian in 1766. A corrected French translation was published in 1768, and an English translation, under the title, *A Treatise on Virtues and Rewards,* London, 1769. This work was written in opposition to the celebrated work of Beccaria on the reform of the penal system, *Trattato dei delitti e delle pene.* In addition, he wrote works on jurisprudence and a historical treatise on the origin of fiefs in Sicily, a work which has been described as full of interesting materials for the history of the Middle Ages. Dragonetti died in 1818.

[20] John Entick, *A New Naval History, or, Compleat View of the British Marine*. London, 1757. "Introduction," page lvi.

[21] Josiah Burchett (1666?-1746) was at an early age taken into the naval office by Samuel Pepys. Throughout much of his life Burchett was connected with English naval affairs, serving from 1698 to 1742 as secretary of the admiralty.

[22] Paine here refers to the French and Indian War (1756-1763), which resulted from the territorial rivalry between England and France.

[23] Philadelphia is located on the Delaware River.

[24] Charles W. Cornwall (1735-1789) held the office of a lord of the treasury from 1774 to 1780 in the government of North.

[25] The King's speech addressed to Parliament may be found in the *Pennsylvania Gazette* for Jan. 10, 1776. The King here averred that he was "anxious to prevent, if it had been possible, the effusion of the blood of my subjects; and the calamities which are inseparable from a state of war; still hoping that my people in America would have discerned the traitorous views of the leader, and have been convinced, that to be a subject of Great Britain, with all its consequences, is to be the freest member of any civil society in the known world. The rebellious war now levied is become more general, and is manifestly carried on for the purpose of establishing an independent empire. I need not dwell upon the fatal effects of the success of such a plan. . . . It is now become the part of wisdom, and (in its effects) of clemency, to put a speedy end to these disorders by the most decisive exertions. For this purpose, I have increased my naval establishment, and greatly augmented my land forces; but in such a manner as may be the least burthensome to my kingdoms. I have also the satisfaction to inform you, that I have received the most friendly offers of foreign assistance. . . ."

[26] Sir John Dalrymple (1726-1810) was "appointed baron of the exchequer" in 1776. He was a writer of history, as well as a pamphleteer. The tract to which Paine here refers is entitled *The Address of the People of Great-Britain to the Inhabitants of America* (London, 1775). The quotation, with slight variations in phrasing, may be found on page 31 of the pamphlet.

[27] Charles Watson-Wentworth, second Marquis of Rockingham (1730-1782), was lord of the treasury and prime minister, 1765-66. In politics he was a Whig and favored independence for the American Colonies. Under his administration the Stamp Act was repealed. In 1782 he succeeded Lord North as prime minister, but died within three months after taking office.

²⁸ Paine here refers again to the French and Indian War (1756-1763).

²⁹ Paine here refers to the Quebec Act passed by the British Parliament in 1774. One of the provisions of this act placed the territory northwest of the Ohio under the control of Quebec.

³⁰ The American Tories were the political party that remained loyal to the Crown and opposed the independence of the Colonies, whereas the Whigs desired greater independence from England—home rule or even complete separation from the British Commonwealth. Although the names were borrowed from the two major political parties of England, the political division which they signified in America differed from that in England. The Tory party in England was the successor of the Court party and upheld the prerogative of the Crown over Parliament, while the Whigs defended the sovereignty of Parliament. The English Tories were mostly titled landowners and, as to their religious affiliation, Episcopalians. The Whigs drew their strength from the urban elements, especially the merchants, and from the small landowners. They were Puritans, either Presbyterians or Independents.

³¹ Reference here is probably to a budget of news from England which appeared on December 11, 1775, in the *New-York Gazette and the Weekly Mercury,* a paper published by Hugh Gaine, who throughout much of his career was a Tory printer. One of the items reads: "A bill for settling an unalterable compact between this country and America for the future government and tranquility of the latter country, is now under the consideration of the cabinet. . . . The general object of the proposed regulation is to put the Americans on the same footing of freedom, and under the same advantages, with the rest of his Majesty's subjects. The whole continent is to be divided into large districts, each of which is to send a representative to the British Parliament. The number of the representatives at first is to be rendered proportionable to the revenue that is expected to be raised by the introduction of the same laws of custom and excise, and the same privileges of trade prevailing in Great-Britain. In proportion as that revenue shall increase, their number is to be enlarged." One must agree with Paine in calling this plan "hypocritical." It is plainly an attempt to disrupt the unity of the colonies and, by the proposed method of taxation and representation, to create a rivalry among the colonial factions.

³² The date "1763" marked the close of the French and Indian War, which for seven years had drained the resources of the colonies. In the light of the passage of the notorious Stamp Act two years

later, the Americans looked back upon this date as marking the beginning of a period of relative freedom from British oppression.

THE AMERICAN CRISIS: I

[1] Paine is here quoting loosely from the Declaratory Act passed by Parliament in 1766. With the repeal of the Stamp Act, an act was passed which declared that the king possessed the right "to make laws and statutes of sufficient force and validity to bind the colonies and people of America, subjects of the crown of Great Britain, in all cases whatsoever."

[2] Late in 1775 and early in 1776 numerous clashes took place in the Jerseys (now called New Jersey) between the Tories and the patriots. Actual fighting in New Jersey started in the summer of 1776. See Leonard Lundin, *Cockpit of the Revolution: the War for Independence in New Jersey* (Princeton, N.J., 1940). Paine himself took part in the Jersey campaign as described in the next paragraph of this number of *The Crisis*. Sir William Howe was the commander-in-chief of the British forces in America from 1775 to 1778.

[3] Fort Lee is located on the Jersey side of the Hudson River approximately opposite what is now 125th Street, New York City.

[4] The North River is now more often called the Hudson.

[5] Nathanael Greene (1742-1786) served as a general of varying ranks throughout most of the American Revolution. The complex military moves here described may be more fully studied in Leonard Lundin, *Cockpit of the Revolution*.

[6] François Arouet, called Voltaire (1694-1778), the French poet, historian, and philosopher.

[7] Probably William I of England. See *Common Sense*, note 5.

[8] A paraphrase of Isaiah 39:8: "He said moreover, For there shall be peace and truth in my days."

[9] Cf. James 2:18: "Yea, a man may say, Thou hast faith, and I have works: show me thy faith without thy works, and I will show thee my faith by my works."

[10] Thomas Gage was commander-in-chief of the British forces in America from 1763 to 1775.

[11] Cf. Philippians 4:7: "And the peace of God, which passeth all understanding, shall keep your hearts and minds through Christ Jesus."

12 "Hessians" was the name applied to the German mercenary soldiers which the British hired during the American Revolution.

13 The first of the *Crisis* papers appeared originally in the *Pennsylvania Journal* for December 19, 1776. The date here given at the close of the paper is the date of its publication as a pamphlet.

THE AMERICAN CRISIS: XIII

1 Paine was not always scrupulously accurate in his statements of fact. From 1777 to 1779 he had been secretary of the Congressional committee on foreign affairs. He was also for a brief period clerk of the Pennsylvania Assembly.

2 On April 19, 1783, the eighth anniversary of the battles of Lexington and Concord, Washington issued a proclamation announcing the end of the war and the discharge of the armies.

RIGHTS OF MAN: PART ONE

1 Dr. Richard Price (1723-1791) was a dissenting clergyman of England, who published in 1776 a brilliant defense of America, followed by other pro-American pamphlets. The sermon here referred to is entitled *A Discourse on the Love of Our Country, Delivered on Nov. 4, 1789, at the Meeting House in the Old Jewry, to the Society for the Commemorating the Revolution in Great Britain* (London, 1790). The three "fundamental rights" are stated on pp. 28-29.

2 The purpose of the Revolution Society was to commemorate the English revolution of 1688 and to preserve and disseminate "the principles of Civil and Religious Liberty." See *An Abstract of the History and Proceedings of the Revolution Society in London* (London, 1789). The Society sent to the French National Assembly a congratulatory address which aroused the indignation of Burke. See *Correspondence of the Revolution Society in London, with the National Assembly, and with Various Societies of the Friends of Liberty in France and England* (London, 1792).

The aim of the Society for Constitutional Information was "to revive in the minds of their fellow citizens, THE COMMONALTY AT LARGE, a knowledge of their lost Rights." See *An Address to the Public From the Society for Constitutional Information* (London, 1780). The House of Commons ordered an investigation of the papers of this and other similar societies. The result of the investigation revealed, it was affirmed, that the activities of these organizations "appear to become every day more and more likely to affect the internal peace and security of these kingdoms, and to require, in the most urgent manner, the immediate and vigilant attention of Parliament." See *The First Report of the Committee of Secrecy of the House of Commons, on the Papers Belonging to the Society for Constitutional Information, and the London Corresponding Society* (London, 1794).

[3] Upon the death of Charles II in 1685, James II ascended the throne. Three years of violent conflict with Church and Parliament led to his expulsion in 1688. Parliament invited William, Prince of Orange, who had married James' daughter, Mary, to occupy the English throne.

[4] The "writer of some antiquity" is St. Paul. Cf. I Corinthians 13:11: "When I was a child, I spake as a child, I understood as a child, I thought as a child: but when I became a man, I put away childish things."

[5] The Marquis de Lafayette (1757-1834), whose memory all Americans hold in reverence, came to this country in 1777 to volunteer his services in the cause of the Revolution. His military assistance proved of great value to the colonies. His friendship with Washington exerted a great influence on Lafayette's mind, and after the establishment of peace, he returned to France, where he played a significant part in the earlier phases of the French Revolution. Paine refers to Lafayette several times in the course of the *Rights of Man,* dedicating Part II of this work to the Frenchman.

[6] Smithfield is the name of a once celebrated cattle market in London. It was here that numerous Protestant martyrs met their death from 1400 to 1558.

[7] The term "Dissenter," as here used, refers to one who has denied the authority of the Church of England. The Quakers, or Society of Friends, an important group of dissenters founded by George Fox in the seventeenth century, asserted the source of religious authority to lie in the "inner voice," or the voice of God speaking directly to the individual without mediation of church or creed.

[8] The Edict of Nantes was a decree issued in the city of that name by Henry IV of France in 1598. This edict secured to French Protestants freedom of religious worship. The decree was revoked by Louis XIV in 1685.

[9] At the conclusion of the American Revolution, when Lafayette was about to return to France, a committee of Congress was charged with the duty of bidding the French general farewell and of expressing to him the gratitude of the nation. Part of Lafayette's reply, in words slightly different from those quoted by Paine, may be found

in John Quincy Adams' *Oration on the Life and Character of Gilbert Motier de Lafayette* (Washington, 1835), p. 39: "May this immense Temple of Freedom ever stand, a lesson to oppressors, an example to the oppressed, a sanctuary for the rights of mankind!"

[10] Henry IV, King of France (reigned 1589-1610), who was responsible for the Edict of Nantes, did much to improve economic conditions in France and was an idol of the lower classes. (See also note 8.)

RIGHTS OF MAN: PART-TWO

[1] In 1778 certain Catholic disabilities in England were removed by act of Parliament. Lord George Gordon as president of the Protestant Association sought in 1780 a repeal of this act. Gordon's cause was soon taken up by the masses, and riots ensued involving the destruction of many Catholic churches, as well as the burning of Newgate prison.

[2] The Abbé Emmanuel Joseph Sieyès (1748-1836) played an active part in the early stages of the French Revolution, although he advocated the retention of the monarchy. In the issue of the *Gazette nationale, ou le Moniteur universal* for July 6, 1791, Sieyès (who signs himself "Emm. Syeyes") defends the institution of monarchy thus:

Ce n'est ni pour caresser d'anciennes habitudes, ni par aucun sentiment superstitieux de royalisme, que je préfère la monarchie. Je la préfère, parce qu'il m' est démontré qu'il y a plus de liberté pour le citoyen dans la monarchie que dans la république.

He later presents a challenge: "J'entrerai en lice avec les républicains de bonne foi."

In a "Lettre de M. Thomas Paine, à M. Emmanuel Syeyes. Paris, le 8 juillet 1791," which appeared in the *Supplément à la Gazette nationale* for July 16, Paine promises to accept the challenge of Sieyès and to defend a republican form of government against the monarchical system. A translation of this letter appears in Foner II, 519-520. Paine fulfills his obligation to Sieyès in this section of *Rights of Man*. The quotation (in English translation) from Sieyès on p. 123 is not a part of Sieyès' article in the *Gazette nationale* for July 6, 1791, though probably from another work of the French author.

[3] In using the date "1715" Paine has in mind the Treaty of Utrecht (actually signed in 1713) which brought to a close the war of the Spanish succession.

The date "1745" probably refers to the victory of the Orange party over the republicans, whereby in 1747 William IV became stadtholder of the Seven United Provinces (Netherlands).

[4] Paine here expresses himself inaccurately. The President is not a member of Congress. In the light of the following sentence, Paine apparently means that the President possesses extraordinary executive power, which cannot be entrusted to an immature mind, as is sometimes the case with a king in a hereditary monarchy.

[5] Born in Boston in 1706, Benjamin Franklin went to Philadelphia in 1723 as a printer, and he practiced that vocation for many years. His political career started in 1748 when he became a member of the city council. After 1750, when he was elected a delegate to the Pennsylvania Assembly, he was increasingly involved in state and colonial politics. He was a signer of the Declaration in 1776, and later in the same year went to France to seek the aid of that country on behalf of the American Revolution—a mission which he accomplished with honor. For a text of Franklin's autobiography and other writings, as well as a study of his life and thought, see *Benjamin Franklin. The Autobiography and Selections from His Other Writings*. Edited by Herbert W. Schneider (Liberal Arts Press, New York, 1952).

[6] Paine is here referring to William of Orange, who in 1688 came from Holland to be King of England (see *Rights of Man*, Part I, note 3); and to George I, elector of Hanover, who assumed the English throne in 1714.

[7] That is, nine out of the original thirteen states.

[8] Paine here refers once more to the ascension to the throne of England by George I, elector of Hanover, in 1714.

[9] Charles James Fox (1749-1806) was a celebrated Whig statesman, who held numerous positions of importance in the English government. His speeches in the House of Commons have been collected in six volumes.

DISSERTATION ON FIRST PRINCIPLES OF GOVERNMENT

[1] As a republican, Paine remained throughout his life opposed to any form of mixed government, although his references are usually to the mixed government of a legislature composed of elected representatives of the people and a hereditary monarchy with special prerogatives over that legislature, such as in England and Holland.

[2] Paine is probably referring here to the general uprising of the Poles, in 1794, under the leadership of General Thaddeus Kosciusko.

The war ended in 1795 with the defeat of General Kosciusko's forces and the third and final partition of Poland.

[3] Maximilien de Robespierre (1758-1794) was the son of an unsuccessful French advocate and had himself studied law. He was elected a member of the National Assembly in 1789 and thereafter played an increasingly important role in the French Revolution. He was the leader of the Jacobins, the radical club which was in a large degree responsible for the Reign of Terror. Robespierre was overthrown in 1794 by the Revolutionary Tribunal and guillotined on June 28 of that year.

[4] Capet was the name of a French royal house which is said to have provided Europe with 118 sovereigns. Louis XVI, by remote descent a Capet, was indicted by the National Convention in 1792 under the name of Louis Capet.

The Guelphs and the Ghibellines were two opposing political factions in Italy and Germany. Between the twelfth and the fourteenth centuries the conflict between these parties was responsible for much of the history of the two countries. The term "Guelph" has since been used with various significations. According to *Haydn's Dictionary of Dates* (New York, 1898), "Guelph (of uncertain origin) is the popular name of the present royal family of England."

Jean Paul Marat, a friend of Robespierre, was intimately connected during the French Revolution with the Reign of Terror.

[5] Philip Dormer Stanhope (1694-1773), Earl of Chesterfield, was an English statesman and a man of brilliant wit, distinguished for his polished manner. He is best known for his *Letters to his Son* (first published, 1774). His other writings include *Letters to his Godson* (first published, 1890), addressed to his adopted son.

THE AMERICAN HERITAGE SERIES

THE COLONIAL PERIOD

THE REVOLUTIONARY ERA

THE YOUNG NATION

THE MIDDLE PERIOD

THE LATE NINETEENTH CENTURY

THE TWENTIETH CENTURY